How to
A Musician's Guide to
Navigating Your Twenties

Nerissa Nields

Illustrated by Katryna Nields

Mercy House Publishing

Northampton, MA
2013

Collective Copies
71 S. Pleasant St
Amherst, MA 01002

www.lifecomposition.com
www.nerissanields.com
www.howtobeanadult.org

ISBN : 9780615845647

Printed in the United States of America

Second Edition

Other Books by Nerissa Nields

Plastic Angel, Scholastic/Orchard 2005

All Together Singing in the Kitchen:
Creative Ways to Make and Listen to Music as a Family,
Shambhala/Roost Books 2011

"If I were called upon to state in a few words the essence of everything I was trying to say both as a novelist and as a preacher, it would be something like this: Listen to your life. See it for the fathomless mystery that it is. In the boredom and pain of it, no less than in the excitement and gladness: touch, taste, smell your way to the holy and hidden heart of it, because in the last analysis, all moments are key moments, and life itself is grace."

Frederick Buechner, from *Listening to Your Life*

"To know what you like is the beginning of wisdom and of old age. Youth is wholly experimental. The essence and charm of that unquiet and delightful epoch is ignorance of self as well as ignorance of life."

Robert Louis Stevenson

Acknowledgments and Thanks

Thanks first and foremost to Katryna Nields for coming up with the idea, painting the cover and doing all the marvelous illustrations, for serving as editor, Big Idea getter, collaborator in all things, and most of all, teacher. Thanks to my parents for their support, enthusiasm and especially to my mother Gail Nields for the obvious, and also for proofreading and for coaching me on the section on democracy. Thanks to my sister Abigail Hillman for her input on the same chapter, and also her living example as an astonishingly competent adult. Thanks to Kate Pritchard, Liz Bedell and Anne Lindley for reading early drafts. Thanks to my Weeding & Pruning class for helping me with sections of this book: Elizabeth Bedell, Elaine Apthorp, Maggie O'Grady, Jennifer Eremeeva, Jennifer Jacobson. Thanks to Ginger Knowlton, my agent. Thanks to Steve and everyone at Collective Copies and Levellers Press; thanks to Lori Shine for editing, to Meghan Dewar for making this book look so beautiful, to Stephen Cebik for his work on the e-book version. Thanks to CREMA, especially Ben Zackheim and Lisa Papademetriou. Thanks to all the contributing "adult" writers: Mary Demerath, Katheryn Geha, John Mark Ockerbloom, Joan Wise, Ed McKeon, Kris McCue, Karen Jasper, Debra Immergut, Michael Biegner, Meredith Tarr, Meredith Killough, Katie Bell, Kate Pritchard, John Riley, Jeff Wasilko, Gayle Huntress, Lee Stokes, Melissa Scott, Elizabeth Lasko, Grace Ma, Aimee Swartz, Courtney Garcia, Gair McCullough, Ellen Finney, Lora Nielsen, Mark Boardman, Trex Proffitt, Ashley King, Ellen Finney, Alan Bloomgarden, Hosie Baskin, Tracie Potochnik, Elizabeth Lasko, Anand Nayak, Enee Abelman, Cady Carroll, Anne-Marie Strohman, Michael Mercurio, Larry Ely, Theresa Marsik, Jennifer Taub, and Patricia Loomis. Thanks to all my Facebook friends for fielding questions and giving me advice all year.

Here is an incomplete list of the smart older people not mentioned above upon whom I leaned heavily in my 20s and beyond—a belated thanks: John Nields, Elizabeth Nields, Sarah Tenney, Laura Page, Jenifer Nields, Lila Nields, Midge Tenney, David Nields, Marcia Jones, Gwendolyn Pierce, Susan Chua, Katherine Nevius, Stuart Davis, John Sonnenday, Patty Romanoff, Michaela O'Brien, Gay Daly, Kathleen Denney, Charlie Hunter, Anna Kirwan, Ken Talan, Dar Williams, Pam Houston, Sara Rose, Peter Ives, Stephen

Philbrick, Judy Hooper, and all the writers in my Monday and Thursday groups. Thank you for teaching me *how to be an adult*, or at least fake it well.

Thanks to Lila and Johnny for entertaining themselves while I pored over printouts and ignored them to finish the second edition. And in advance for reading to me in my dotage—I'm counting on that.

And most of all, thanks to Tom Nields-Duffy: my partner, best friend, guide, student, teacher, fellow adult, fellow foil for our children, reader, cheerleader, inspiration and incidentally, love of my life. It's because of you that I was finally willing to grow up.

For Lila and Johnny

Table of Contents

BOOK TWO
Vocation and Avocation

BOOK THREE
Bloom Where You Are Planted

BOOK FIVE
Other People

Preface to the 2013 Edition

In the five years since this book has come out, I have wanted, almost daily, to revise *How to Be an Adult*. This is natural, of course, as Adulthood is not a static state: one never arrives. New insights, new ways of changing car tires, organizing one's finances, even new ways of roasting a chicken emerge, and I as an extroverted blabbermouth feel compelled to trumpet the new findings to the masses. Moreover, as the mother of two children (ages 7 and almost 5 as of this writing), I've had some good practice with some adultish skills that helped me to refine my perspective since the first edition, which was mostly written before motherhood, though edited and published when Lila was just two and Johnny was three months from being born. Those two kids have taught me more than all my life experiences to date combined. Also, as I am fond of saying, I was *this* close to enlightenment before I had kids. All that forgiveness work and cultivation of a relaxed attitude about the things that really matter, which I spout on about in the earlier edition—well, let's just say I have been put to the test. And failed miserably. But as I have also written, it's in the failing that we learn most.

When I asked for suggestions for the new edition, here were the requests:

- An expanded Vocation/Avocation section, especially with the advent of Facebook and Twitter and LinkedIn.
- Advice on resumés and interviewing
- more on time management (er, consciousness)
- A section on common illnesses and what to do about them
- A discussion of the importance of getting enough sleep
- A handy domestic toolbox full of tips
- Eggs and egg recipes
- More healthy recipes
- Skin care suggestions

I wrote this book because I love to give advice. I love to get advice too, and it's extremely gratifying for me to find out the answers to the nagging questions—my own, and those of my friends.

To this end, I regularly annoy my family by grabbing my iPhone as soon as anyone says, "I wonder how..." or "I wonder when..." or "I wonder what..." and then Googling like a madwoman. In my work as a life coach, I work with many twenty-somethings. I love it when they ask me basic questions to which I know the answers. But I love it even more when we work together to figure out some of the deeper problems we all confront—like how to break an addiction, or how to figure out what career would bring the most joy, or whether or not to marry the guy (or girl). I wanted to condense some of my coaching experience, too, in this new edition.

It can be lonely to be in one's twenties. Not always, and not for everyone—sometimes the twenties are a rowdy extension of those bright college years. Some twenty-somethings are already married. But even then, even so, many folks I have spoken with confess to a sinking feeling of being alone with their cluelessness. *Everyone else seems to know what to do. Why don't I?*

In her book *The Gifts of Imperfection*, Brené Brown talks about the important distinction between "fitting in" and "belonging." We think these terms are synonyms, but actually they are worlds apart. "Fitting in," to my mind, has always been about trimming off objectionable parts of myself so that I take up less space and don't stand out in any way. I think that if I can do this, more people will love me. "Belonging" is the feeling I get when I'm among people who see my whole self—all the parts of me—and love me anyway. In fact, in many cases, it's exactly those objectionable parts that create bonds between people[1]. For me, my twenties were a journey that began as a "fitter-inner" and ended with a profound sense of belonging, and the way I got to this brave new place was through embracing my own objectionable parts. In doing so, I found my people, my Tribe, and through their collective wisdom, I got my answers, at least most of the time. When they failed me, when I had to strike out on my own, I came back with answers for them.

In this age of easy access to all kinds of information, we are training ourselves to Google things like, "Will my daughter have friends in Junior High School?" and "Is my neighbor stockpiling weapons of mass destruction?" as if Google were an oracle. The answers to many questions, in ancient Greece and modern-day America, are equally unknowable, but my sense is that when we're compelled to reach out to the faceless unknown for answers, what we really want is to connect with the Tribe.

This book is in large part about identifying and finding that Tribe. In the beginning, you might start by looking among others who are equally clueless, and begin to commiserate with them. And then, ask questions. To that end, please join the conversation this book has launched at www.howtobeanadult.org where I will be posting regularly. Here, you can actually ask questions and get answers. We need your input!

In the meantime, I hope you enjoy this book. I hope I have kept the very best aspects of the original and added and improved where it was lacking. If you have suggestions on other topics, send them my way. And of course, if you have better ideas on how to manage time, organize a budget, roast a chicken or change a tire, let me know.

Introduction

On the occasion of my college graduation, I received my diploma and immediately began to examine it. It was written, unhelpfully, in Latin, a language I studied for one year at age thirteen. Undaunted, I flipped it over in the hopes that somewhere among the *ovems* and the *isimuses* there would be some final directive, some code that would tell me what to do next. I'd been an English major in college, taking the advice of my favorite high-school teacher who told me the purpose of college was to read all the books you'd never get around to reading otherwise. So while my roommates were studying pre-med, pre-law and economics, I was immersed in Shakespeare, Elizabeth Bishop, and Samuel Beckett. In March, Jenny was accepted to medical school, Susan was off to Stanford Law, and Giselle had a job offer on Wall Street. When anyone asked me what I was going to do, I said something vague about bringing my acoustic guitar to England, where I was planning to become a famous folk singer.

As the snow melted and the hackysackers returned to the green in the spring of my senior year, I noticed a consistent shortness of breath accompanied by a low buzzing in the back of my head. The approximate content of the low buzz was something along the lines of, *"What the hell am I supposed to do now?"* How, for example, was I supposed to find an apartment? What exactly *was* a down payment? Or a security deposit? For how long could I live solely off peanut butter and jelly sandwiches and ramen noodles? What was the difference between a premium and a deductible? Were they really serious about that whole filing taxes thing? That just seemed mean.

Hence the frantic fumbling with the diploma. There were no instructions on the diploma, just the smudged signature of the college president and some unintelligible Latin. So I did what any sensible, practical-minded person would do; I married my current boyfriend, David, who happened to be seven years older than I and, in my mind, a bona fide adult.

This worked out well for a while. David was happy to deal with what I termed the "grown-up stuff": security deposits, medical insurance, bill-paying, and yes, taxes. My twenties rolled by pleasantly enough: I started a rock band along with David and my younger sister Katryna, and we drove around the country in a fifteen-passenger van.

Although in the early days of the band, I'd had to do a lot of what seemed like pretty "adult" stuff—booking gigs, putting together press kits, opening and maintaining a checking  account—eventually, we hired a manager to do all that for us. Once again, I was off the hook. "Your job," said our new manager Dennis, "is to write songs, stay in good shape, and rest up for your performances. Let me take care of everything else. After all, that's why you pay me 16.67% of your gross income."

So I spent my days in a kind of prolonged adolescent summer vacation: writing, reading, shopping for clothes that would make me look like a hot rock star (and running up credit card debt), exercising like a maniac so I would fit into said clothes, and driving around the country performing at festivals, coffeehouses, theaters and rock clubs. It was a blissful existence.

But nothing lasts forever, and by September 2001 the band had broken up, David and I had separated, and I was thirty-four years old—clearly an adult no matter how you did the math. I needed to learn how to function on my own and fast.

What We Learned About Life in 20 Years on the Road

Katryna first got the idea to write a book called *How to Be an Adult* after graduating college. She felt clueless, living with her sister and brother-in-law in a prep-school dorm and eating the prepschool's free food, while trying to figure out things like how to get health insurance and how to pay her taxes on the non-existent income of a budding folk singer. She pronounced, "Someone should write a book called *How to Be an Adult*. How are we supposed to know any of this stuff? We all need a manual. Someone should write it, and since no one else will, I guess it's got to be me. Except I don't know how to be an adult, so why don't you do it?"

We had grand plans to research the topic, but we never followed through. Over the years, we'd revive the project and toss around some ideas, but mostly the concept of either of us writing a book about how to be an adult reduced us to fits of tearful laughter. Who would take a couple of folk singers as their models for responsible adulthood?

But by my mid-thirties, I had observed two things. First of all, somehow along the way, like everyone else, I'd figured it out, mostly, and so had Katryna. It took years, and we made lots of painful and hilarious mistakes. But many of those mistakes were wonderful lessons.

Secondly, what I hadn't figured out (taxes, insurance, retirement accounts, bill-paying) were easily deciphered by the simple act of homing in on someone who clearly appeared to be a competent adult and asking that person how she did what she did. Believe me, if you ask enough people, someone will have a strong opinion on this topic and feel it's their mission in life to sit you down and set you straight.

There Is Always Someone Who Can Help, So Ask

Beware: this is a spiritual lesson as well as a practical one. *There is always someone out there who can help you.* If he or she doesn't respond to your call for help right away, keep calling. Eventually someone will, and in the meantime, you will have made lots of connections. Ask questions. *How to Be an Adult* Golden Rule: If you want to do something well, find someone who is doing it beautifully (or at least adequately) and ask her how she does it. People love to give advice. They love to feel like they know something you don't know. You aren't bothering them. Figure out the channels. And thank God for Google. *When we were your age, there was no internet!* (At least, not that I nor any of my friends knew about, though of course, Al Gore and people at NASA did.) Today, finding out information is as easy as typing, "How do I change my oil?" into the search box.

And thank God (or whatever you think runs this ship) that we live in a world where we're supposed to intermingle and get to know each other. Ignorance and abject terror are wonderful prods toward this end.

Speaking of God, I should let you know that I believe in God. I don't mind at all if you don't, but you should know this about me, because it informs all of the advice in this series. The older I get, the less confidence I have in the aging, creaky body that used to be able to leap from the top bunk halfway across the room unharmed, and more confidence in 1. the wisdom of those who have gone before me, 2. the wisdom of the ages, 3. what actually works, and 4. what I know resonates in my bones as true. All this fits into my definition of God. So if God talk bugs you, feel free to translate the "G" word to "the Universe" or "Truth" or "The Great Reality" or "Presence" or "Big Cheese" or "Yo Mama" for all I care. Or else—and I give you my permission—just roll your eyes when I bring up God.

Missing Owner's Manual

But regardless of your spiritual beliefs, *you* don't need to suffer the way we did! Because Katryna and I have put everything you need to know into one handy volume, with each book highlighting a different delightful area of adultification. Within these pages, we address: time management (er...consciousness), goal-setting and goal-resistance, mental and physical health, jobs and work life, home, food, money, cars, insurance, getting along with others, voting, marriage, divorce, remarriage, and parenthood.

Even though I probably would have ignored it, I wish I'd had a manual like this back when I was 21. When I went to the bookstore looking for how-to books, they inevitably intimidated me with their length and writing style. Things with numbers threw me for a loop. Some people really do have a knack for navigating their way through the world and finding out how it works as they go—like my friends Jenny, Susan and Giselle. But others of us would much rather spend our time reading *The New Yorker* or Ann Patchett novels and have someone else figure out the quarterly taxes.

So for those of us who are artists or marchers to the beat of a different drummer, I attempted to create a series that speaks in the language we can understand: the language of poetry, humor, literature—a set of right-brained manuals. There is some concrete practical advice about money and insurance and stuff like that (think of this part of the book as the raisins in the cookie). The cookie part of the book is a series of how-tos in essay form, told through anecdote, in a way that is (I hope) palatable and memorable. A portable older sister, if you will. And like an older sister, it is full of partisan opinions. Other so-called adults will surely take issue with me on many of my claims, especially when I bash consumerism or blow the horn for the environment. I am sure I will annoy you at times; feel free to ignore me when I do. Also like an older sister, I will probably change my mind and do things differently a few years from now; after all, adulthood is not a static state any more than adolescence is. I've given you a lot of my own stories and life experiences because it's the life I know best. When I had scant experience, I asked all my smart friends on your behalf. Thus, it's the absolute best advice I can give you today. It's the book I wish I'd been given at my graduation, or better yet, it's the instructions my Latin diploma should have included, scrawled on the back like the Dead Sea scrolls.

Who Am I and Why Should You Listen to Me?

I am a musician, novelist, blogger, creative counselor and General Aficionado of Life (GAL). With a brief two-year exception, I have only ever worked for my band and myself. I am a person who has gotten wildly interested in many disparate topics for about ten minutes at a time, so I can say enough to appear knowledgeable about a lot of things up to a certain point. I am a severely right-brained person who has somehow managed to cobble together a vague understanding of finances and how the world works, but really what I know how to do is come up with creative solutions, look for the  reasons why we don't do what's in our own best interests, and make peace with reality. I also live in the town of Northampton Massachusetts, a progressive enclave of students, academics, musicians, writers, and fuzzy-haired aging hippies. We name our kids things like "River" and "Happy." We raise chickens in our backyards and make our own yogurt. Having few corporations here, I can't tell you how to climb the corporate ladder, but I can tell you how to make a ladder for a tree fort.

The best advice I can give you is to find a group of people who will act as your tribe. There is strength in numbers, and there are answers in the shared experience. A group of people getting together to solve a common problem is a lot more productive than one person floundering around on her own. Look for the people who are doing well what you want to do well. If being a millionaire is your goal, hang out with very wealthy people and see how happy they are. If, after a few years, you still want what they have, ask them to teach you how they did it. If you want to be a great parent, make friends with the parents who seem to derive great joy from being with their kids. If you want to be a writer, find someone who is happily making a living doing just that. Then see how she spends her days.

In the name of gathering wisdom from a tribe, I have interviewed over 50 actual adults and included some of their observations, comments and suggestions. Because there are many areas where I as an adult still totally fly by the seat of my pants and mutter "there but for the grace of my friends go I," I have relied heavily on their testimony, especially on matters financial, or in the arena of "real jobs." This works out nicely for me in general; they tend to rely on me for matters of culinary, health, and emotional import. Also for good fiction and movie recommendations.

It has famously been stated that it takes a village to raise a child. I think that's because it takes a village of grown-ups to form what we think of as just one competent adult. It's also been said that organizations survive because on any given day, not everyone is insane. Part of my journey toward adulthood has been the acceptance that I will never be able to "know it all" or certainly, thank God, do it all. I get by with a little help from my friends. We all do. That's the secret behind this book. Figure out what you do well, share it with your friends. Ask for help for the things you don't do well.

Improvement makes straight roads, but the crooked roads without improvement are roads of genius.—William Blake

Life would not be fun or worthwhile if we never had to struggle, never took a wrong turn. Not only that, ask anyone and they will tell you that some of the best things that happened to them were the result of "wrong turns." Three such examples off the top of my head:

1. All the people who got pregnant by accident and ended up madly in love with their children.
2. The guy who screwed up the glue recipe and ended up inventing Post-its[2].
3. Joni Mitchell inventing all her own chords because she never learned how to properly play the guitar.

Finally, almost all the names here have been changed to protect the innocent. I fictionalized a lot of anecdotes. Contributing "adults" have been credited by first name and age only.

The books in this *How to Be an Adult* series are:

1. Taking Care of the Vehicle That Is You
2. Vocation and Avocation
3. Bloom Where You Are Planted
4. Money, Insurance, Cars and a Bunch of Other Boring Stuff
5. Relationships

Feel free to read all the way through this series in order, or to jump around and choose books that interest you. And if you want it all condensed, Cliffs-Notes-style, here is a Cheat Sheet.

Cheat Sheet:
What I Know About Being an Adult

1. Work hard, be disciplined, have courage to change the things you can, tie your camel, etc.
2. Trust God (the Universe, your Inner Light, Krishna, Jesus, Allah, Gaia, etc.), relax, accept the things you cannot change. Also, take regular days off, a.k.a. a Sabbath.
3. Follow Your Bliss.
4. Bloom where you are planted.
5. Make and maintain friendships. Be loyal. Be kind. Show up when you say you are going to.
6. Don't cling to friends or lovers. There are other fish in the sea.
7. Pay your taxes joyfully. If you can't do this, read *One Day in the Life of Ivan Denisovitch*. Or read an article about Darfur, Iran or Saudi Arabia. Freedom is not just another word for nothing left to lose.
8. Be your own best friend, or as Anne Lamott says, become militantly and maternally on your own side. God dwells within us as us.
9. Minimize crap in your life, be it substandard food, entertainment, gadgetry or experiences.
10. Be honest.
11. Question your thoughts and stories.
12. Forgive your enemies.
13. Forgive yourself.
14. Cultivate your own garden.
15. Reach for the stars.
16. All the terrible things that happen to you will be extremely helpful if you get through them and then use your experience to help another person. My friends and I call this "going through the fire." At some point in your life, you will go through the fire, after which you will never be the same again.

17. Don't gossip, try not to criticize, because it will make you sick, and try not to complain because it will zap your energy.
18. Practice gratitude. This is The Secret of the universe, so you may as well join in.
19. Don't postpone joy. Or put another way: when you find a chance to feel really great without using a substance, abusing a person or doing anything clearly illegal and immoral, don't hesitate. Jump in. Splash around and live, for God's sake! Or, to quote the rabbi, "If you're going to eat pork, relish it and let the grease drip over your fingers."
20. Exercise daily.

Adult Checklist

...For Your First Year Out of College

1. Find a roommate or housemates
2. Get health insurance as soon as possible
3. Register to vote as soon as you settle in a town
4. Figure out your trash situation: where can you recycle?
5. Set up phone service, or be miserly and just use your cell phone
6. Set up cable or be miserly and just get a DVD player and join Netflix or Hulu
7. Find a Primary Care Physician
8. If you're a woman, get a pap smear
9. Open a checking account with an attached savings account, preferably a money market if you have enough money.
10. Get high-speed internet
11. Find a store nearby that sells organic produce and meats
12. Get auto insurance as soon as you get a car
13. Register your car with the DMV or RMV, and if you've moved to a new state, get new license plates
14. Have your car inspected
15. Line up someone to help you with your taxes by February

Book One
Taking Care of the Vehicle That Is You

Tools and Rules:

- Know thyself
- Work with the currency of time
- Set goals, but hold them loosely
- Wrestle with resistance
- Don't let the perfect be the enemy of the good
- Take care of yourself—body, mind and soul. Once you're twelve, it's no one's job but yours

HEALTH

Time, Resistance and Priorities

This chapter starts with what I consider some important skills to develop when moving from the carefree, fake-cheese eating world of adolescence to the kale omelet world of Adulthood. These skills are:

1. An ability to know who you are, so you know what you like, so you know what you want, so you know what you need, so you know what you must do.
2. An ability to work with the currency of Time
3. An ability to deal with the related issue of inner resistance, otherwise known as DPI (Desire to Procrastinate Indefinitely)

Now, some of you soon-to-be-adults will have no need for the chapters that follow, and if that be the case, skip ahead to the practical sections on exercise, food and sleep, and knock yourselves out. Your problems (if you have any) may have more to do with sitting back and relaxing rather than kicking your own butt, which may be sore from all the lunges and squats you've done over the years. There's a section just for you a little later on. It's called "Eight Cheap

Forms of Therapy." For the rest of us who know a little something about sitting in front of the TV for five days straight eating nothing but microwave popcorn and diet Shasta, read on.

Know Thyself

> *Be yourself; no base imitator of another, but your best self.*
> *There is something which you can do better than another.*
> *Listen to the inward voice and bravely obey that.*
>
>   —*Ralph Waldo Emerson, "Self-Reliance"*

Everyone seems to know that Shakespeare said, "To thine own self be true." Very well. What most people ignore is that the character who says this oft-quoted line is the big blowhard and hypocrite and oh, by the way, *spy*, Polonius. In the context of the scene within the play *Hamlet*, what he really means by this bit of wisdom adopted by the New Age, is, "Make sure whatever you do, you look appropriate and protect your interests." Still, there's a reason the New Agers (and many Hallmarky-type cards and refrigerator magnets) have sold this quote. It's valuable advice. Even so, because as a teenager I really hated Polonius, I prefer Socrates's "Know Thyself," which is more succinct.

How do you know who you are, anyway? Until you do, you can't really do much. You just kind of whirl around in circles, following whatever is the most sparkly (or safe) person, situation, trend, idea, diatribe, religion. You get your idea of self (usually) from your family of origin, or perhaps from your social group at school or elsewhere. But what if they are all saying things that don't ring true to you?

Get out of the house, and get out of town. Or at least, begin to question: what feels unharmonious to you about the messages you're getting from these people? Are they walking their talk? More importantly, are you? When you listen to that core set of values deep inside yourself, does it match how you are behaving on the outside? When your inside matches your outside, we call this "integrity." Look for others with this quality. Get to know them. These people are the real deal. As Gandhi says, "Happiness is when what you think, what you say, and what you do are in harmony."

Figuring out who you are and what you like and what you want and what you need is a lifelong pursuit. Some get clarity earlier than others; you might already have a very good idea of who you are and what you do best and what you like and what you want and (sometimes hardest of all) what you need. If you know these things about yourself already, use your knowledge to be—to paraphrase Dr. Seuss— the Youest You you can possibly be. If you don't, take some time to find out. It does take that most valuable resource: *time*. I first took this kind of time the summer I turned fourteen and was leaving the school I'd attended for seven years to move on to high school. I lay in my bed every morning, thinking, "who am I really?" And by the end of the summer I'd made some important discoveries. First, that (like my heroes, John Lennon and Bob Dylan) I was an artist, and therefore (necessarily) different from everyone else. And second, that therefore I didn't need to worry about "fitting in" anymore. Eventually everyone would catch on that I was hip, but for now, I could march to the proverbial beat of a different drummer. With these empowering discoveries, I had a huge surge of energy and creativity. I began writing songs; I spoke out about what I believed; I started to wear a lot of red and purple, and also strange hippie garb from the Salvation Army. "I have found myself!" I announced audaciously to anyone who cared to listen. (I really impressed my mom, but my sisters told me later that they were horribly embarrassed for me.)

And indeed, I *had* found myself. But then "myself" changed, and I realized I looked terrible in red and that I wasn't really a hippie. We discover ourselves like the layers of the onion. It's an ever-evolving process. We have to keep asking ourselves what we really love, and make sure we are not swayed by the opinions of others. If all our friends were suddenly abducted on a spaceship and we were left with a totally different crowd, would we adopt the new crowd's preferences and predilections? Would we stay true to what we loved now that we are a part of the (now Martian) crowd? Or are we secretly glad our old buddies have moved onward and upward? In fact, you might want to listen carefully to those outside your strongest spheres of influence. If you are a diehard Christian, read the Koran. If you are a lifelong Democrat, read *Atlas Shrugged*. If you grew up listening only to classical music, try some hip-hop. Don't let others define you. Make up your own mind. See for yourself.

Play a game of "What Do You Like Better?" Oatmeal or choco-late chip? Red or blue? Liberty or Justice? Urban or Rural? When in the day is your energy strongest? What makes you lose your temper? Which is harder for you: anger or sadness? Which is harder for you: your own feelings or the feelings of others? Do you really like jazz? Big drooly dogs? Ernest Hemingway? Short hair? Sci-Fi? Downhill skiing? Or do you just wish you were that kind of person?

To some of you who have strong, healthy egos these ques-tions might seem ridiculous. But I must confess that when I was in my teens I "put on" a lot of likes, dislikes and opinions that were not quite true to who I really was—and I certainly believed I had a healthy ego, and I came across to my friends as a leader. Looking back, here are some of my "should likes."

- Camping
- Rush (the band)
- Charles Dickens' novels
- Soccer
- Lord of the Rings

And some "should not likes."

- Tiny cuddly dogs
- Peter Paul & Mary
- Makeup
- Woody Allen (I know I'm supposed to hate him, but...)
- iPhones
- Starbucks

Some of these are things I realized as a young girl. I should definitely not like:

- To play with dolls
- To like fairy tales
- To wear pink
- To watch *The Brady Bunch*
- To re-read the *Little House* books when I was in 7th grade

And so I did these things in secret. I "put on" being a tomboy instead.

Even as I write this, I am cringing. I don't want anyone to know some of my true likes and dislikes. But one of my favorite parts of Gretchen Rubin's wonderful *Happiness Project*[3] is her First Commandment (to "Be Gretchen.") This reminds me of the Hindu observation that God dwells within us *as us*. Those quirks we can't stand about ourselves—they are divinely wrought. And our work is not to eradicate them but to learn to love them.

The older I get, the more permission I give myself to love what I really love. Our twenties are a time when we start to put down the masks and stop trying on different personae. By the time you hit thirty, you should be well on your way in a lifelong game of Hot/Cold ("Warmer....warmer...hot! Hot! Hot! You've found it!").

"Why try to be a Pekingese if you are a Greyhound?"[4] Listen to the still small voice within. Get to know it. Take it out on dates. Write to it. Talk to it, but also listen. See if it has any better ideas. Some people have an Inner Child. (More on this coming up.) In addition to my Inner Child, I seem to have been gifted with an Inner Sneering Older Brother, whom I probably acquired from reading too much *Creem* Magazine when I was a teen. Some of my work today involves standing up to that Inner Sneering Older Brother (ISOB) and singing, "I decided long ago never to walk in anyone's shadow!" or some similar drippy 80s ballad. (ISOBs hate 80s ballads, 100% of the time.)

Now is the time to do something wild and crazy. Join the Peace Corps, Teach for America, or teach English abroad. Move to New York City or Los Angeles and live the life of a starving artist. Move to Bhutan and become a monk or nun. Go to Europe and be the founder of a political movement. Start a rock band like I did and travel around the country. Or, if you know you are going to end up being an artist, take a few years to do something totally different. (One of my friends from college became a cop. He's now a writer. What amazing material he got during those years!) You will never be this unencumbered and free again! And your back will never enjoy sleeping on other people's floors as much as it does now! Seize your moment!

This of course assumes you have your college loan situation under control. Mindful of paying off the bills, do so—in the most adventurous way possible within your comfort zone. And use your weekends for exploration. Take a weekend to be alone. Go on a Vision Quest. In Native American tradition, youths are sent away with no food (usually) to spend a period of time communing with their spirit guide. At the end of this period, they come back to the tribe clear on what direction their future will take.

Can you find a way to do something similar? I am only asking because, adult though (I think) I am, I wish I could say that I have done a Vision Quest. Everything about it terrifies me: the wilderness, the fasting, the insects, the boredom. That's why I think it might be necessary. Next edition, I hope to report back.

One more thing about my crazy vision quest idea: it is worth noting that in every ancient tradition on every continent the young males went through some kind of initiation rite (the young females did not because they were usually impregnated at that point and/or breastfeeding, and believe me, motherhood is a pretty thorough initiation rite in and of itself). The point is, people have known for millennia the necessity of taking time apart to know oneself so that one can find one's place in the community, make choices that are true and right and not end up like Zelig, the famous Woody Allen character who, chameleon-like, became whoever the people he encountered wanted him to be. Too many of us fail to buck peer pressure even when we're well beyond Junior High. "Know thyself" is an ongoing project; the work of a lifetime.

Time Consciousness

I like the term "time consciousness" better than "time management" because we don't really manage our time. We think we can, and this causes all sorts of frustrations and forms of mental illness. It's the illusion of time management that leads to all manner of anxiety and uptight behavior. How can you manage the sun rising and setting? You just have to surrender to it. Besides, as an artist, one of the first rules I learned was that serendipity (which is, by definition, that which is out of one's control) was the very best song-giver. At the same time, I found early on that the way to be open to serendipity was to leave myself designated times to create, to even go so far as schedule "write songs" into my day planner. We'd be in the van driving around, and I'd start to get that anxious feeling that I always get when I haven't written a song in awhile. I'd look around quickly and confirm that it would be impossible for me to pull a guitar out of the attached trailer while driving 65 mph down Route 80, and instead sigh and write "songwriting week" into my calendar during the second week of March, the next time we were off the road.

Ben Franklin

The week of March would arrive; I would come downstairs first thing in the morning with my cup of coffee, notebook, and guitar, and I would write all week until the songs were written. It seemed to work pretty well. But during the interim, I acted like a little video camcorder, taking everything in, jotting down ideas, and humming tunes into a tape recorder. Whatever crossed my path turned into potential material for my songs. This is still pretty much the way I write. I go around figuring the universe is trying to tell me something, so I'd better listen.

The other reason I like the term "time consciousness" is the way it connects to the marvelous truth that all we ever have is this moment, and another way of saying *that* is all we really have is time. And maybe not as much of it as we assume. I try to hold this loosely, so that I'm not neurotically thinking "must get this done before I die" in a freaked-out, Type A kind of way; neither am I just lolling about eating bon bons and watching *American Idol* (though Katryna might be). I try to keep a schedule and also an eye open to the plans of others, in case they have a better idea of what I should be doing with my time than I do. Sort of like that excellent 38 Special song "Hold On Loosely."

Setting Goals

Goal-setting is probably not new to you. Who hasn't at some point tried to achieve something just beyond one's reach? How does one do such a thing? By working a little harder, a little longer, a little more often, in a focused way. We can set goals for ourselves around almost anything: making it through school, training for a race, mastering an instrument, achieving a social status, winning a chess ranking, winning first prize at a Rubik's Cube tournament. When I was 22, my goals were: to never have to feel lonely again; to start a band that would be the next Beatles; to write a hit song; to look great in a Betsey Johnson dress; to have a daily yoga practice; to run every day; to keep a daily journal; to (eventually—many years in the future) have a family; to go to Harvard Divinity School and be a minister living in western Massachusetts.

Dealing With Resistance

The problem with setting goals is that as soon as we do, 95% of us come up against the source of all evil: Resistance. Resistance, as I am defining it here, means *not doing something you know you want to do, ought to do, love to do, and* won't *do—yet have no logical reason for not doing.* There is something about the nature of resistance that speaks to the very heart of this question of maturity. We all know resistance in some aspect of our lives; we all know that huge creature slouching toward the mall, if not Bethlehem, this three-toed sloth who sleeps all day in the cool of the trees and rouses itself only to eat and excrete. We all know the frustration of setting a goal—to keep our living room tidier, to jog three miles in the morning, to practice the guitar, to send out that resumé, to straighten out our finances—only to watch as the weeks go by and helplessly observe that sickening refusal in some deep part of ourselves to participate. What is it? Where does it come from?

I have no idea. All I know is that I recognize this sloth in myself, and it baffles me that I have accomplished as much as I have, given its hegemony over me. But I do have some observations.

Of course, if we never set goals, we'd never have to deal with resistance. I tend to see the whole issue of resistance to goals in myself as a conversation between a very willful, creative child and a very ambitious parent with the "Real You" stuck somewhere in the middle.

Sigmund Freud uses the terms "id," "superego" and "ego" here, but some of us have problems with old Siggy, so I've provided some alternative jargon for you. Perhaps your resistance is actually healthy and self-protective. What if the goals you are setting for yourself are the wrong goals anyway? What if these particular goals do not support your true dreams and desires? What if the Real You—your true self before socialization, the unique person you were meant to be during your brief sojourn on this planet—what if this You does not care about glamour and fame and money? The Real You might think your perfect manifestation to be a gardener in the town of Ogunquit, Maine. The Real You might fall in love with an overweight, illiterate cab driver with eyes like Tom Hanks' and a heart as big as Canada. The Real You might just want what it is meant to want.

Willful Child   **You**   **Inner Ambitious Parent**

Your Inner Ambitious Parent (IAP), on the other hand, is who and what our peers, *People* magazine, *The New York Times* and perhaps our actual ambitious parents tell us we should be—what we should look like, how much money we should make and what we should accomplish in our lifetime. Your IAP has been told to follow in the family business, or to be a doctor or a lawyer or something (please, God) that will provide our parents with some security upon retirement. Your IAP might want you to be straight, though sometimes, in some communities, gay. Your IAP wants you to contain your feelings (unless it's Italian, which means it wants you to be extremely emotive, operatic, and a good cook and lover to boot. Pardon the "boot" pun). In short, the Real You and your IAP might be worlds apart.

Maybe the reason you keep procrastinating on your screenplay or sleeping through your morning workout is that you don't really want to be an award winning documentary filmmaker or a triathlete.

Maybe your house continues to be a disaster area, even though you subscribe religiously to FlyLady[5], because you don't really want your house to look like it sprung from the pages of *House Beautiful*. Maybe this resistance is some kind of divine protection, a cry from the dark saying, "This is not me!"

The Willful Child on the other hand is not that helpful either, though some of us in our teens and twenties champion our WC and follow her on a long goose chase to degradation (see The Prodigal Son and a bazillion other characters in literature). The Willful Child is not that keen on making money, friends, or attending to personal hygiene. She's fun for awhile, but not for a lifetime. You really don't want her running the show, or you'll end up like one of my *actual* willful children who, on occasion, refuses TV and candy simply because their actual IAP (me) is offering it to him or her. Or in my case, the WC is that same sloth spoken of earlier who doesn't so much stamp her foot but rather curls up on the couch for an entire season if left undisturbed. Life, of course, is a process of finding that balance between chaos and rigidity. The balance point changes over time, which is why we need to practice balancing a lot.

The Problem (For Some of Us) About Setting Goals

The trick for me is to get the IAP and the Willful Child talking calmly to each other instead of having one of them throw a tsunami-size tantrum while the other one nags like a critical op-ed writer. For this is the challenge. As soon as I set a goal—like getting in shape so I can look great in a Betsey Johnson dress—my inner six(teen) year old (WC) immediately rolls her eyes and curls up in bed with a book. Meanwhile, my IAP goes ballistic on the poor reader, screaming, "Your thighs! That bulge above your triceps! Not to mention you're going to get osteoporosis and heart disease! Get out of bed and do forty laps around the park!"

Eventually I learned to treat these two opposing personalities the way I would treat a cat. Cats (at least the ones I lived with) don't respond well to direct orders or being scooped up and cuddled. They like to be wooed, approached at a 45 degree angle. Slyly. Gently. Coyly. And so when I am feeling listless, I have my IAP say, ever so slyly, gently, and coyly, "Wow, remember how nice it was to go for a run? You used to bring your iPod and listen to *Anna Karenina*. That was fun. Hmmm. Maybe if we go back to running, we can down-load *Middlemarch*. You could start by just walking, and call Susan on your cell phone… no pressure." The six(teen)-year-old responds much better this way (though she negotiates for Patti Smith's *Just Kids* in lieu of *Middlemarch*), and there is peace, harmony and fitness in the kingdom once again.

But this diplomacy has been long in negotiation. This should give you hope: in order to meet my second goal (to be the next Beatles) I knew I would have to practice my guitar a lot more. (I am undisciplined about practicing my guitar, and I pretty much always have been.) When I started at age eleven, that directive: "I should practice more!" rang in my ears every time I came home from school and saw my little nylon string guitar safely tucked away in its black pleather case. What did I do? Sometimes felt kind   of sick and guilty and stuck the guitar in the nether regions   of my closet. But often the desire to make music would   come and pull at my heartstrings, and I would pull   the guitar out of the case and open my *Beatles*   *for Easy Guitar* book, sit down on the carpet   a n d painfully play a few songs with especially easy chords. But I'd get so frustrated because the songs sounded nothing like the Beatles LPs I'd put on the record player that I'd slam the book shut in frustration and lock my guitar up in its case, to be ignored for the next few weeks. Still, the IAP had *some* effect, as I eventually played the guitar for my living.

Wormholes

And here's where the concept of Wormholes comes in. Wormholes, as I define them, are these little breaks of opportunity in my great wall of resistance. They're the moments when I feel like maybe, if the circumstances were just right, I might possibly be talked into:

- Giving up bananas (they are SO not local)
- Organizing my office
- Writing a new song
- Doing more than just my one sun salutation in the morning

- Doing more than just 2 miles in my morning run
- Doing whatever totally heinous chore has been on my
  To Do list since two years ago Christmas (Today it's
  finding a new stylus for our aged turntable; last week
  it was filling out copyright forms to register the songs
  on our new CD)

Now, if I take advantage of these miraculous wormholes, the impossible not only can happen, but usually does with remarkable ease, especially if I have a little grace and humility about it. I resist playing the guitar until I stop telling myself I'm *supposed* to be playing the guitar. Then, usually, I want to play it. I go through phases with it, and today I know that about myself. Some years I practice diligently, with love and great enthusiasm and creativity. Other years, I coast along. Even though I have made my living as a singer-songwriter who plays the guitar, I know I will never be a virtuoso. What I *have* done is evolved my own style, and today it's good enough for me. And I got that style from a certain amount of "just doing it," as a certain shoe company would say. Just showing up and gritting my teeth and pushing that Sloth to play scales and figure out songs. On the most wonderful days, actual enthusiasm would appear in the middle of a practice session, and I know there's nothing I'd rather be doing than just joyfully banging away at my guitar.

Best Trick Beating Resistance

> *"Play till you feel like resting.*
> *Then rest till you feel like playing."*
>
> —*Martha Beck*

When I have a lot to do and I don't feel like doing anything, I make a deal with myself. I say, "Okay, then: do nothing. But *really* do nothing."

Doing nothing involves reclining on my couch and staring into space. I do not get to talk on the phone, read, check my email, or sleep. On the other hand, I do not have to meditate, count my breaths or practice any kind of spiritual discipline whatever. All I do is space out. Somehow, this always relaxes and refreshes me, and before too long, my spinning mind has a million things it wants my body to do. I jump up and start accomplishing all the tasks I was fixing to resist[6].

Perfectionism is the Enemy

So when I look back on my "goals" list, my IAP sees all the things I haven't done and won't ever do. (Not going to be the next Beatles. I am clear on that. Don't think Harvard Div's in my future either, but that's another story.) My IAP can sometimes be quite disappointed. But the truth is, I played the guitar well enough to make a career that has sustained me emotionally and financially and artistically for the past 22 years. Instead of becoming the next Beatles, I have this fantastic patchwork life: a manageable, wonderful music career, and a life as a freelance teacher of writing, music and life. I get to write books, go to my kids' assemblies, and have date night with my husband once a week.

Like the person who really wanted to be a gardener in Ogunquit, the Real Me chooses the life I have made over the life I thought I should have when I was 22. This life, as they say, is right-sized. But I am also glad I gave it my all and "went for it."

Twelve Time-Consciousness Suggestions

As severely right-brained as I am, I have somehow become a pretty good time manager. I have about five full-time jobs, play three instruments, run every day and raise two kids. Here's how:

1. Take morning quiet time
2. Make a time map
3. Be loyal to only *one* planner
4. Make To-Do Lists and Checklists
5. Make planner and to-do list play nicely with each other
6. Maximize high energy times
7. Schedule down time and family time
8. Leave space for God/Chance/*Lila*/Sh*t Happens
9. Wisely use small pockets of time
10. Don't kill your TV
11. Do It Now
12. Give Perfectionism the boot

1. Morning Quiet Time

There is something magical about that first hour of the day. Trust me on this, even though you might be a night owl who thinks the day should start at noon. Maybe it should—but even so, take that first half hour or so to greet yourself, remember your priorities and think about the day ahead. This can be done by lying in your bed with your eyes closed, gently sitting up and propping your back on multiple pillows, watching the sky lighten and change. Or you might meet yourself on the couch with a steaming cup of coffee and a journal. You might do a little yoga or go for a walk or a run. But make this time *your* time, and if possible, avoid other people, including those on the other end of your iPhone or computer. Use this time to connect with yourself. Think through the day. What most needs doing? What did you promise someone you'd do? What did you promise yourself you'd do?

Getting clear on priorities is actually the hardest part of time management. For me, it helped to keep a journal (another thing I wanted to do but couldn't--until I took advantage of a wormhole). I read Julia Cameron's *The Artist's Way* and started doing Morning Pages. It was like having a therapy session with myself. The writing was awkward at first, but over time I got to like it. And more importantly, I got to like me. I got to see, over time, what mattered most to me, what I really cared about accomplishing during my time on earth. Over and over, I'd ask myself "what do I want?" Over and over, I'd see: a family. A soul mate. A writing career. A singing career. A community of friends. A community to serve. Health. Work that Matters.

2. Make a Time Map

Conversely, to find out what doesn't matter, do this exercise: make a graph of a week and systematically write down exactly how you spend your waking hours (and how much you sleep, for that matter). Don't try to edit your actions. *Honesty is key here.* If you spend 14 hours a week watching TV, write it down. At the end of the week, see how much time you actually spent working, exercising, emailing, Facebooking (who knew that word would become a gerund? Sorry about that). See where your "lost" time is. With this knowledge, you can move forward and make the changes necessary to do the activities you really want to be doing. When I do my weekly

Time Map, I can see graphically where I am putting the time in to fulfill my commitment to my priorities (family, soulmate, friends, singing, writing, health etc.)

3. Find just one planner and get married to it.

Julie Morgenstern, author of *Time Management from the Inside Out* strongly suggests choosing just one, and I couldn't agree more. It's when I write the kids' friends' birthday parties down on my wall calendar and neglect to put it on iCal that I get into trouble by double booking myself at a reading in Brookline. Keep all dates and to do lists in one place.

4. To Do Lists and Checklists

I loves me a To-Do list. I scribble them on scrap paper. I have official notebooks for them. I have them on my iPhone, and now they bounce up at me also on my MacBook Pro. When I've done an item, I check them off all devices and go searching for the scrap paper so I can check the item off of there, too. Inspired by my kids' Suzuki teacher, Emily Greene, I have a nightly check in with my Ben-Franklin-Virtue-Charts for weekly resolutions. My resolutions, too, are copied on my iPhone, which is especially funny this week, as one of my resolutions is "Resist iPhone." So this bounces up at me, once a day or so, and I get to check it off, and then go, "D'oh!"

5. Your datebook and your to-do list are like Donnie & Marie.

Apologies to those born after 1977. What I mean by this is that your to-do list is useless if you don't schedule in when you are going to do each to-do. To this end, the first event you need to honor is an hour a week of planning time, and then five minutes a day following that up, with calendar and to-do lists in hand. I look at my week on Sunday night, and I write down what needs to get done and when I am going to do it. I refine this process each morning, going day by day[7]. Inevitably there are surprises: my manager will email me to remind me that I need to send out a newsletter to our fans, and then my two hours to write my novel or find my summer clothes in the attic is postponed. I go through phases where housekeeping is more important, and phases where it takes the back seat. Ditto the amount of time I spend trying to look presentable. But I always make time for family, exercise, writing, music and reflection. In fact, there usually ends up little time for anything else. Oh, well. Time mapping can be a sobering endeavor.

6. Maximize Your High-Energy Time Zones.

You might already know when in the day you have the most energy. Then again, you might regulate yourself by dosing up with caffeine and vodka. This might work for now while your body is at its vigorous peak, but sooner or later your circadian rhythms will take over, and at this point it will be very helpful to (in unison, please): Know yourself.

One miserable summer between sophomore and junior year, I decided I might as well sleep between 1-6, whether a.m. or p.m. I seemed to thrive from sunrise to about lunch, and then wilt until dinnertime, get a second wind, and then crash after midnight. Undaunted, I just drank some more caffeine.

Later, I solved this problem by taking a fifteen-minute power nap at about 12:30.p.m. And then drinking some caffeine. But I still tend not to schedule anything very important during what I think of as my low energy zones: 11-1 p.m. and after 9 p.m. (though if we have a gig, I am usually still onstage at 9 p.m. This is kind of too bad. Caffeine has its limits).

I do notice that my energy is highest when I first get up. (I recognize that this is not true for everyone). So I like to use this high-energy time to do something I might not have the wherewithal to do later. In the beginning, I chose to journal every day first thing. Later, this switched to meditation and exercise. After many years, I know that I write best in the morning and evening, and that midday is a great time to read or watch a portion of a video. My appetite peaks at 7 a.m., 11:30 a.m. and 5p.m., so that's when I eat. I used to eat dinner at 7pm when my parents always ate, but this meant I was "dalling down" (my daughter's phrase for starving to death) and snacked like crazy in the late afternoon. Now I just cut to the chase and serve everyone dinner at 5:30 p.m. It seems almost boorish to eat so early, but actually, once one has small children, 5:30 is a reasonable meal time.

Notice your own high and low energy zones. Eat when you're hungry, rest when you're tired. Don't hitch your rhythms to anyone else's and see what comes naturally.

7. Schedule Down Time and Family Time or Risk Burnout and Fallout. And Possibly Divorce.
You need to rest. Sarasponda—the pulsation at the heart of the universe—is a basic principle. Working all the time is like trying to make a body breath through only inhalation. So even though you *can* work 80 hours per week, don't do it. Although this is exactly what I did during my twenties, and I refused to listen to those who told me to rest more and take more vacations, so I understand if you choose to ignore me. Still, you heard it here.

8. Leave Space for God/Chance/*Lila*/Sh*t Happens.
Whenever I schedule myself to the minute, I get tripped up. I am not running the show. If I don't give myself big margins in between the things I want to do, nothing in my life seems to work. I have a strong sense that God wants me to help out. So I leave space to make phone calls, take phone calls, make a meal for a friend in need, pick up someone's kid for a play date (and this means leaving space and margins in my kids' schedules), have an impromptu date with my husband, veer off course. *Lila*, by the way, is a Sanskrit term meaning "Divine Play." It's the concept we're talking about here: stuff happens. Good stuff, bad stuff, but all sorts of stuff happens that has nothing to do with you, your karma, your good or bad efforts or your date planner. You can't control everything. If you try, the Universe might make you its divine plaything. Not only that, the very best breadcrumbs have come in the margins. That's inevitably where inspiration strikes.

9. Wisely Use Small Pockets of Time.
For things I don't like to do, I work well in tiny increments, say fifteen minutes or less. Any more makes me anxious. So I trick myself by saying, "I don't feel like cleaning up the dishes right now, but I'll just do it for five minutes." Then I set the timer and go. Usually, if/when the timer goes off, I ignore it because by then I am immersed in my task, it's almost done and I have a rage to finish it. Here are some things I can do in small pockets/packets of time, of 5-15 minutes:

-make one phone call
-meditate
-run around the park

-ablutions
-dishes
-my kids' violin practice (30 minutes, though I trick us all
     by saying "short practice today")
-guitar or bass practice
-check in with husband on the couch (never long enough)
-"reading" audiobook on iPhone (every chance I get,
     especially while cleaning or running)
-yoga (5-7 minutes are enough for one sun salutation or
     the stomach series in Pilates)
-journaling (Dar Williams gave me a Five Year Journal
     five years ago. It's the best. I can only write about 1"
     by 2" worth of text per day. But over time, I can look
     back and see what I was doing the previous year(s). I
     used to write three pages of long hand every day. Not
     so much since having kids.)
-write a part of a scene or a verse of a song

10. Don't Kill Your TV

That's what I did. Yes, I'm way more productive, but I miss out on all the cool shows. I am hopelessly behind on *Downton Abbey*, and I have never even seen *Mad Men*. When I used to watch TV, I would multitask. I would knit and mend clothes and sew on buttons, or I'd prepare a mailing. Since I don't have TV, I don't have any pockets of time to do these sorts of tasks, and so I don't do them at all. Plus, there's something really great about watching a show with your honey. Then again, there's something really great about actually *talking* to your honey, which is what I get to do.

I'm being a bit facetious, of course; and partly I am reacting from having just read Laura Vanderkam's awesome book *168 Hours: You Have More Time Than You Think*[8] in which she makes many good arguments for killing one's TV. I did stop watching TV, about ten years ago, and I don't miss it (that much). Vanderkam's book is excellent at showing how to minimize wasted time, and she defines wasted time as driving around to do errands, cleaning up one's house, making meals, doing laundry. She says that if you can afford to, offload all these chores onto someone else. But I'd argue that some of these tasks can become "found" time, the way I used to "find" time to do my knitting while I watched TV. Here is what I do while simultaneously doing housework, including laundry.

-listen to an audiobook like Laura Vanderkam's
-listen to music or a podcast or the radio
-catch up with myself
-think about a song idea or plot for a novel
-cultivate mindfulness
-talk to my husband or child
-make a phone call
-plan my week

11. Do It Now.

My parents taught Katryna and me this major life lesson when we were wee lassies. They had it embossed on some Scotch glasses (naturally), and I must say, they modeled that behavior pretty darn well. The idea behind Do It Now is that you are and you will be busy. So busy that if you don't do it now ("it" being, let's say, a bill from the phone company, and "do" being "pay it"), it will become an annoying piece of paper in your inbox whose little burst of energy has been lost. It won't get paid on time, and you will end up paying a penalty. Same with answering email: if I read the email and don't respond right away, I inevitably lose a bit of my enthusiasm for the response. (Though sometimes, if the email invokes a too-strong response from me, it's probably better for me not to do it now.)

Whenever you get the idea to do something worthy, at least *consider* doing it now. This works really well if you're in the kitchen and have just finished a meal and there's not a lot else going on and you remember that you need to call the plumber to fix your toilet. It doesn't work so well if you're in bed with your lover and you suddenly think about alphabetizing your books.

The other big time management life lesson my parents taught is "you'll feel really good about yourself if you do what you're supposed to do when you said you would do it." Of course, this might come under the category of "brainwashing," but it was an effective way to internalize a strong parental directive.

One caveat: I am especially keen to organize my systems—RIGHT NOW—when I have a project due, especially a book. If I am supposed to be writing, I suddenly become very interested in organizing my spice rack and sorting through my children's clothes. The creative part of one's brain feels safer when it's in a structured environment. I have no idea if this is true, but I do know that every writer I've met agrees that they feel compelled to clean house before they sit down to write. It seems the very act of cleaning and sorting gives the brain a burst of serotonin and energy. After de-cluttering, I write like a fiend, have fantastic conversations, and am prone to do spontaneous handstands.

12. Give Perfectionism the Boot.

Perfectionism, says Anne Lamott, is the enemy of the people. It's a sad, evil lie, the single worst foe of all creative types. Perfectionism is the Devil incarnate. Perfectionism whispers to us, "This is your one and only chance. Don't blow it." And then we're stymied. God tells us, "I've got your back. Go for it. You'll learn from your mistakes. There are no wrong turns, as long as you follow the dictates of your heart and stay honest." Katryna said to me the other day that she thinks my biggest gift is that I don't let the perfect be the enemy of the good. (Voltaire said this.) This is true. I would rather get something done—anything done—than have it dangle indefinitely. Hence, this book in all its roughshod, imperfect, self-published glory.

Body

You will never again in your life be so young. But you can live very long and happily in that body of yours if you take care of it. Here are some basic bits of information on maximizing your physical health.

Exercise

This chapter is not aimed at those of you who are varsity track racers, tri-athletes or climbers of Mt. Kilimanjaro. This is not aimed at those of you who go out dancing for three hours every night and wake up ready to do half an hour of crunches. This is for those of you who don't remember the last time you tied sneakers onto your feet.

It's true what everyone says. You should exercise. Every day, if possible. Why? Here are some reasons.

1. You'll feel better. Exercise releases endorphins and serotonins in the brain that literally act as antidepressants. Studies show 45 minutes of daily exercise to be as effective as 45 mg of Zoloft.

2. You'll look better. Or at least more muscular and fit and trim, if that is the look you are aiming for. If you think you look better a bit zaftig—which people did about a hundred years ago—then ignore this reason. And seriously, you might want to consider ignoring this reason. We live in a particularly Buff Is Beautiful kind of era and it's just a matter of aesthetics that the zeitgeist is hovering around the look of Cameron Diaz instead of Camryn Manheim. You really can buck the system and stay round, and I would encourage you to, except there are other good reasons to exercise.

3. It's good for your heart, which is a muscle that likes to be exercised and does better when its owner makes it beat a little faster once a day. (Note: it actually

increases your chances of heart attacks to exercise on
an extreme level.)

4. It's good for your brain. Scientists are now saying
that exercise can help stroke patients recover faster
and more completely. It's even said to stave off
Alzheimer's and dementia. I always
get good creative ideas when I am
running or walking.

5. It's good for your bones. Women
who lift weights and do moderate
aerobics have lower levels of osteoporosis.

6. It's good for your digestion. People
who exercise have fewer problems with constipation.

7. You will sleep better at night.

8. It will increase your energy.

Basically, people are supposed to move around and lift things
every day. That's how we evolved. Even though in about a million years (if the human race is still around by then) we may have
evolved into creatures with really strong digits and huge brains and
tiny useless legs and abdominals, for now we are stuck with the machinery we've inherited, and that machinery likes to be exercised,
creaky joints and stiff necks notwithstanding.

Enough! you say. I am convinced. But what kind of exercise
do I have to do?

Three kinds: aerobic, anaerobic and stretching. But don't put
this book down and take off to join a gym just yet.

The most important attribute your plan should have
is likability. In other words, if you think it would be good
for you to take up cross-country skiing because your boyfriend likes to ski—only the thought of getting up at 6
a.m., bundling up against the winter in Gore-Tex and wool
socks, and fitting your feet into those annoying boots with
the infernal hooks which only sometime click onto the skis
leaves you wanting to curl up and go back to bed, then
don't choose skiing as your form of exercise. Choose something you
would be drawn to anyway. Maybe you'd prefer a team sport like
basketball or softball, or dancing with a group of people. My friend

Ruth loves to contra dance and she met her fiancé Paul that way (two birds, one stone). Walking is an easy and ever-available option. There's also ballet, boxing, biking, kayaking, rollerblading. Do you have the money to join a gym? This can be a great way to meet people, if you are the social type. Or maybe plan running dates or walking dates with friends. Or if you are more of an introvert, choose something solitary. Get an iPod and download some audiobooks and  give yourself a 45 minute break with a novel you've been wanting to read. Get yourself into a routine. If the social thing works, make dates with people; that way, when that sudden feeling that your feet weigh two hundred pounds hits you right before you're supposed to hit the road (or gym or yoga studio), you'll have a harder time backing out.

Consider biking to work. Get in shape, save money, and save the planet, all in one bold life change.

Ideally, every day you would do some aerobic exercise, some kind of muscle building exercise (anaerobic), and some kind of stretching. Again, self-knowledge is the key here. Are you drawn to yoga? Yoga professes to be the "yoking" of body and mind, but honestly, all athletics and exercise can be this way, given the right mindset. And getting your body and mind in sync is one of the greatest pleasures life has to offer. This isn't a *"How to Be an Adult"* issue, though, it's a "how to remember the right things you did as a child" issue. Children instinctively know that it's pleasant and necessary to move their bodies and shake their booties. As we age, many people get sedentary and tired and generally uninterested in their bodies until, that is, the body stops working the way it's supposed to. So pick a sport or activity and at least part of the time, give your mind as well as your body to the activity. Be with yourself.

But back to yoga, if the real thing is what you're after. There are many branches of yoga available to the western consumer, some geared toward strengthening, some more about stretching and relaxing, some purely spiritual. And yoga studios are a good place to meet people. They're so pretty and pleasant, and you can either go with the frank desire to check other people out in stretchy clingy clothes or you can pretend to rise above it all and transcend the physical experience. I personally love yoga and think it essential to my well-being. I found a studio that is just right—not too mellow, not too extreme, and I don't leave with my clothes soaking wet. When I leave, I feel that I've been challenged, stretched and relaxed.

Maybe pumping iron is more your style. For this, you will probably have to join a gym, but fees are cheap at YMCAs, which tend to have fairly good equipment. I personally love to go to my Pilates studio[9] with my iPod and listen to a book on mp3 as I go through the circuit of Pilates machines, which resemble nothing so much as medieval torture devices, but which feel wonderful on my body. Pilates combines strengthening with stretching in a very efficient way.

There are also good old calisthenics, which you can do for free with just a few feet of carpeted space in your own apartment. Buy a couple of dumbbells and a pair of those ankle weights, and read some ridiculous articles about how to firm your abs in thirty days or trim your thighs by bikini season and take the time to learn the exercises in them. Voila! Instant gym in your own home for under twenty bucks.

Speaking of instant gym, I noticed after I bought my house that just doing yard work and gardening was practically the equivalent of having my own gym. Add a couple of cartwheels to leaf raking and you're there. Now that I have children old enough to be left alone in the house (but too young still for me to leave the property) I have been known to jog 40 times around my house when I am desperate for exercise.

I am not at all—and never have been—a fan of boxing, karate, tae kwon do, wrestling, fencing, jousting, polo—basically anything that involves two or more people at odds with each other. I like situations where one person is wrestling with inner demons. Or where big groups of people are having a really great time saving the earth or playing in a rock band. Even so, I was kind of obsessed with fitness in my late twenties. This was during the years in which my band was on the road 340 days a year, and something about the daily routine of running first thing in the morning was grounding and comforting. I might be in Des Moines one day and Chicago the next, but it was the same running shoes, running parka and jog bra every morning. I ran for a half hour to an hour every day, and I can vouch for the purported "runner's high." I felt exceedingly powerful and strong as I covered my miles in all the strange cities, even if I was just running along the access roads near the Comfort Inns and Motel 6s of this fine continent, noticing the difference between the spongy Iowa ground and the dry Arizona dirt. But there were also the runs in Stanley Park in Vancouver, in Blue Hill Maine, up Blueberry Mountain on a perfect August day, the run around Cold Spring Harbor, New York in July, along the Red River in Winnipeg in early October. Not to mention that, trapped as I normally was in the van, long distance training allowed me to trot on over to the grocery store and get whatever I needed for the day and be back for load-out of the hotel by 10 a.m. Running came to equal freedom. And therefore fitness came to equal freedom.

Conversely, I now know that lack of fitness equals a kind of slavery. In 1997, when we were on tour constantly, we were in Charleston, South Carolina at a club called the Music Farm. It was completely pitch black and there was a lot of equipment on the periphery of the stage. I put my foot where there was no stage and fell about four feet. I knew instantly I'd broken something, and the visit to the emergency room confirmed this (after I'd played our show standing on one foot).

The stage

I got a cast and was told to stay off my foot for eight weeks. Eight weeks! An eternity! I got so stir crazy (and was just slightly eating disordered at the time) that I took to daily forty-five minute sessions of "crutching" as fast as I could, sometimes losing my balance on the February ice and stepping down hard again on the injured foot. (Life lesson: when you've broken a bone, it's really a bad idea to walk on it. It heals when it heals.)

While I was pregnant, I preferred the more leisurely pace of a half-hour morning walk through the park across the street from my house. I brought my cell phone and made phone calls to all the people I wanted to catch up with. Now I jog around my neighborhood and spy on the gardens, dodge the dogs, nod to the cats, try to be Zen and wordless and instead plot my plots. And after a decade of paying lip service to stretching (doing the quick twenty-second quad and hamstring stretch after my hour-long run), I am now a convert. Stretching just plain feels good, and though it may just be because I am old now and need it a whole lot more, I make time for stretching at the end of my workouts. Stretching[10] is a controversial subject these days, but I find empirically that if I do stretch, I feel good all day, and if I go for my run and skip my stretches, I feel tight and cranky. I'm also a believer in stretching for its own sake.

1. You may injure yourself sooner or later if you don't maintain a supple body. Stretching leads to supple.
2. Vanity. If you don't, your muscles will be all bunchy and short and knotty looking like the evil apple trees in the Wizard of Oz.
3. It's a great metaphor. Limber and flexible people are a lot more pleasant than uptight, I-don't-have-time-for-stretching types of people.
4. Your sex life will improve. Enough said.

Skin Care

> *Eye cream: the big deal is wrinkles! I spent my early twenties*
> *generally trying to dry out my face, but the key is actually to*
> *moisturize. The skin by the eyes is particularly delicate and*
> *prone to wrinkles, and you're supposed to apply the eye cream*
> *with your ring finger so you don't unnecessarily pull/tug it*
> *and make things worse. At twenty-two you may not care about*
> *people thinking you're ten years younger, but when you're 36*
> *it's awesome.*
>
> —*Tracie Potochnik, 36*

I have added this for the 2013 edition of this book, because so many of my readers suggested that taking care of one's skin in one's youth was of vital importance, and they wanted to make sure I passed this on to you. Of course, they are in their thirties now, these particular readers, and they are just beginning to notice the tiny lines around their eyes and mouth, and they have the mistaken belief that if they had only applied moisturizer rigorously from age sixteen onward, these lines today would not exist. Not so much. Once you get to be my advanced age (45 at the moment) you get that there's an inevitability to wrinkles, and your only hope really is to make peace with them. So save your money on the expensive eye cream, but I'm going to argue that you go ahead and slather your face and body with moisturizer anyway.

Attending to one's body is a radical act of self-love, as important as all the inner work I suggest later in the "Soul" portion of this book. Ayurveda, an ancient Indian practice that has gained popularity in recent times, has a practice called abhyanga, which entails giving oneself a massage with regular old vegetable oil first thing in the morning. When I first heard about this practice, I thought it was ridiculous. Who has time for this? Who wants to get greasy first thing in the morning? Before the shower? Waste of oil! After the shower? Are you kidding me? Then I'll have grease stains on my clothes!

But then again, who has time for any kind of meditation or profound self-care? No one. And yet when we take care of ourselves, we gain something beyond the actual service. We gain connection. After doing some research and becoming sold on the benefits of

ِ, it occurred to me that spending five minutes lovingly slath-
 ِ, moisturizer all over your arms, legs and torso could be a very
sweet and deep meditation and a pretty nice way to let yourself
know you…well, you *care*. So I visited my friend Brooksley Williams at our nearby Valley Ayurveda[11], got my doshas diagnosed (I
am a Vata with a touch of Pitta) and left with a bottle of almond oil.
For the past year, I have been giving myself a massage every day,
and I have to say I feel profoundly fabulous. The whole process
takes about a minute, and it feels so good. My skin is soft and tender
and looks glowing and radiant. As I attend to my toes and my lower
back and my elbows and all those places one doesn't regularly com-
mune with, I feel as though I am mothering my own body. And I
always think of the passage in the Bible (Matthew 26: 6-13) where
a woman anoints Jesus with costly oil and the disciples get mad,
saying that oil could have been sold and proceeds could have fed the
poor. The way I read it, Jesus responds by saying, "I'm worth it."
Okay, maybe some would say this is a moment presaging his burial,
but I sense in this scene a definite leaning towards the poetic, the
Now, and the mingling of the sensual and the divine and how one
can find the latter in the corporeal. Rubbing oil into my body feels
like a profound act of self-love, if I do it with awareness and not on
auto-pilot. Same with applying eye-cream. (See "ablutions.")

Even though you might now have oily skin, put on moisturizer
every morning. Believe it or not, part of the reason your skin is oily
is because it's trying to overcompensate for dryness. Keeping your
skin soft and supple now will pay huge dividends in your forties and
fifties. Trust me on this.

Be aware of the damaging effects of too much sun. Truth is,
the jury is out about the safety of sunscreen versus the ill effects
of sun exposure. My best advice today is to stay out of the midday
sun altogether, don't cover yourself with coconut oil and then lie in
the sun, as much as possible wear a hat, and in the winter take your
vitamin D.

Sickness

You are going to get sick. At some point, your body will be run
down and you will be susceptible to the common cold. Scientists
still haven't found a cure for this little bugger, though I am count-

ing on your generation to come up with something better than what we've got now. Some crackpots[12] think that common colds are actually healthy; that they are nature's way of clearing us out (witness the copious mucus and other bodily expulsions). As I write this, I am battling a sinus infection and its accompanying self-pity, and I am trying mightily to see the bright side. But in case you'd like to speed up the process of being cleared out, here are some suggestions:

Wash your hands whenever you come into contact with anything other than yourself. This includes doorknobs, the steering wheel of your car (if you share the driving with someone), your sister, your sister's child's toys, the table at a restaurant; pretty much anything. Yes, you will be washing your hands a lot. Don't bother with the anti-bacterial soap. That just wreaks havoc on the environment and destroys the power of antibiotics when they are actually necessary to save someone's life. When washing your hands, use soap. When opening the door to the bathroom you just used to wash your hands, don't actually touch the door with your just-washed hands. Use a paper towel, or your wrists.

"Cough into the cave," the crook of your arm—if you don't know what I mean by this, find a four-year-old and ask her how to do it. Sleep for ten hours straight.

When you get a cold, the best things you can do for yourself are to rest and drink a lot of water. Go ahead and take some zinc and vitamin C. Do the Lion pose (open your eyes really wide, open your hands so that all the digits are stretching out, stick your tongue out and breath out with a forceful breath, making the sound "haaaaah." Hold for 15 seconds. Do three times). Gargle with salt: Dissolve 1 tsp of salt into 8 oz. very warm water. Take a mouthful in and gargle, counting to thirty in your head. Spit. Repeat until glass is empty. Rest some more. Your body might be telling you that you need a break, so take it, gratefully if you can.

If you go to the doctor and she prescribes antibiotics (which she should only do if there is strong evidence of infection—a positive strep test, ear infection, sinus infection), be sure to take every last pill. Why? Because if you don't, you are strengthening the germs that caused your infection and weakening the power of the antibiotic so that the next time you get sick and need antibiotics, they might not work as well. Moreover, they might not work for your friends, your kids, your nieces and nephews and some kid you don't know on the other side of the globe[13]. Part of being an adult is recognizing that you are one among many, and that your actions have consequences for everyone else on the planet. Taking all your antibiotics is like refraining from tossing your empty soda can out the window of your car.

I hate being sick. And I get sick all the time these days, probably because I have two small children who are in contact with other small children, and because I teach music to kids who are constantly rubbing me with their sweet little hands, fresh from picking their sweet little noses. I wash my hands like a maniac, but I still get sick sometimes. I try to see these passages as opportunities to slow down, turn inward, and do less. And, in the name of practicing gratitude, I give thanks that I don't have lice. I also try to focus on how healthy I actually am, and give thanks for the parts of my body that do not hurt or ache.

Sleep

I learned, shortly after the birth of my second child, that the difference between psychosis and neurosis was just two hours of sleep a night. It's vital to get your ZZZ's! And while it's pure torture for me to put down my reading material at 10 p.m. to try to get my requisite eight hours of sleep (the standard for most people, and empirically for me), I do it because, as with exercising, I love the results. When I get eight hours of sleep, I feel brighter, lighter, more energetic, less addicted to caffeine, more sweet-tempered and optimistic. In short, everything in my life goes better. But sometimes it's not possible to get eight hours.

Insomnia

Something rouses you from your slumber; maybe you have to pee, or perhaps there was a loud noise outside. Maybe you share a bed with someone who snores. (Sorry, don't have any advice on that one.) But for many of you, you will have to deal with those longest hours that come somewhere between 11 p.m. and 7 a.m. Wide awake.

There are different kinds of insomniacs. Some have trouble falling asleep, tossing and turning as soon as they turn out the lights.

This is called sleep-onset insomnia. The other kind—which I've just described—is called "nocturnal awakenings," visiting us in the so-called wee hours. There are all sorts of remedies and suggestions for treatment, everything from getting more exercise, abstaining from alcohol and caffeine, limiting access to TV and technology in general (and the internet in particular), meditating, sleeping with ear plugs and/or eye masks, foot massages, yoga, eating turkey sandwiches, drinking chamomile tea to taking sleep meds. If you are going through a phase of sleeplessness, you will probably try all of these. (My father has memorized *The Baseball Encyclopedia*, and when he has insomnia he goes through the statistics one by one. This makes him pass out in short order. But it seems like an awful lot of preparation to me. Then again, it would make me pass out just to *read The Baseball Encyclopedia*.)

Here is what works for me. When I am awakened, I think about my poor nervous system and all I ask it to do every day. No wonder it's wired! No wonder that it goes "on" in the middle of the night, frothy with concerns and opinions. So what I have learned to do is to say to it, very gently, "My dear, there is nothing to be done about that now. Go to sleep."

Fat chance, right? But at least I've been polite.

The next thing I do is imagine I am standing in front of the thermostat in my dining room. I lift my hand (in my mind's eye) to the controls, and I gently bring the temperature down. The way I really do this is to breathe extremely slowly, so slowly that if you were to clock it, it would be about five inhales and exhales per minute.

Once I've slowed my breathing, which slows the heart rate and activates the parasympathetic nervous system—and this part is the most important—I soften my eyes, imagining them going from being hard-boiled eggs to raw ones. Then I imagine the space between my eyes. (Try this right now—you'll see that this relaxes you immediately.) Why does this work? I think it has something to do with losing the part of me that is predator and becoming more like a prey animal. Predators have their eyes in the very front of their heads (imagine lions and coyotes) where they are very focused on tracking their prey. Prey animals, on the other hand, have their eyes on the sides of their head (sheep, cows). I like to think of cows when I am trying to go to sleep, and of course I would not be at all original if I wrote about counting sheep, but you certainly could do that too. Try imagining yourself as the sheep. (IMPORTANT: do not actually use the word "prey" as you are doing this exercise or you will start to worry about becoming someone's dinner.)

My method is not easy, because the real trick is calming down the mind that is buzzing at 120 miles per second after it's been awakened. Breathing and softening is meditative, and you have to sometimes force your mind to focus on this exercise, yanking it away from its contemplation of your finances and your presentation tomorrow and that thing you shouldn't have said to the cute boy in the office. Keep bringing your attention back to the breath and the softening.

Putting these two practices together has pretty much solved my sleep disorder. Try it for yourself, and if it doesn't work, do whatever it takes to get your sleep. Being well-rested is the basis for all that you do. Or, you could always just look at those wakeful moments as found time and go sort your in-box. (Sometimes I threaten my insomniac self with that chore. That prospect alone can send me back to dreamland.)

> *I read in a sleep-training book for toddlers that if your little one gets out of bed in the middle of the night repeatedly and comes to you, you are to just gently, calmly take their hand and walk them back to bed with as little interaction as possible. Over and over again, as many times as needed, without speaking. With this approach, the toddler is said to get bored and stay in bed. When I wake up in the middle of the night and can't get back to sleep, I do the focusing on my breath thing. And when my racing, wandering thoughts intrude, I am both the mother and the toddler, gently, without judgment or stimulation, walking my straying mind back to the breath, over and over again. Works for me.*
>
> *—Lori, 38*

Naps

If all anti-insomnia methods fail, or if you regularly get less than eight hours of sleep a night, I highly recommend taking a short nap every day right after lunch. Siestas, of course, are a time-honored tradition in southern Europe and the South-of-USA Americas, for good reason. Our energy tends to peak around 10 or 11 a.m., then drops until 4 p.m. North of the Rio Grande, we just dose ourselves up with lattes, but it's probably healthier to take a little rest. Twenty minutes of shut-eye can work miracles, if you can train your body to do this. Even five minutes, if you actually fall asleep, can be like restarting your computer. Even just lying on your back with your eyes closed is helpful!

Ingredients for the perfect nap:

1. Flat place to recline, off the floor if possible, on a couch, bed, or even the bench seat of a car
2. Eye pillow[14]
3. Blanket (your temperature will drop if you fall asleep)
4. Ear plugs
5. Timer set for 20 minutes
6. Phones turned off
7. Mug of tea to drink as soon as you wake up

Soul

This section is about the part of you that you can't see, at least not in the same way that you can see your body. But ramifications of soul-care do become visible. Just look into any adult's eyes, or see how the mouth is formed. You can see pretty quickly from these features how the owner's soul journey has been going. Here are some thoughts about care of the interior.

God

You may as well believe in God. Why? Because if God exists, you certainly want to take advantage of The Eternal One's benevolence, right? And if God doesn't exist, you haven't lost anything. Except maybe the favor of the atheists who might snub you, but even that doesn't have to be—just don't tell them you believe. Make it your and God's little secret. After all, Jesus said to pray in private in a closet and not on the street.

What you might not want to do is sign on hook, line and sinker to an established religion where you run the risk of being excommunicated (kicked out) if you don't toe the line on everything from diet to dress code and hairstyles. (All the major religions are guilty of legislating these at some time or another in their history—apologies if you feel I'm picking on your particular religion.)

Here's what I know about God: I'm not It. Or rather, my ego is not It, and by ego I mean that part of me that gets notions to do things for the purpose of making myself look good, or to make money or feel safe. And yet, the other thing I believe about God is that God dwells inside me, as me, as the famous Hindu teaching goes. That doesn't mean that I always hear the still small voice— sometimes it's a really loud voice, and sometimes it seems to remain annoyingly silent when I need it most.

The Sufi poet Abu Yazid wrote, "For 30 years I sought God until I realized that God was the seeker and I was the sought." How cool is that? God *wants* to be in relationship with us, and God will do almost anything to get our attention. Emerson wrote, "There is a crack in everything God has made,"[15] and Leonard Cohen finishes the sentence: "That's where the light gets in."[16] People in recovery speak of a "God-shaped hole." We're all like puzzles missing one

piece. Nothing but God will fit that space. Not only that, God probably put that defect there just so you would seek God. If you believe
your Hebrew Bible, God is a jealous god and doesn't put up with
rivals. When I put down whatever it is that I think will fill that hole,
and instead ask God to please show up, God always does. I feel God
as a kindness, a presence, a calmness. And somehow, whenever I
ask, God does show up.

The other thing I know about God is that God loves all of us—
all of us, even the murderers and the dictators and the Republicans
(or the Democrats). Even the sex abusers, even the mosquitoes, even
the hypocritical church leaders, even the terrorists, even the second-
grade bullies, the talk-show bullies, the runaway dads, the manipu-
lative mothers, the polluters, the corporate bandits, and the animal
torturers. God might not like what these people do, but God still
loves them.

It's often said that God is Love. I like to think of God as more
verb than noun. If you are stuck on the Old-Man-in-a-Cloud version
of God, try to reframe and think of God as something more abstract,
like Truth, Love, Righteousness, or Good Orderly Direction. Sometimes it helps me to think of God as Presence: something we all can
achieve. Being Here Now, wide awake—this is at least a portal to
the Divine, if not Yo Mama Herself.

I don't believe in a God who answers prayers the way *O* magazine answers letters from readers or the way Senators try to please
their constituents by giving them what they want. I believe God
hears prayers, and that if I am listening carefully and creatively, I
can hear the response. But it's an overcrowded planet, and death and
disease are a part of life. I don't think if we get it just right we get
to escape from the worst of these. I do believe that when we are in
distress, God comes and sits by our side and feels sad right along
with us, and doesn't leave until we kick God out. I also think the
most effective prayer I've ever heard or said is this: "Hi, God. No,
I'm good. Don't need a thing, because I know you are taking care of
it all. How can I be helpful to you?" Try it sometime. You might be
surprised by how much stronger and more helpful you feel. It turns
out, God doesn't care that much about what we accomplish. God's
much more impressed by how we treat other people.

Sometimes in my more agnostic moments, I think of God as simply What Is. The ancient Hebrews called God "The Great I Am." If God is the river that flows from North to South, you can choose to fight God by swimming upstream, but you'll just exhaust yourself and not get to where you want to go on time. This (basically Taoist) idea appeals to me, but I also believe in the God who frees slaves— and how can you go with the flow and fight the powers that be at the same time?

People in recovery talk about being a slave to whatever it is they're addicted to. I was certainly a slave to my notions of thinness and success and fame. I defined them the way *Us* magazine defined them: have a BMI of 18, sell a lot of CDs and get good reviews, and have everyone know who you are and like and respect you to boot. It seemed like a pretty straightforward plan, and in my twenties I pursued this vision of myself with every dram of my power and talents. But whenever you try to get your self-worth from other people, you are doomed. Why? Because people are only interested in other people for a few minutes. Most of us are really self-centered and have short attention spans. After a few years, the new girl with a BMI of 18 knocks Jennifer Aniston off the block and now Jen has to stay thin *and* not be *People's* Number One Sexiest Woman of the Year. Your first record sells well, and the next gets panned, or maybe it gets praised and even so it only sells a third as many as the first one. No one sits at the top of the mountain forever. Sooner or later, the most successful person has to deal with disappointment, and for some of us, disappointment is an intolerable feeling.

God can help with this the way a really great friend can help with this. God's got a really long view, and if you try to see the situation through God's eyes instead of your own squinty ones, you might feel less disappointed and you will certainly feel less alone.

Organized Religion

Some religions are more organized than others. Some religions require more discipline and authority than others, and some require less. This is because there are some *people* who require more discipline and authority, while others require less. Try to be patient with yourself and other people. My friend

Ken Talan[17] came up with a great analogy: It's as though emotionally each of us is either a vertebrate or an invertebrate, and we're all walking around the world seemingly normal. But the vertebrates look at the invertebrates and wonder, "Why do they need that ridiculous exterior structure? Don't they have a backbone?" The answer is: maybe not. Whereas the invertebrates look at the vertebrates and think, "How are those people standing up at *all*?"

The important thing to remember is that everyone has a religion. Even if we are atheists, we believe in something, and surely will love something, some principle or idea that is bigger than ourselves, with all our hearts. The essence of religion is a system of beliefs and values by which we explain the universe and its inhabitants to ourselves and to those we want to convert. So the question isn't whether you have a religion, it's how you practice it.

Many people have an idea that religion is connected to an institution, like a church or synagogue or mosque; or a set of beliefs; or a book like the Bible or the Koran or the Bhagavad Gita. But some of the most dedicated, ideological, reverent and disciplined people I know are actually vague agnostics. Their religion is a kind of Leftist political crusade, a love of the world and a deep desire to change it for the better, to give to their great-grandchildren a world that is as good as or better than the one we're living in today. They tithe to the Sierra Club or to Occupy Wall Street, or to the Green Party. They get up early not to pray but to compost. Their hymns are "We Shall Overcome" and "It's the End of the World As We Know It."

Capitalism is a religion, too, and there are many devoted capitalists who truly believe that a free market is a divine mechanism for bettering the world and that morality is connected to wealth; the devil is in regulation. Music is a religion to many of the musicians I worked with over the years; practicing scales becomes their meditation, studying the greats their exegesis. Anything becomes a religion when a person loves it and believes it has the power to help the individual transcend his or her circumstances and the power to heal and enlighten: film criticism, exercise, astrology, mathematics, environmentalism, psychotherapy, science, the law, video games, alcohol, caffeine, your career, your new girlfriend, your parents, your children—the list is endless. People are built to believe in and (maybe even) worship something greater than themselves. There's a term for those who don't: *narcissist*. Or worse, *psychopath*. There

doesn't need to be a God figure in your religion, though if you look closely enough, you can often see one. As the great religions of old have taught us, we make God in our own image, so it is not surprising that Noam Chomsky is a god to the Left, just as Thelonius Monk is a god to jazz aficionados and Antonin Scalia is a god to those on the Right.

Many of you already belong to a specific religion. If this is the case, may I suggest that one of the first things you do when you've moved into your new town is to check out the churches, synagogues, mosques, Buddhist or Hindu temples, Gurdjieff foundation, yoga kulas, and see if you can find one you like. You will meet lots of people and have all sorts of opportunities to get involved with the inner and outer community.

Many people in their twenties are not particularly interested in organized religion. Saturdays and Sundays are meant for sleeping late or catching up on much needed "me" time, or for spending with friends and lovers, a good book or sports team. I for one had no interest in spending my Sunday morning at church. It wouldn't have mattered if I had, because I was usually out of town on Saturday night playing a gig, and Sunday morning found me in the car or van making the trip back home. But I did experience yearnings toward spirituality after I turned twenty-eight. I have a theory that in this day and age, those of us who are not plugged into a traditional form of organized religion replace what we get from the church, synagogue, mosque and temple with some other place and set of values.

Therapy

I truly believe that therapy is the new religion for a lot of the urban elite (and by "elite" I mean anyone making over $35,000 a year). People use their therapist as confessor, certainly, but they also use him or her as a kind of guru or guide, an elder from whom to derive wisdom and to trust with their souls. And the poor therapists, like the clergy before them, have to deal with being put up on pedestals and seen as wise, untainted, kindly advisors with no agenda of their own other than bringing the words of God (disguised as Freud, Jung, Adler, or whomever) to the broken and needy disciples. No wonder preachers' kids and therapists' kids often have such a tough time; when you're entrusted with the improvement of people's souls, it's kind of hard to be a regular mom or dad who roots outrageously and embarrassingly for their kid at a soccer game or a school play.

I'm a big believer in therapy, but only if the patient goes in knowing the limits and promises of the experience. Therapy is only as good as the patient's honesty and forthrightness and willingness to grow and change. Therapy, as I understand it, is a chance to revisit your past, share the horror stories with a competent, trustworthy individual, and then (and this is the key) re-enact the "traumas" and issues of the past *with* that therapist. In other words, one must be brave enough to have a relationship with the therapist. And a relationship is about resolving conflict and expressing love, maintaining boundaries while occasionally pushing the envelope.

The theory goes like this: we got screwed up by our parents and brothers and sisters and teachers, and these rotten role models left us deficient in some way in terms of being able to have fulfilling intimate relationships with others now that we are adults. Once we identify—with the help and insights of the therapist—the ways in which we were poorly guided, we can begin to practice healthy behaviors *with our therapist*. It's sort of like a miniature playground where we get a second chance, this time with a qualified professional and not Billy the Playground Bully.

The problem is, sometimes this process goes wrong. Sometimes therapists are dealing with weird issues themselves; they haven't worked through their own background issues sufficiently; they have what's called counter-transference. Transference is when you "transfer" your feelings about your father and/or mother to your therapist; this is good and part of the process, but not good if you do it with your lover or your boss. Counter-transference is when the therapist transfers *their* issues about their parents, lovers and bosses onto the patient. The therapist's job is to stay very centered and grounded, aware and conscious. But that's easier said than done. When a therapist starts calling you at home with ideas about your healing journey and questions about that risotto recipe you mentioned in session, you know you have a problem.

Mostly though, therapy helps, even if you have a mediocre therapist, because the act of talking and telling your stories is a powerful one for healing. Humans have a deep-seated need to talk and express themselves, and they will do it anyway, even if they don't have a therapist; the trouble is, if there is no healthy outlet for talking about our problems, we will begin to spill them out of ourselves in all sorts of harmful and colorful ways: self-mutilation, abuse, overeating, overspending, overdependence on an individual, working too hard at our jobs, playing video games for hours a day, abusing drugs or alcohol or gambling. To name a few.

Addictions

Which brings us to addictions. An addiction is when you give yourself habitually or compulsively to a substance, behavior, or even a person. It's a spiritual hunger gone awry. It's trying to find peace, happiness and/or an end to our pain through something "out there" as opposed to within; another way of saying this is that we're seeking ourselves in something or someone else.

We live in a particularly addictive culture, and many believe it's a direct result of the busyness of our daily lives. Others think the busyness is a reaction to the pain we are trying to avoid, and thus another addiction. Addiction is about unwillingness to feel pain and discomfort, avoidance at all costs. Because we are a wealthy society, we are in large measure successful in our endeavors to avoid pain and discomfort. You would think the fact that we tend to get through life with a lot less physical pain than our ancestors did would allow us to accept the inevitable pain more graciously, but it doesn't. Instead, we just work harder at developing more ways to try to avoid it.

Recently I looked up from my iPhone and caught a glimpse of all the other adults surrounding me. I was at an airport, and the vision suddenly struck me as very 1960—everyone had a cigarette in his or her hand, except instead of a ciggie it was a smartphone.

We've all become addicted to that quick hit we get from checking Facebook, our Twitter feed, our email, our messages, or whatever new thing it is that consumes our attention and feeds our self worth when this edition comes out. We are the wealthiest society in the history of the world. So what is it we're so eager to escape?

If you suspect you are addicted to something, someone, or a behavior, one of the most successful methods of dealing with these problems can be found in church basements around the country. Twelve-Step groups are fellowships of individuals who recognize a powerlessness over an addiction or behavior, and through a kind of behavior-modification program, peer pressure, support from each other, and trust and reliance on a Higher Power, learn to live without the substance or behavior. In the best of these groups there is camaraderie, deep friendship and real recovery. But again, as with therapy, the cure is only as good as the sincerity with which the seeker approaches it.

Impression Management

I know I'm going into a state of anxiety when I catch myself engaging in what I call Impression Management. This is when I duck into a restroom to apply lipstick, or start obsessing about fitting into the jeans I wore when I was fourteen, or catching myself wanting to mention that I went to an Ivy League school, or name drop some pop star I met back in the day. And not Kevin Bacon, Natalie Merchant, Dar Williams, or James Taylor either. Nope, when I am feeling particularly insecure, it's Bonnie Raitt's name I want to drop. In fact, when I am particularly fixated on concerns about my future, which is, after all what anxiety is, I start to mention Bonnie Raitt at every turn. Did you know Bonnie Raitt had the same birthday as my ex-husband? And that I met her? It was at a party where shrimp was served, and sometimes, when I'm anxious, I mention Bonnie Raitt whenever I see shrimp. Or sometimes I'll invite people over and serve shrimp just so I can mention Bonnie Raitt.

Since I know you are DYING to know, here's the story of how we met Bonnie Raitt. We were at a Grammy party at Tavern on the Green in New York City. Our record company president (RCP) Steve Murphy was on a mission to introduce us, his newly signed band, to all the celebrities at the event.

ME

(to RCP) There's Bonnie Raitt! She'd be a good celebrity for us to meet! I love her!

RCP

Uh, sure. I sort of know her.

DAVID

Oh, my God! She and I have the same birthday, did you know that?

RCP

Excuse me, excuse me, Ms. Raitt?
(Bonnie Raitt keeps her back to him; in fact, if anything, edges farther away. Our record company's publicist sidles over.)

PUBLICIST

(*sotto voce*) Steve! It's your cigar! Put it out and she'll turn around!

RCP

(puts out his cigar): Ms. Raitt...(she turns and smiles graciously). I'm Steve Murphy from Angel Records? And I just want to introduce you to some members of a band we recently signed.

BONNIE RAITT

Oh. (smiles more). How do you do?

DAVID

You are shorter than I expected!

ME

(pointing to David) He has the same birthday as you!

DAVID

(nods eagerly)

BONNIE RAITT

(smile has hardened) Oh, is that right?
(We all look kind of blank and BR wanders off towards the shrimp. Michael Stipe saunters by. We poke Steve and each other. Our manager Patty comes over squealing.)

PATTY

I just met Bernadette Peters! My life is complete!

RCP

Hey, there's Kevin Bacon! Will you guys introduce me?

Anxiety and Somatic Experiencing

Anxiety. As in, "we live in the age of." Everyone knows this is a stressful time to be an adult. As a matter of fact, there has never been so stressful a time to be a child, either. So you, now, are seasoned stress muffins. Have you heard of "boiling frog syndrome"? If you drop a frog in a beaker of hot water, he will immediately jump out, so as not to experience the pain of boiling water. But if you put him in a lukewarm beaker and then place the beaker over a hot flame, he will languish with half-closed dreamy-looking eyes (at least the frog in *An Inconvenient Truth* did) until he boils to death. That's kind of like the level of stress we all live with now.

Many teens I know get up at the crack of dawn, bust ass at school, spend their afternoon doing enriching extracurricular activities, eat dinner in a hurry, blast through homework, and spend as much of their in-between time as possible trying to keep up with their friends via text messages, Tweets and Facebooking, and even the good old-fashioned telephone.

No wonder approximately four million Americans are on some form of anti-anxiety medicine.[18]

There are other ways of dealing with anxiety. Most have to do with being in the Present Moment. Anxiety, put simply, is fear about the future. We get tense and nervous about the presentation we have to do tomorrow or about the date with the guy who could be the One, or about climate change, or about whether Bonnie Raitt remembers our name. But Bonnie Raitt isn't here right now (unless you are her best friend and you happen to be reading this. More likely, Bonnie Raitt's best friend—whom I did *not* meet—is an actual adult and has no need for this book). Tomorrow and its presentations, commitments, and even its fluctuating temperatures are not here. We are probably just fine right now, but no one would know it from the way we are fidgeting and perspiring.

The best way I have found to leave the future and return to the present involves getting into my body again. Try this as an experiment: sit still and do nothing for ten minutes. Just focus on your body. (Almost no one can do this.) After a minute or so, you will probably start to get agitated, irritated, annoyed, and feel the urge to jump up and water your plants or surf the Internet.

In a process called Somatic Experiencing[19], here's how I calm down when I find myself obsessively planning my seven-year-old daughter's wedding or how I'm going to deal with her potential future desire to get a tattoo (will show her photos of women who tattooed their abdomens and then got pregnant):

1. Sit still with your eyes closed. Notice your breathing, notice how your body *feels*—are there aches and pains? Hunger? Thirst? Now notice your emotional body. Do you feel happy? Sad? Angry? Afraid? (Those are the Big Four emotions. Most other so-called emotions are really versions of these titans.)

2. Now find the place(s) in your body where there isn't much pain, where you might feel comfortable. In women, it's often the pelvic region; in men, it tends to be the abdomen. Keep breathing. You will probably feel like you are beginning to relax. You may feel some tingling in your fingers—that's the parasympathetic nervous system expelling your stress in the form of excess energy.

3. Now notice if that feeling of relaxation is spreading. Don't try to force it; your body will do it naturally. You may find yourself smiling a tiny bit. This is good. Again, don't force it, but allow it to happen if it's happening. When stressful thoughts come up, notice how your body reacts. For most people, they get all tense and achy again. Let the thought go and see if you feel better. If you don't, by all means, please continue to think that stressful thought! But if you do, ask yourself this: will you be more effective at dealing with your life as a stress muffin or all mellowed out? Is it possible that you don't need to think the stressful thought? Keep going back to your breath. It's the key.

Big Feelings Leave Footprints.

It used to be that people would tell me how sad they were about something that happened in their lives, and I'd want to say, "Hey, I've got a trick to help you with that. It's called Not Feeling."

I was an expert at not feeling. I'd get really hard and I could take anything. Like Superman. Like a snowman. And secretly, I'd feel sorry for all the poor saps who had to go through life feeling pain. I knew I was immune.

I don't want to do that anymore, and anyway, I'm not sure I even can. It's a high price to have to feel your feelings, because part of what that entails is connecting with other people. If you're going to feel sad and angry, you probably will need to talk to some other people. As Audrey Hepburn said in *Breakfast at Tiffany's*, "Quelle drag." But I've lived the alternative: I've been a Brain With Feet, someone who races around with a tiny little body and a great big head, accomplishing things and staying above the waters of the emotions. It looks good, it's neat and tidy, but it means the only pleasure you get to feel is at the level of Disney World or a hot fudge sundae. Nothing that lasts.

Many of us were encouraged not to feel our feelings. When we were little, it was pretty inconvenient for our parents when we had a tantrum or freaked out about the neighborhood pit bull who lunged toward us from behind a chain-link fence, or even when we were insanely joyful about the Happy Meal we were consuming that compelled us to dance wildly around McDonald's, bumping into other patrons as we careened. Many of us got the message that it wasn't the behavior that was the problem; it was the feeling in the first place. So we squelched our feelings and blended into a nice shade of beige; we ate some sugar or drank a lot of coffee when we were down and drank a few beers when we were manic, and generally kept ourselves under control. This is all right once in a while, but for some of us sensitive artist types, this kind of mood control doesn't work very well. Artists are *supposed* to feel things deeply; that's our raw clay, as it were. "I use my rage to act!" says my friend Dougie. "Without it, I'd be painting in just shades of black and white."

There are many theories as to why we so often get separated from our bodies. Some say it's a form of Post Traumatic Stress Disorder caused by some event early in our childhoods. Some say it's the fault of TV. Some say it's the nature of our post-industrial non-agrarian age. Many of us no longer use our bodies that much anymore, except our brains and our fingertips, and so we have a kind of divorce from our bodies, or at least an "understanding" which goes something like this: "you stay healthy and don't bother me and don't feel strong feelings and I in turn will feed you lots of nachos and beer."

I do find after re-connecting with my body in one of the ways I will outline below that there's some aspect of my life that I'm at odds with, that I wish were different and that I cannot change. What I've learned after years of self-study and research and experience is that I do best when I (to use Marsha Linehan's wonderful term) *radically accept* whatever the situation or person is, in the present moment. After I do so, I usually feel better, though sometimes a little sad. Acceptance is the cerebral version of sadness. Sadness is the emotional version of acceptance.

Eight Cheap Forms of Therapy

Below are Eight Cheap Forms of Therapy that have helped me and many others to connect with themselves, uniting body, mind and emotions. Have fun and be sure to sing, "Reunited and it feels so good…"

1. Meditation

To paraphrase Swami Satchidananda, "Meditation can't calm the waves, but it can teach you how to surf." There are lots of methods of meditation, just as there are lots of kinds of therapy, yoga, exercise, etc. But most forms follow a similar idea: sit without moving for a period of time and concentrate on a fixed object. Many traditions use the breath because it is so readily available, but you can choose a word, a phrase, or focus on a visible object, too. Though many people think the point of meditation is to empty the mind, it's more accurate to say the point is to become aware of the many pointless, unhelpful thoughts we think on an almost continuous basis. The greatest gift meditation has given me is the training to "drop the thought."

Meditators learn to develop an attribute called "mindfulness." Mindfulness means being aware of what is going on around you, keeping a perspective that you, the observer, are just a piece of a larger puzzle and not the center of the universe. So that when someone steps on your toe, you don't react by yelling at the person, but reflect first that perhaps he was shoved by someone else; or perhaps he didn't see your foot there; or perhaps he stepped on your toe because you just kicked him in the shins. It's taking in a larger context than we usually allow. Another word that comes to mind as a goal of meditation is "understanding."

When I meditate, I try to access my inner Compassionate Witness. We all have one, somewhere deep inside ourselves. This is the part of ourselves that doesn't judge, doesn't condemn, doesn't form opinions—it just observes calmly and notices, and accepts. It gathers information.

The kind of meditation I was first taught is called Vipassana, which means "insight." The idea is that by sitting and observing your mind, over time, you will see its habitual patterns and stop be-

lieving that it always has the right answers. My mind, for example,
is particularly fearful and thinks that something terrible is probably
about to happen at all times. But after meditating for years, I began
to get wind of the fact that usually my mind wasn't correct. I came to
relax in the knowledge that I just have a kind of jumpy mind. It's not
that my mind got less nervous and jumpy through meditation; just
that I wasn't taken in nearly as often by the stories it told. Our minds
are masterful storytellers, which is a good thing if you are a writer.
But trouble sets in when we begin to believe all the stories our mind
spins. It's taken me many many years, but I am now, finally, on to
myself. When I catch myself thinking judgmental, critical or self-
critical thoughts, my practice is to just drop them. Not to analyze,
not to deconstruct and not to fondle them; just to drop them, the way
you train your puppy to drop the slipper he's been chewing on. I
can't begin to tell you how much happier this has made me.

How to meditate: Start by sitting in a comfortable position. The
classic one is cross-legged with your hips raised a little on a cushion
so that your knees are lower than your butt. Close (or partly close)
your eyes and just follow your breath. Notice the inhalations and
the exhalations. Try not to think about anything but your breathing.
You will find this impossible for more than five or ten seconds, after
which your mind will wander outrageously, to the point where it
might take you five minutes or so before you remember you're supposed to be not thinking, but following your breath. That's okay! At
this point, bring your attention back to your breath, without judging
or beating yourself up. *It's the act of bringing your attention back
to the breath that strengthens the muscle of insight and mindfulness.*
So when your mind wanders, be glad; it's a chance to exercise that
muscle and voila! Congratulations! You are meditating as soon as
you notice the lapse.

Set a timer for 15 minutes to start with. Once you can deal with
15 minutes (or I should say, *if* you can deal with 15 minutes—some
days, I can't) go up to 20, 25, 30, up to an hour a day. You may
not see results for a long time, but practitioners who stick with the
practice report that the fruits of meditation are peace, greater love,
release from addictions and addictive behaviors, and best of all, a
general amusement and tolerance for their own worst attributes. I
can vouch for this. After fifteen years of meditation, I don't beat

myself up nearly as much. I am much more likely to giggle at myself when I get angry or sullen or hurt or outraged. I still have all those emotions, but I can now recognize them as emotions, and again, not take them too seriously. "And this, too," is a well-loved mantra of meditators.

Real meditators might draw and quarter me for what I'm about to say (well, actually, they won't because they're dedicated to harboring good, non-harming intentions for all beings): honestly, there are many days when I sit for my 10 or 15 minutes and I can't say what's going on inside in any way matches the above description. But I find the exercise still to be of value. At the very least, I am being with myself. I am sometimes catching up on my thoughts. I am sometimes feeling emotions I've been unaware of or holding back all day. Sometimes I pray. Sometimes I'm thinking of a song I want to write, or a portion of a novel I'm developing. Sometimes I'm realizing that I've scheduled way too much that day and need to cancel something. Sometimes I remember a friend's birthday. I don't berate myself for being a bad meditator. I figure that if the Buddhists are right, I am establishing a good intention this time around; next lifetime maybe I'll be more focused.

Other words to substitute if you hate the word "meditate":

- Sitting
- Waiting
- Listening to the sounds around you as though someone composed them on purpose
- Practicing not doing anything (this also works when you're experiencing resistance)
- Daydreaming
- Collecting your thoughts
- Feeling your feelings or Carpet Therapy (see below)
- Relaxing, or as Tom likes to say, "chillaxing"
- The "relaxation response"
- Holding the yoga pose "padmasana" for an extra long time
- Quiet Time
- Wordlessness
- Helping your brain develop "open focus"[20]

When I catch myself thinking a useless habitual thought—like comparing myself (unfavorably) to Sheryl Crow or Joyce Carol Oates, I call this a "Dead End," and I drop the thought. Any form of meditation can help us not only to identify our Dead Ends, but even more helpfully, meditation can help us to stay away from them and live with a delicious amount of inner freedom.

2. Carpet Therapy

Now that I am willing to feel my feelings, I get inundated with emotions on a fairly regular basis. What I've learned over time is to welcome them when they come, occasionally with a little Carpet Therapy. I had a friend who referred to this practice as "stretching out on the rug with your feelings." Here's how to do it: close the door, if there's a door. Lie on the carpet on your stomach and think about what's painful, or if you don't know what's painful—you just know you feel sad and miserable—let the feeling wash over you until you cry. Then cry. Cry as long as you want to, and then just rest.[21]

3. Smile Yoga

Humor is a lamp we can take with us into the darkness. When you're scared, turn it on.

The corollary to Carpet Therapy for me is Smile Yoga. This is a practice also known as Acting As If. As in, "acting as if you are in fact calm and full of equanimity when you are instead seething with rage and depression and acute fear." This is, I admit, paradoxical. Didn't I just tell you to feel your feelings? "To everything there is a season." There are times for tears and confrontation, and there are times for containing the feelings and looking within for solutions. Very frequently I find that feelings pass, and I am glad I didn't try to get someone else to "make me" feel better.

Thich Nhat Hanh, the Vietnamese Buddhist monk and poet, says about smiling, "If in our daily lives we can smile, if we can be peaceful and happy, not only we, but everyone will profit from it.... A tiny bud of a smile on our lips nourishes awareness and calms us miraculously. It returns us to the peace we thought we had lost."[22] Smiling reduces stress and relaxes the face. It is well known that just exercising the facial muscles into the "pose" of a smile actually makes a person feel happier. I try to remember to unclench my jaw and smile as I'm making my breakfast in the morning, although sometimes I catch myself scowling down on my oatmeal for no reason whatsoever.

There is an actual school of yoga called Yoga Ho Ho Ha Ha Ha, with very detailed practices and asanas involving chanting "ho ho ha ha" and simulating laughter until it catches on and becomes real (which it inevitably does). This school comes from India, where there are actual Laughing Clubs running on the principle, "Laughter is the Best Medicine." Really. Founded by a Dr. Madan Kataria, a doctor from Mumbai, India, participants get together and lie on the floor. One person starts laughing and pretty soon everyone has joined in, since laughing is like yawning and very contagious.[23]

I tried this once. It was my wedding day. My favorite people were gathering around me. I was about to marry the man of my dreams, my soulmate for whom I'd been waiting my whole life. I was surrounded by love, flowers, good food, large wrapped packages. I was about to go to California on a two-week honeymoon. So why was I in such a bad mood?

Well, there really was a good reason, theoretically. When in doubt, blame the weather (at least if you live in New England). During the week leading up to the big day I was mysteriously compelled to keep checking the weather forecast, as in, once an hour. When, the September before, Tom and I had chosen May 14 as Le Grand Jour, we knew the weather could be iffy. Sometimes in New England, it's 90 degrees in May; other times it's in the low 50s. I had no idea if I should buy a strapless dress or wear fake fur. Ten days out, both AOL Weather and The Weather Channel predicted 62 degrees and rain. We planned on an outdoor wedding, with tent, but with the knowledge and accompanying trepidation that we might really, deeply (and muddily) regret it.

The morning of May 14 it was 58 degrees and raining. To make matters worse, my head felt like it was being compressed in a vise, the familiar symptoms of a soon-to-be raging migraine. I was in a passive-aggressive fury at myself for not being more spiritually evolved so as to rise above the unfortunate circumstances. I called some friends and met them in the morning, and as they sat with me and listened quietly and calmly, I raged, wailed, and sobbed. Then I went up to Goshen to get my hair done. I thought I would feel better with my up-do, ringlets and all, but instead, looking in the mirror, I felt like the fat old duchess from *Alice in Wonderland* and not like the dainty wisp of a bride I wished to be. Next stop was the minister's house where I was to meet my family for a final luncheon, my last meal as a single chick.

As I drove up, I cried some more. Why did I feel so bad? Why would I be cursed with a migraine on today of all days? And why did God hate me so much that He would make it 58 and raining? And why, most of all, did I care about such trivialities on such a momentous spiritual day? It was going to be fine; I knew that somewhere inside me. Why did I have to have such negative aversive feelings?

I put Martha Beck's *The Joy Diet* into the tape player of my car. Somehow I had a sense that her wry sense of humor might lift me out of my current pit of despair. "Laugh 30 times a day," she admonished on the tape. Minimum. If you need external stimulation, fine: rent some Christopher Guest videos or hang around your funniest friends. But more importantly, learn to laugh "without any discernable cause."[24]

And so, having nothing to lose and being alone in the car, I let it rip. I laughed from the deepest part of my belly, with the same fervor with which I would have practiced Ashtanga yoga. And wouldn't you know it? It was infectious and addictive. I continued to giggle the rest of the way up to Cummington.

I'll never know for certain whether it was Yoga Ho Ho Ha Ha Ha or the fact that the sun came out a half hour before the ceremony, and that for the rest of the day it was 69 degrees and lovely, but my migraine and bad mood went away. My niece Amelia dropped rose petals before me as I walked down the aisle. My mother was my maid of honor. My father escorted me while my Aunt Jenifer played Schubert's "Ave Maria," singing like an angel. My beautiful, heartful, soulful groom Tom stood waiting for me.

After we exchanged our rings, Tom and I exited the church to the congregation singing the Hallelujah Chorus from Handel's *Messiah*. And then, Tom and I rang the church bells. I took hold of the rope and pulled with all my might. The bell rang, and the rope pulled me up, off my feet, high up above the ground, and there I hung, for just a second or two. Enough time for me to laugh and laugh.

4. Keeping a Journal

As I said before, one of the great values of therapy, even if your therapist isn't top notch, is the opportunity to tell your story out loud and be heard. My friend Elizabeth (who, for reasons I cannot divulge, was renamed "Juice" for the year she was seventeen) taught me that a cheaper and ever-available form of this comes in keeping a daily journal. Here is a place to put your anger, confusion, grief, excitement, hopes, dreams, or simply the day-to-day events that you might want to remember in the future. It's wonderful to keep a journal when you're single, because sometimes you just really need to express yourself and there's no one around to hear you. When I was single, I wrote every day, faithfully. It was an act of deep support for myself. Now that I am married, I still write frequently. Often, this involves putting my difficulties with my partner down on paper so that I can take a virtual "count to one hundred" before I react to some implied slight or outrage to his face. Usually if I am angry it's better to write about it than say something in the moment of anger. (Another form of containment.)

By the way, Elisabeth Kubler-Ross, the great grief guru, says that anger lasts only a few seconds and is entirely normal, natural, and healthy. What is not so healthy is resentment—that slow burning fury that can last for years. Grouchiness. Holding a grudge. Pissiness. These are the forms of anger we could work on letting go of.

In his wonderful book *Peace is Every Step*, Thich Nhat Hanh talks about "cooking our potatoes."[25] What he means by this is that anger is a natural reaction and emotion and our job is not to get rid of it. Rather, our work is to transform the emotion from something harmful to something helpful. Raw potatoes and boiling water are not much good; the potatoes are inedible and the boiling water can scald you. But if you carefully (mindfully) put the potatoes in the boiling water and watch them and let time take its course, you will end up with a meal that will feed and sustain you and be of some benefit. I think of my journal as my stove. I put down all the indignities that have occurred by way of stupid, careless and just plain mean other people. Once I've written them down and really looked at them—and seen, inevitably, where my logic is wrong, where maybe perhaps I was just a tiny bit at fault or might be overreacting, or that so-and-so did exactly the same thing last week and I didn't mind at all then—time has passed, and usually my anger passes too.

Another great way to get some free therapy—and this time with an audience, and potential feedback—is the modern blog. Anyone can start one; there are several free services out there, like Blogger.com or WordPress.com. Just be careful with that whole "journal as transformative stove" metaphor: the stove thing only works in private. You might scald a whole bunch of people, including yourself, by blogging recklessly. In the '70s they said, "Don't drink and drive." In the '90s it was "don't drink and dial." Nowadays it's "don't drink and go anywhere near an Internet connection."

5. Art, Music and Literature

Art saves. Music heals. Literature transports. Maybe that's because these forms bypass our left brains—or, more poetically, they bypass our brains entirely and communicate directly with our hearts. They move us past our logical selves and speak to those parts of us that come from a different, perhaps otherworldly address.

I am a sucker for the self-help aisle. When I'm going through something difficult, I want to use my expensively educated noggin to get me out of whatever hot water I'm in, and it would stand to reason that if I have a problem with X, I should go find a book entitled, "X No More!" Or "How to Deal With X and His Terrible Breath" or "My X, Myself." So I go to my local bookstore (independent, naturally) and browse the self-help aisle. I seize a couple of books and sometimes buy them, sometimes just crouch down anonymously in the corner of the store and furtively read. I usually get a sick-to-my-stomach kind of feeling pretty quickly. (Not always—some of my all-time favorite books, indeed many that I included in this book's bibliography, are technically self-help.) That's when I slowly get up, revive my cramped legs and mosey over to the fiction aisle.

Art, Music, + Literature

Have a question about marriage? It'll be answered by Tolstoy in *War and Peace* or *Anna Karenina*, by Wallace Stegner in *Crossing to Safety*, or O. Henry in "The Gift of the Magi." Dating? Listen to the great advice Rosalind gives Audrey in *As You Like It* ("You are not for all markets"). Obsessed? Check out *Lolita*. Or *The Great Gatsby*. Or *Othello*. I just spent the morning reading the Annie Proulx story "Brokeback Mountain" and felt sane and cleansed when I closed the book. There's a reason we read; the ancient Greeks called it *catharsis*; Aristotle said watching tragedy purges the spectator of his own demons. So for me, mission accomplished. I find that I *need* to read fiction, that if I go too long without it, I become a bit ungrounded.

When I was going through my divorce, I would hit patches where I seemed completely emotionally dry. I felt rotten inside, but somehow I couldn't manage to cry. I knew that if I only could, crying would wash away the plague of moroseness building up inside. All I had to do to shake up that state was listen to Bob Dylan's *Blood on the Tracks*. I'd be weeping by the third verse of "Tangled Up in Blue," and by "Buckets of Rain," my head was screwed on right again.

Movies have a similar effect, though for me they really are more escapist than cathartic. Still, I was very grateful to laugh my head off at *There's Something About Mary* and the last scene of *The 40 Year Old Virgin*.

6. Recycling (Yes, Recycling)

I'm counting recycling as a cheap form of therapy because it is a practice that brings an abundance of good feeling and relief. Given that the planet contains limited resources, and that landfills are quickly filling up in this country, and that the average American generates 4.6 pounds of solid trash per day (for a grand total of 1,460 pounds per year), and that Americans, who represent 5% of the world's population, contribute over 40% of its garbage, you can consider yourself a patriot and a good citizen of the earth if you just take the time to recycle.[26]

Most states will accept paper products and all sorts of plastics, aluminum cans, and other containers. In addition, you can start a compost heap for solid food wastes (minus meat, bread, and dairy). Designate an area in your house or apartment for bins: paper, containers, and regular garbage, and a small closed bin to keep next to the sink (Keep it closed! Compost stinks! In fact, if you live in an apartment and can't get to your compost heap easily, you may even want to freeze it, especially in warmer months). Then when you take your trash out to the dump, it will already be separated. I used to keep three small trash cans in my office: one for paper, one for garbage and one for the bazillion plastic bottles of Poland Spring water I consumed. (I know, eco-cowboys, I know. I was bad. But now I'm reborn, and I use only Mason jars and aluminum water bottles.)

I love recycling because I don't have to do it perfectly. If the motto is "reduce, reuse, recycle," I figure I get three chances to get it right. It's about batting averages. Every bit helps.

7. Forgiveness

The weak can never forgive.
Forgiveness is an attribute of the strong.

—*Mohandas K. Gandhi*[27]

Adults forgive. It's a benchmark of maturity. Nothing feels better, and you cannot have peace without forgiving your enemies. Yes, you can hang on to your anger and resentment, and it's pretty fun for a while. You feel righteous and justified. I personally love to get worked up by a good Michael Moore film. It gets my blood boiling and I get to feel smug and hateful towards the powers-that-be and also vaguely guilty for the fact that I over-consume, which I vow on the spot never to do again.

But the buzz doesn't last, and in the end, if the world is going to be destroyed by our errant ways anyhow, I may as well choose to see the people in power as a bunch of innocent two-year-olds, try to see the humanity in them, as in all beings, and do the annoyingly painful and slow work of forgiveness.

Forgiveness can't be something one does because one is forced to. Forgiveness has an organic quality; it bubbles up once the raw anger is gone. But sometimes nature needs a nudge. We can get stuck in our resentments and judgments against others if we aren't challenged to think outside the box of our own point of view.

I came up with a kind of mental hygiene exercise on forgiveness, which is derived in equal parts from Twelve Step work, Buddhist psychology, and Byron Katie.[28] I do a version of this every night. I think of it as my spiritual ablutions.[29] It goes like this:

- Write down whom you are angry with and why.
- Then, like a "boomerang" flying back at you, see where you manifest one or more of the following three symptoms of illness, or what the Buddhists call "the three poisons": greed, aversion, and delusion.
- Next, list the skillful or unskillful actions you've taken so far, if any.

Example:

I resent Tom for not doing the dishes this morning and instead working on the kayak he is building.

He should not work on his kayak when there are dishes to be done!

I should not have let him go without a fight.

Instead, I should have asked him to do the dishes and he should have said yes. In fact, I shouldn't have had to ask him! He should just *know*.

BOOMERANG!

Here's where you turn your thoughts around.

Greed: I want Tom to do the dishes so I can go check my email, read the paper, and play my guitar.

Delusion: It's deluded to think it's Tom's job to do the dishes. That it isn't good for me to take the time to do the dishes. That the world will end if I have to do the dishes. That Tom "should" do the dishes. That just because Tom isn't doing the dishes now, he will never do the dishes. Besides, there are lots of times I leave dishes in the sink and he cleans them up. In fact, truthfully, he probably does the dishes more frequently than I do. Also, I am trying to play God by thinking Tom should be other than who he is—i.e. a mind-reader. (I am not God. Tom is not a mind-reader.)

Aversion: This is the feeling of dislike and scorn that creeps in: "Tom's kayaking thing is so selfish and stupid! How could he be so selfish?"

Action: I made a passive-aggressive comment about kayaking; I did all the dishes except for his coffee maker, which I left, full of grinds, in the sink.

After reading what I wrote, I ask myself if there was anything good that came out of my having to do the dishes. Where is the potential growth, where's the potential gift? I realized:

Yes! I noticed the sky as I looked out the window. I had some interesting thoughts. When I do the dishes, they get done the way I like them to. Generally we take turns, so therefore, I got my turn out of the way. Next time, he will probably do them.

Byron Katie, a veritable forgiveness expert, has a whole system, which she calls "The Work," which asks four questions of the angry person.[30] First she has the angry person put their grievance in the form of a statement. For example:

"Tom should have done the dishes instead of working on his kayak after breakfast."

The questions are:

1. Is this true?
2. Are you absolutely sure this is true?
3. How do you feel when you think this thought?
4. How would you feel if it were impossible for you to think this thought?

And then she encourages the angry person to do a "turn around" for the statement, usually stating some form of its opposite:

Tom should not have done the dishes. He should work on his kayak.
Or
I should do the dishes.
Or
I should work on the equivalent of my kayak, which for me would be playing guitar.

Byron Katie's philosophy is that all of our misery stems from struggling with What Is. The fact is, Tom really loves working on his kayak, and he will do so whenever he's not blocked by his own ideas of what he should be doing. So that's What Is. If I believe the statement *Tom should do the dishes and not work on his kayak*, I am fighting a powerful reality. Besides, why *should* Tom do the dishes? Does he ever do the dishes? (Yes.) Does he ever *not* work on his kayak? (Yes.) Can I be absolutely sure I'm right about the idea that this morning he should have done the dishes instead of working on his kayak? (Um. No.)

If you are angry with someone, it's helpful to write about it in this way. Writing takes us out of ourselves for a second, to do what my mom taught my sister and me to do when we were squabbling little kids: to see the situation from the other person's point of view, just for a moment. Would I like it if Katryna grabbed my doll out of my hands and refused to give it back even after I started to cry? No. Well, then, what makes me think she likes it any better when I do the same to her? This made sense even to five-year-old me and yet still, I have to stop and ask myself today, would I like it if I left the dishes in the sink just once, and went into the next room to play my guitar, and Tom sighed all passive-aggressively and banged around the dishes as he sacrificingly cleaned them? Well, no. Remembering that saved me from being an ass this morning.

Not to put too fine a point on it, but this daily mental hygiene—working daily with these so-called "turnarounds"—has changed the architecture of my brain, and made me an immanently nicer, more reasonable and happy person. It is a lot of work, and it can seem tedious at times. But if there is one thing you take from this book, and only one thing, I hope it will be this: Challenging and changing—and, as I said earlier, even just dropping— your thoughts will make everything else in your life work better. To find a practice sheet, please see Appendix A. Or visit http://www.thework.org.

The corollary to forgiveness of course, is apologizing, or making amends. In any spiritual tradition I've ever heard of, this step is essential. Whom have you harmed? What do you wish you hadn't done? What do you wish you *had* done? Have you stolen from anyone? Been mildly dishonest? Say you're sorry. But don't just go through the motions; for an apology to be real and valid, the person to whom you are apologizing must believe that you are sincere. So get sincere. Think about how you would have felt if that person hurt you the way you hurt her. Then go to her and look her in the eye and say that you are sorry, that you wish you had behaved differently and that you intend to behave differently in the future.

Making amends goes even further. In this case, you are actually trying to make right what you once made wrong. The clearest example of this is when you have stolen money or an object from someone. Here, you simply return it. (With interest.) But what if you spent a lifetime ignoring your doting father and now he's got an incurable disease? You go to him, sit with him, tell him you love him, and continue to do this until you feel that mysterious process begin to work in you (I think it's called love.) Hearts really do change if we change our behavior.

8. Gratitude

"Nothing is more helpful than an attitude of gratitude," goes the platitude. It's true, though. Think about it. Is there any emotion that feels better, cleaner, more wholesome than gratitude? Gratitude is about looking at your life and seeing the good in it, the grace in it, the luck and joy. When we feel grateful, we also feel generous and magnanimous. We hold the door open for strangers and smile at people who usually annoy us. It's almost impossible to feel envy, self-pity, hatred or bitterness when you've worked up a good head of gratitude.

One really easy way to access gratitude is to make lists—gratitude lists. Sometimes, when I'm stuck, I just make a list A to Z. "I am grateful for Apples in the fall. I am grateful for Babies. I am grateful for Compassion. I am grateful for my Dad." Like that. If you are feeling despairing or even just a little sorry for yourself, this trick works wonders.

The best advice I ever got was this: when something terrible happens, ask yourself, "Why is this the best thing that could have happened to me? It's my job to figure that out." In 2010, the beautiful circa 1835 church where Tom and I were married burned to the ground, overnight, in about three hours time. (Faulty 1835 furnace, and not, as we first feared, the work of the arsonist who had recently ravaged our town, burning down many family homes.) It was a devastating loss to us, to our community, and we were facing an $800,000 bill to rebuild. How could this, in any way, be good?

Well, it turned out, in the end, to be more good than bad. It was also sad. There was an undeniable loss, but there were so many good things that came out of the experience.

1. We banded together as a congregation.
2. Our minister kicked ass from the pulpit during that
    time.
3. The original church had no bathrooms. After rebuild-
    ing, we had two bathrooms, and this in turn makes
    our church more habitable for potential future mem-
    bers.
4. My then 3-year-old daughter said, "I could be a good
    helping builder of the new church. Can I paint it
    pink?"
5. We discovered how much the community loved us,
    how loyal the family of congregational churches was
    (they sent us much in terms of hymnals, a pulpit,
    pews, and money).
6. We now have a beautiful new building which looks
    identical to the old building from the outside. Inside,
    it is luminous, clean, comfortable, and yes—it has
    two bathrooms.

In the end, there is always something to be grateful for. And
the more grateful we are, the more lovable we are, and the more we
are able to see the path in front of us. In the words of former slave
ship owner turned minister/songwriter John Newton, "Was blind,
but now I see."

Book Two
Vocation and Avocation

VOCATION

AVOCATION

Tools and Rules

- Do what you love; love what you do
- Are you someone who lives to work or someone who works to live?
- Vocation? Avocation? What's the difference anyway?
- How do you know? Flow
- Find work that matters
- Don't text while interviewing for a job
- No kissing on the job
- Learn to fail (well)

Do What You Love; Love What You Do

"When you are no longer compelled by desire or fear...when you have seen the radiance of eternity in all forms of time... when you follow your bliss...doors will open where you would not have thought there were doors...and the world will step in and help."

—*Joseph Campbell*

What does it mean to follow your bliss? First of all, I don't think you can follow your bliss unless you know yourself well enough to know what you really like, which is why I am so big on that "Know thyself" stuff. After that, bliss is a lot easier to spot. As you get to know yourself, you can begin to envision your future. Martha Beck talks about looking forward on two levels: with eagle vision and with mouse vision. Eagle vision is seeing from above, the big picture, the big lofty goals. "I want to be a musician and write songs that kids sing on the back of school buses 100 years from now!" Or "I want to be a doctor and cure patients of cancer!" Mouse vision is back here on earth, taking the next small step towards your goal. Want to be a musician? 1. Choose an instrument. 2. Purchase it. 3. Practice it for 10,000 hours until you master it. 4. Write some songs. 5. Make some cold calls to seedy bars and try to get them to pay you. Etcetera. Want to be a doctor curing cancer? 1. Take pre-med. 2. Survive Orgo. 3. Apply to med schools. 4. Choose one (I'm being flagrantly optimistic here). 5. Survive med school. 6. Get a lot of sleep so your brain works properly; after all, it needs to figure out how to cure cancer. Etcetera.

Though it often doesn't work quite this neatly. Actually, it almost never does, and each one of these mouse steps might take multiple mini-mouse steps. You might choose five different instruments and "date" them for months or years before committing to one. You might major in English or Physics before the calling toward medicine arrives, at which point you might finally attempt to stomach the dreaded pre-meds. (My friend and fellow folk singer Hugh Blumenfeld went to med school in his early 40s after becoming a father to two boys. Today, he brings his guitar on his rounds and sings to his patients.)

I think of following my bliss as akin to the way Hansel and Gretel left a trail of breadcrumbs so they could make it back from the gingerbread house. You just look for the next sparkly bit on the premises and see where it leads you. Of course, as with Hansel and Gretel who were, after all, lost in the woods and in danger of being eaten by a witch, a wee bit of anxiety can sometimes help—it's useful to have some directive like "pay rent, student loans, and grocery bill" to prod one along, but just a bit. And it also helps to have faith—to trust that someone really did put down those breadcrumbs just for you—in fact, *you* put down those breadcrumbs just for you.

Sometimes the breadcrumbs lead you in a completely different direction from the one you thought you were supposed to be taking.

It's all very well to say, "Follow your bliss," but remember, in order to do this, you have to really know what your bliss is. You might think it's painting, but when you add into the equation "long hours alone," or "potential to never make any money until fifty years after death," you may decide that following your bliss really is *teaching* painting at a university, or doing portraits of your family on weekends, or supplementing your job as an architect with painting on the weekends. Or maybe what you really love is the physical movement of painting, and instead of landscapes you opt to paint the interiors of houses. Or maybe following your bliss means building dollhouses for your children. Don't get locked into someone else's idea of bliss any more than you would get locked into someone else's idea of success. You might be really happy to sing in a local choir, or take guitar lessons, or teach guitar lessons, or read about other people finding a cure for cancer.

Do You Work To Live, or Live To Work?

How do you decide what you want to be when you grow up? What kind of career do you want? I think that career is huge for us twenty-somethings—feeling like we have to have a calling. What if you don't have a calling?¬¬

—Kat, age 27

Well, what *if* you don't have a calling? I know plenty of people who think working for a good paycheck and benefits at a job they aren't particularly interested in is a fine way to get along. They want to put a down payment on a house, buy a car, and spend the rest of their time living a full and satisfying life replete with passions and friendships and activities. "I work to pay for my lifestyle," said our friend Melinda, who answered phones, filed papers, and in general assisted higher-ups in a law firm in downtown Washington. She went out with her friends every night and spent her paycheck on margaritas and fajitas. My bandmates and I scorned her at the time. "She works to live," we said to each other smugly, "while we live to work!"

Our friends Priscilla and Richard also had jobs they didn't totally dig. They too worked to live, building up an amazing group of
friends and saving up to buy a house and start a family of their own.
We'd visit them, watch *Northern Exposure* episodes and eat hot
artichoke crab dip and wonder how they could be content leading
such boring lives. They, on the other hand, came to our early shows
in rooms where both the floors and walls were painted chalkboard
black, where we would make $150 a night to a walk-up crowd and
wonder how we kept our sanity.

Katryna and I had a conversation this month about this very
issue. While we still feel that our work is central to our lives—she
actually married one of our bandmates and has two children with
him, while I married a fellow writer and force my sweet children
to practice violin every day—we have moved beyond this dialectic.
"Process Not Product" has been our mantra of late. We work to live
as much as we live to work. On the other hand, plenty of our friends
who worked to live in their twenties had a career change, a new
calling later in life, and are now firmly in the live to work category.
My college roommate Susan, the one who went to law school, had
always wanted to be a grade-school teacher. But somewhere during
her senior year, she was strongly advised otherwise. So she did the
sensible thing and leveraged her Yale degree for a coveted Stanford
Law School slot and practiced law for many years. But I heard from
her recently: she'd just finished her master's in teaching and was
opening the doors to her very own first grade class. And she's never
been happier.

What is the Difference Between Vocation and Avocation?

Most people understand vocation as *the work you get paid for.*
I like to think of vocation as that magic place where your talents
and gifts meet the world's need, and so the world compensates you
for your gifts. Avocation is the work of your heart, which may or
may not be remunerative, *the work you would pay someone to allow
you to do it.* Often, a person has a vocation (day job) and an avocation (hobby, passion, calling), which have nothing to do with each
other. My parents were a lawyer and a teacher, respectively, but they
joined together every weekend to play competitive tennis. They had
their three daughters on the tennis court from the time we were mo-

bile, whacking at balls and chasing them around the courts, and they spent every vacation playing in tennis tournaments.

In another way, music was my father's avocation. Though he never got paid for it, he played his guitar every chance he got: in our kitchen, around campfires in the Adirondacks, at our church, at friends' parties. And we girls grew up knowing how to sing because our mother always read out the alto part in the church hymnal, or harmonized with our dad. As I thought about it, daydreaming during my Music 210 lectures on obscure Baroque cantatas, it made a lot more sense to put all my eggs into one basket. Why not make my passion my main occupation? Robert Frost famously called for us to unite our vocation and avocation "as two eyes make one in sight." And so I did. But the problem I faced as I moved through my twenties into my thirties was that as wonderful as it is to have two eyes making one, occasionally I want to wink a little bit. When all one's play is work and all one's work is play, one sometimes gets confused.

Better to Strive in One's Own Dharma Than to Succeed in the Dharma of Another

I love my job. It is, after all, my dream job. I have wanted to be a singer since I was seven. I am one of the lucky ones who got to do what she wanted. I love singing for a living, love writing songs, love traveling around the country with my sister. But at the height of my career, I found myself clandestinely purchasing *Martha Stewart Living* and reading it in secret in the back of the van, hiding its cover behind *Rolling Stone*. (I referred to *Martha Stewart Living* as my "porn.") And sometime around the time I met Tom and we got married, I began having fantasies about having health insurance and weekends off. I began to wish that I didn't have to rely on my wits so much. If I were someone with an honest trade, like a plumber or a nurse, I thought, I'd always have work to do. If I run out of ideas, I have nothing. This can make a person anxious, or at the least, give them Stiff Neck Virus. Stiff Neck Virus is my father's term for what happens when suddenly your shoulders creep up to your ears and you have to turn your whole body in order to converse with the person sitting next to you in the car. I always seemed to get Stiff Neck

Virus after a long weekend on the road or a plane trip where I had to lug my six-thousand-pound guitar.

In 2004, Katryna took her second maternity leave, and I did a solo tour with Lisa Loeb and Carrie Newcomer called "Folk The Vote." (It was fun, but apparently we didn't Folk enough because George W. Bush won a second term.) On that trip, my friend Jill Stratton suggested that I become a life coach. "A *what*?" I said. But I was intrigued. I'd heard of Martha Beck; I'd even read one of her books. I went home, did some research, made some applications, flew out to Arizona, and within a few months was fully certified in her program. I had a full client roster, and I discovered an entire continent of myself. Day after day, week after week, I sat in my sunny office at home, talking on the phone to men and women about their lives, their careers, their struggles. I listened, challenged, questioned, probed, got excited about their successes and grieved with them about their setbacks. I loved coaching. And I began to think I could do it for the rest of my life. It was fun and creative work, after all. It was especially fun to help them with time management (er, consciousness) and forgiveness work. Most interesting of all for me was exploring the mind-body nexus—getting clients (and myself) to feel feelings in our bodies and using a tool called "wordlessness" to make sense of them; to stay with feelings and not run. As this is not my strong suit—I am the proverbial helium balloon, constantly floating up above as a thought takes me away from the present moment—it was great practice to work with others.

But something nagged at me. There were many times when clients came to me with issues that were frankly above my head. There were many times when I wished I'd had more training. Should I go to grad school for social work? Divinity school? Become a "Master Coach"? But how could I get more training when I still had a music career, a writing career and a family to hang out with?

After the birth of my second child, the director of my favorite yoga studio[31] started coming to the children's music classes Katryna and I run. "Oh," I said to her one day. "I have always wanted to do a yoga teacher training. But who has the time?"

"I will teach you privately!" she said.

Yes! I thought. Not only is yoga teacher training on my Bucket List, this is just what my coaching practice needs! I will become even better at being present, being embodied. I will help my clients so much—not to mention fulfill a lifelong dream to create a daily yoga practice. This was IT! The next breadcrumb.

And so for a year and a half, I met with her privately, went to several classes a week, practiced on my own in the mornings, read books on anatomy and medieval yogic philosophy. I learned to do a handstand, twisted my body till I saw things from an entirely different point of view, lost my baby fat, felt a new centeredness and groundedness. The training was half over. I looked ahead to an even more intense period of study and practice. Meanwhile, Katryna and I were writing a book[32] for families, to teach them to make music with their young children; and we were also attempting to record our 16th CD *The Full Catastrophe*. Friday was our only day to work in the studio. Friday was also a yoga day. Every Friday, I found myself torn between my commitments. Usually I did both.

My teacher assigned *The Bhagavad Gita*, an ancient text that tells the story of Arjuna, a warrior who is about to enter the battlefield but has suddenly panicked. The poem is a conversation between himself and his charioteer who turns out secretly to be the god Krishna. At one point, Arjuna begs Krishna to reveal himself—to get out of his disguise as charioteer. So Krishna does. But the vision is overwhelming—full of monsters and blood and gore and so much raw beauty and horror that Arjuna is overwhelmed. He wants Krishna to put his Halloween costume back on to finish the conversation. He simply can't bear to see God in all His glory. It's like staring into the sun: for us humans, this is a recipe for going blind. And so Krishna takes pity on his poor human charge, and resumes his disguise as charioteer.

Towards the end of the poem, Krishna tells Arjuna, "One's own dharma, performed imperfectly, is better than another's dharma well performed. Destruction in one's own dharma is better, for to perform another's dharma leads to danger."[33]

Something profound shifted in me as I read this. My dharma, for better or for worse, is my career as an artist: musician and writer. And, as I understand it, we don't choose our dharma—which means vocation, among other things. It chooses us. All these months of *studying* yoga felt very much to me, in that moment, like *my* dharma. But *teaching* yoga—that belonged to someone else. Like

Arjuna, I was avoiding the "battle" involved in the business of living by one's wits, by one's muse—in short, as an artist—by turning to alternative ideas about how to make a living. When I read the *Gita*, I related to Arjuna throughout; as wanting to get out of the battle, not go forward into my fate—of appearing to others (if not myself) as an aging musician who never had a hit, or of laboring to write a book that might not even make a splash.

Looking backwards at my career, I alighted at my 23-year-old self. If could talk to that 23-year-old, who was safely working in a boarding school as an administrator, just married, with just a dream to be a folk singer, and I, Krishna-like, revealed to her what would be in store for her/me for the next twenty years if I chose this path, that 23-year-old would not have chosen it. That 23-year-old's idea was to try this music thing, succeed at the level of the Beatles, with the plan that, if she failed, she'd go to Divinity school in her forties. Given a reasonable back-up plan, who would choose to stay in a "failed" career? Who would choose to strive so hard and so long for a goal (world famous singer/songwriter) and not achieve it?

The problem was, I didn't fail. We weren't the next Beatles, but we have a very successful music career, landing in the gray area between world famous and sub-karaoke. Moreover, looking back, I would not change a single thing. I can't say I have a single regret. I am so glad to have exactly the amount of fame and success I do have. Even the disappointments have made me who I am today. Every year, I am so glad I continue to make music, continue to perform. What a life I have had! Music chose me, wooed me, won me, in the end.

And I am glad I didn't know how it would turn out. I am so glad I had those big dreams as a young person. Young people need to have big dreams, and their work is to mine those dreams, work hard to reach for the big brass ring. It's none of our business whether or not we succeed in wrestling it down, but it is our business to reach.

We can't ever stand to know what our future will hold. It is too much, just as the vision of Krishna in the *Gita* is too much for Arjuna. We think we can't possibly live through what we end up living through. But we do live through it, and if we are awake and kind—to others and ourselves—we come out the better for it.

Yoga is a process of making one's inner intentions match one's actions. To make my inner intention match my actions, I needed to admit that as hard as it was to go forward as an artist, I had to because it was my dharma. Also, as hard as it is to keep showing up on stages around the country, I do love it. I do believe I still have much to give. And if I am awake, I notice that after shows, over and over, people say things along the lines of "Thank you for sharing your gift. Thank you for bringing your message to North Carolina/ St. Louis/Winnipeg/Seattle—thank you for traveling so far to sing to us." In other words, I got, post-*Gita*, that we are actually doing a *service* by sharing our music. I still often feel just so grateful that anyone pays any attention to us at all. It feels like a gift to get to make this music. I feel as amazed as Willie Mays when he found out that he could be paid to play baseball. Most days, I would pay to play. Good thing our manager won't let me.

> *Only by single-minded devotion*
> *can I be known*
> *as I truly am, Arjuna—*
> *can I be seen and entered.*[34]

I went back to the studio. I needed to take a leap of faith in my music career: devote more time to it, even though it might not be remunerative. Rather than get a degree or a certification, I needed to take a hiatus from my life coaching practice. I needed to continue to give myself, my artist—my Willful Child if you will—margins to play in and explore. I needed to write for the sake of writing again. And I needed my IAP to cultivate single-minded devotion. (Not to just one thing; that's not possible for me. But whatever it is I am doing, being, whomever I am loving, I must do this with devotion, focus and attention.) Our book, *All Together Singing in the Kitchen: Creative Ways to Make and Listen to Music as a Family* came out in September, 2011. *The Full Catastrophe* came out in April 2012. Neither shot to number one. No matter. We are so happy with both projects, so delighted when people let us know that they read and use the book, listen to the CDs. And of course, making *The Full Catastrophe* proved to us that *we* still love making CDs, layering our harmonies in the studio, working with guest musicians. And our long-time fans repeatedly let us know that they love it; that they play it; that they are learning the songs and singing them with their families. We have a book that stands as a teaching tool and memoir, rolled into one. And we have another CD to represent a phase of our lives, of our career. Process, not product. This, to me, is success.

And finally, since my yoga training, the first thing I do every day is a single humble sun salutation. I can officially say that I have a yoga practice.

How to Decide What You Want to Be When You Grow Up

In the big picture, I think I was surprised that even though I had just left sixteen years of education behind, I had no idea what I wanted to do with my life. It felt like I should have been planning for this whole life-after-college thing, but really I didn't have any direction.

—*Courtney, age 29*

If you are wondering what to do after college, a good place to start is with your avocations. What do you like to do for fun? Play parlor games? Participate in outdoor activities? Paint walls? Landscapes? Do those things in your spare time and look for the next series of breadcrumbs. See where they lead you. They might turn into a career. If not, you can still knit together a life that includes ways to make money *and* ways to make your heart sing. In the end, it will add up to a life with two eyes, seeing together. Do everything as if it were for the highest purpose, as though it were your true calling. The wise old people all say this is the point of life anyway: not to have riches and acclaim, but to be in the moment with your task, whether it be threading a needle, diapering a child, chopping wood, carrying water, or finishing the last sentence of your latest manuscript. "We can do no great things, only small things with great love," said Mother Teresa.

And be open to *lila*/serendipity/180° turns. My friend Emily Greene majored in sociology at Amherst College and was very clear that her career would be in the field of social justice. A life-long Suzuki-taught violinist, the three things she was sure of upon leaving college was that she would never a. teach b. have anything to do with the violin or c. work with kids. (She had also ruled out medicine and the military). But when the neighborhood music school contacted her to see if she'd be willing to step in as the violin teacher ("just for a year; we promise!"), she grudgingly said yes. After her first day of teaching bow holds to five-year-olds and watching their faces light up, she changed her tune (har har). "I just couldn't get over the joy in their faces when I gave them these simple tools," she told me. Thirteen years later, she is the most beloved and respected Suzuki violin teacher in the area, and her studio has a several-year-long wait list.

Flow

Here's how you'll know that you've found work you love: while you are doing it, you lose track of time. You are so immersed in your task that you are not thinking about the clock, your hungry belly, the text messages dinging on your phone, or your problems with your girlfriend. Flow, according to Mihaly Csikszentmihalyi, who coined the term, is "a state of concentration so focused that it amounts to absolute absorption in an activity. People typically feel strong, alert, in effortless control, unselfconscious, and at the peak of their abilities. Both a sense of time and emotional problems seem to disappear, and there is an exhilarating feeling of transcendence."[35] You know you are on the right track in your work life when you find yourself in this mode. If your work does not ever come close to providing you with this feeling, don't despair. Pay attention and notice when, if ever, you achieve this. Flow is one of the three levels of happiness, according to Martin Seligman, author of *Authentic Happiness* and the world's foremost Happiologist. According to Seligman, Flow, or Engagement, is the second level of happiness. The first is Hedonism, or Pleasure—lots of sex, drugs, Rock & Roll and chocolate. The third is about service towards something one believes to be greater or more important than oneself.[36] Flow is essential for a happy life. So if you can't find it in your work, and you know you never will, at least find it in your hobbies, or your avocations.

Keep a Dreams List (some call this a Bucket List). List everything you would like to do, everything from writing a *New York Times* bestseller to seeing every Oscar-nominated film annually. Check off the items you've achieved. Review your list regularly. Cross off anything that no longer rings your bell. Add your new passions. In the end, most people find that the things they most love to do are also the things they do best. This is the sweet spot we're going for.

Work That Matters

At some point, I am guessing, you are going to want to find work that matters. Work that makes you feel engaged and also of service in the world—Martin Seligman's third stage of happiness (and the highest). I certainly didn't think being a musician would qualify; that seemed utterly hedonistic when we first started out. But after 22 years of concerts and CDs, we have witnessed countless fans fall in love, marry, get divorced, remarry, even leave this earth. We have seen people have babies, and we have watched these babies grow up. We have sung to many of them and even taught them. We have heard countless times that we are the soundtrack for portions of lives. So I guess that matters. For me, when I think about how the Beatles and Bob Dylan, and also lesser-known artists like Catie Curtis, Moxy Früvous, and Dar Williams have provided a soundtrack for my life, I would certainly say they and their work matters. If you have any kind of job where you encounter people on a regular basis, if you do it with your full presence and passion, or even about 80%, my guess is that what you do matters.

The Buddhists speak of "Right Livelihood," and I'd be remiss if I didn't mention this concept. Work that causes direct harm to people or animals was considered harmful for one's dharma, so that would include butchers, tanners, soldiers, sellers of intoxicants, and sellers of weapons.[37] But I have to say, our friends who raise chickens, pigs, turkeys, sheep and cattle in a humane and thoughtful way seem to me to be exemplars of Right Livelihood. Those "local" farmers are all about making the world a better place.

Getting a Job

Sometimes instead of calling myself a musician, I tell people I am a Creative Entrepreneur. It has a certain zing to it, don't you think? But the fact that I have (almost never) applied for a job is not much use to you in terms of advising you about procuring a job or (more importantly) keeping one. So for this section, I polled my friends on the best office/workplace advice they could give, and I was amazed how the same principles apply whether one is in an office or a five-piece band.

Network, Network, Network

The advice I'd give is to network, network, network. All of the great jobs I've gotten have been via friends/former co-workers. All of the crappy, soul-sucking jobs I've gotten have been 'cold' leads where I didn't know anyone.

—Jeff, age 36

I wasn't all that interested in getting a job. I wanted to be a rock star. The fly in the ointment was that I didn't want to live with my parents, which is what I would have had to do, given that so far, I'd made about $25 performing on the streets of Alexandria, Virginia. David was in grad school and he was living with his parents, so one of us had to get our own pad, and it looked like it was up to me. So sometime around March of my senior year, I half-heartedly put together a resumé and sent it out to schools in the Washington DC area to see if they wanted an unqualified music teacher. I was unqualified for the following reasons:

- I had no degree in music.
- I sang, played some guitar chords, but could not play the piano and had no knowledge of orchestral instruments.
- I led camp sing-a-longs and ran a folk group at my college, but that was pretty much it.
- I knew every single musical and personal fact about the Beatles, but had only a cursory knowledge of

Mozart and Beethoven (I have not even seen
Immortal Beloved.)

Not surprisingly, I was not offered a job teaching music. But
my fiancé's mother—network—worked at my former high school
as the Assistant Head, and she offered me the position of Assistant
Dean of Students. This job came with an apartment in a girls' dorm
and a monthly check of about $1200, which to me in 1989 seemed
like a small fortune. (Remember, I had no rent to pay, and had I
wanted to, I could have eaten every meal for free at the dreaded
school dining hall. Though that would have meant interacting with
the students.)

Our biggest breaks came through connections. After playing
together for only about five months, we got booked at the Bottom
Line, the premier listening room in New York. Our family friend
Andy Schaffer was friends with the club's landlord—network—so
our cassette went to the top of the pile and into the hands of Al-
lan Pepper, who booked the club and was something of a star-mak-
er. A couple of years later, we made friends with Nalini Jones, a
new teacher at Loomis Chaffee. It turned out—network—that she
worked for Festival Productions, which booked the Newport Folk
Festival. That summer, we hit the stage there, and after we sold more
CDs than any other act on the bill that weekend, we got offered a
record deal with Rounder, our audience spiked, and we were inundated with offers from venues and festivals around the country, not
to mention getting the attention of several managers and booking
agents. And when we were negotiating major label deals, connections once again came in handy. We'd signed with Razor & Tie, an
indie label who was hoping to leverage their cleverness in signing
us by uploading us to a major. It turned out that Razor & Tie's president, Craig Balsam had a son who went to pre-school with the son of
Danny Goldberg, president of Mercury Records. We almost signed
with Mercury, but at the last minute Guardian, a subsidiary of EMI
offered us more money and the prestige of signing with the Beatles
label. We signed with Guardian. And how had they heard of us? Our
bass player's mother had gone to a party with their Vice President
and mentioned that her son had a band and….

Years later, in 2002, I got a call from our manager, Patty Romanoff. I was sitting at my computer working on a draft of my first novel The Big Idea. Patty said, "Do you want to publish a novel, by any chance?" And within a week, I'd signed a contract with Scholastics books. See, the acquisitions editor Randi Reisfeld had college-aged children who had seen us open for Dar Williams at MIT. They'd bought our CDs and made their mom a mix tape. She heard my songs and decided I should write a YA book based on one of them. So in 2005, I published *Plastic Angel* (based on a song called "This Town is Wrong") which in turn made me officially a published writer, which gave me the credentials and confidence to do much of what earns me a living today: help writers, run writing groups and retreats, and write books.[28]

More About How We Found Our Employers

In the winter of 1991, right after the US invaded Kuwait, my sister Katryna, a senior in college, called to tell me that she had not gotten the prestigious Watson fellowship and would therefore not be spending the next year in Nepal. "Let's start our band," she said.

Elated, I told David that Katryna would be moving in with us so the three of us could be in a band together. David played the guitar, it was true, but he was in the midst of trying to launch a career as a stage director and was not at all convinced that playing in a folk-rock trio would advance his dreams. Still, he was a great sport about it all and agreed that Katryna could live with us. "But," he warned me, "I'll give you one year in which I'll support you completely. If after that year the band hasn't taken off, you have to get a job again."

That was enough motivation to fuel me for decades. I had been working at the girls' boarding school for a year and a half at that point and knew several things clearly about myself.

1. I was not cut out to wake up to an alarm clock.
2. I did not like working for other people.
3. I did not like sitting in an office for eight hours straight.

This really made the idea of just about any job somewhat problematic. Don't get me wrong, I was enough of an "adult" to understand that having a job where your health insurance and taxes were taken out for you by your employer (so you didn't have time to mourn the loss of that extra few hundred dollars a month) was a really nice dividend. But at that time in my life, it just wasn't worth it to me. Working for a secure paycheck with benefits was not enough. Having children and "planning for the future" (whatever that was) was nowhere on the horizon. I wanted to put all of my energy into my childhood dream: to be a singer. And so, the following June my sister graduated from college and moved in to our new digs in New England. With nothing but my little Apple Macintosh and my wits, I became the manager and booking agent, publicist, songwriter, and member of our band, The Nields.[39] Mission: to find at least 100,000 people to employ us.

During the years of launching the band, Katryna and I ate, drank, and slept music and the music business. We watched Letterman to learn comic timing and see who the hot new bands were. Also, we watched Letterman because it was the perfect background noise for the task we were most commonly up to: affixing stamps to postcard mailings announcing our next gigs. David had taken a job as a drama teacher at yet another boarding school, this one in Connecticut. I helped out by once again being a dorm adult in a girls' dorm and running an a cappella singing group. Katryna sold clothes at the local mall and helped coach a softball team. On weekends and every single vacation we had, we toured.

In those early years, I would sometimes become paralyzed with fear. Since I wanted to become the most popular band in the history of Rock and Roll, I wanted *everyone* to love everything I wrote. It took me years to understand that I didn't have to please all the people all the time, I just needed to find my audience and make music that was interesting, important, and of use to *some* people. Now we have an audience of tens of thousands, but not hundreds of thousands. We know by face if not by name many of the people who come to our shows. They are our people, and they are enough. When I write my songs, I often have them in mind— individuals and the collective.

Resumé

> *My first real job was also my first temp assignment. I graduated from college and realized I'd kind of forgotten to look for employment (Hey, there was a lot going on!), so after crashing on my sister's floor in New Haven for a month recuperating from academia, I went to a local temp agency and they found me a placement starting the following Monday. I went, they liked me, hired me permanently after the mandatory six-week waiting period was over, and twelve years later I quit to do what I'm doing now. Over those twelve years I did about eighteen different things and ended up with a whole lot of responsibility...none of which I would have thought to do on my own (and none of which had anything to do with my education, whoopsie). If that temp agency hadn't sent me to that place, who knows what would have happened.*
>
> *—Meredith, age 34 (Meredith is now an A&R person for a prestigious indie label.)*

When I first started trying to get us gigs, I had no idea where to begin. So I got the local free paper and looked in the section marked "Nightlife." I circled the names and numbers of all bars and music establishments in the section, called each one of them, called them back until someone returned my call (after a booking agent told me that the squeaky wheel gets the grease). Mostly these were terrible choices—bars that hired cover bands who were supposed to play for four hours a night and whose patrons would probably not be amused by young, earnest, quirky folk singers. Nevertheless, I sent each one of these a press kit.

A press kit is the musician's equivalent of resumé. (Nowadays, I think they are obsolete—most bands now have websites that cover all the bases of a press kit.) I was told it should contain a one-page bio, an 8-by-10 band photo or headshot, a list of venues the band has played, and/or acts the band has opened for, and of course, any press (preferably good) the band has garnered.[40] Of course, when one is just starting out, there isn't any press, but after our first gig, we called the local paper (the *Berkshire Eagle*) and begged them to send a reporter in to review us. Instead, their music critic Seth

Rogovoy (who later became our friend), stuck this into the bottom of the Music Notes section:

> The Nields at the Williams Inn,
> Sunday and Monday evenings.
> And there's never any cover.

Our first year in the business, I quickly discovered how hard it was to get gigs as an unknown band. Believing that we were at least cute, Katryna and I made a photo collage of some performance shots that demonstrated our passion (even as they couldn't prove we sang on key) and arranged them in a border around a white blank space where we'd write the address. This we Xeroxed onto a giant 8-by-10 sticker, which we affixed to the manila envelopes we used to send our press kit to potential venues and festivals. We figured our press kit would stand out from the others even in the pile of mail. We were right—countless promoters confessed to me later that they opened our package right away because of the photos on the outside.

If you are some kind of creative entrepreneur, your resumé will be your website. Take some time to figure out how this "face" reflects who you are. Invest in a good designer, and make sure that you have the know-how to update your site yourself so that you are not dependent on someone else.

The rules for creating a good resumé are basic: don't lie, but put your best face forward. Some employers will fact-check, others won't, and you won't know which kind of employer you've got reviewing your resumé. Take some time with your resumé. It's your calling card, a virtual representative of you.

Hit the Internet to look for jobs, and get tips on how to write a resumé. Some sites to check out: indeed.com for nonprofits; higheredjobs.com for staff jobs at colleges and universities, mediabistro.com for jobs in publishing and advertising, jobsthatareleft.com for a certain bent of political jobs, snagajob.com as a simple aggregator.

Join LinkedIn.com and connect to everyone you know. These days, this is the It place online to find jobs and where recruiters look for and at you. So take some time with your profile there. And when you are looking for a job, put your dream job in your search engine, and surf away—and follow the breadcrumbs.

Have coffee with everyone you know. In this new überconnected world, find the six degrees of separation for the industry in which you want to work. Facebook is excellent for this. If you're clear that you want to work at a specific company or field, be persistent and accept any job you're offered. Work hard and keep your eyes open for any and all opportunities to advance. Jack Nicholson got his start working in the mailroom at MGM. So buy coffees for those in the know, and then pick their brains for an hour. If you still like what you learn from these coffee interviews, ask for an exploratory interview, which is a more formal version of taking someone from the industry out for coffee.

The Interview

Pay attention to how you feel when you walk in an office for a job interview. Ask yourself, "Is this a place I could come every day and be happy? Do I like these surroundings? Are these the type of people I can get along with? Do I get a good vibe from the office?" Get a job description in writing of what your responsibilities will be. It will give you something to return to when you write up your next resumé and negotiate a raise when your tasks go above and beyond what you were hired for.

—Gayle, age 28

I polled my friends who have more experience with interviews and interviewing for advice for that all-important job interview. Along with their advice came some stories of what can go awry:

Here are two stories from post-college job interviews:

1. I had made it to a second-round interview with a nonprofit in DC and was being interviewed by a group of people. At one point an interviewer asked me, "If you could be a tool, what kind of tool would you be?" I panicked. Given time, maybe I could have said something good, but in that moment I couldn't think of any tool that sounded like a good thing (hammer? saw?). That killed (or helped kill) my candidacy for the job, but was a funny story that I've been able to tell for years after. If you're asked a question like that, just

take a breath (time to think) and give the best answer you can. My stunned silence did not really work for me.

2. I had read in one of those interview books that women should not bring a purse into an interview. (Why? I have no idea why.) So I arrived at an interview, put my keys in my purse like always, and then proceeded to put my purse in the trunk of my car (with my cell phone) so that I wouldn't make the "mistake" of bringing a purse into the interview. I sat through that interview just thinking that I had no way to really leave when it was over. (By this time I had made a new move to Knoxville, TN. I knew nobody in the area that I could call.) I ended up going to an office building next door (so that I did not have to tell the interviewer what I'd done) and calling my car insurance company to have Pop-A-Lock come. Then I loitered in the parking lot for about an hour, hoping they weren't looking out their window. (I don't know what the lesson is from that one...Keep your keys with you?) —Kristina, age 33

And for the good advice part:

*   Set up exploratory interviews. If you're interested in a particular field, find people who do this kind of work and interrogate them.—Gayle, age 27
*   Do not look away when spoken to. Do not give a weak handshake, look in the eyes and offer your hand too. Do not slurp, burp or bring a Super Gulp from the 7-11 into the interview. Do not slump. Sit as if you are interested. This is not high school history class.—Enee, age 57
*   Don't check your phone, answer your phone, allow your phone to be visible except if you need to use the calendar feature to see if you will be available to start working on a certain date. But by no means use it to check anything else!—Nerissa, age 45

- Don't say "like," don't chew gum, wear clean and ironed clothes, try not to ramble! —Lauren age 29
- Do research on the position and the organization. Come up with five to ten intelligent questions to ask. Put on a suit. Bring paper copies of your resumé even if you think the interviewer will already have it. Practice interviewing to get comfortable (and eliminate any tics you might have, like "um-ing" or fidgeting with your hair or jewelry). Ask for the interviewer's card and send a thank-you email—but then do not flood their inbox with emails or ask them to be a contact on LinkedIn (or, god forbid, friend them on Facebook).—Michael, age 38
- Do not belittle your accomplishments, even if they were things you did in high school. Do not make yourself small, but not puffed up either. Do not be contrived, remaking yourself, or fake.—Enee, age 57
- You should arrive early to your interview (but don't expect to be seen before your interview time). Also, if I interview a bunch of people at once (like at a college career fair), I frequently look people up on Facebook to remind me which kid is which, so make sure that your cover and profile pic aren't some crazy party pictures and that all other settings are private. —Theresa, age 40
- Do listen. Do not monopolize the conversational space. Be yourself, no job is worth compromising who you know yourself to be at that very moment in time and space (remember, you're still discovering who you are and what you stand for and all of that is subject to change, so be open to new things and listen to your gut and work accordingly). I guess, lastly, I would say—just because it's offered to you in the interview does not mean you have to say yes. You can take some time with the information you have learned about the position and get back to them in a relatively short amount of time.—MaZe, age 30

- Do: talk about how you can add value to the organization or company you are applying to. That's us.
  Don't: only talk about what you want to get out if the job.
  Do: show up 10 min early.
  Don't: be late or show up out of breath just in time. If you aren't familiar with the location, do a dry run the day before and account for traffic.
  Don't: wear perfume or cologne.
  Do: have good questions prepared ahead of time that can't be answered simply by looking at their website.
  Do: be yourself, breathe, and smile.—Naomi, age 48
- Don't bring your mother to the interview!—Jill, age 42
- If you don't know the answer to something, first make sure you understand the question fully, then be honest but talk (briefly) about how you would go about finding/learning the answer. Be optimistic—explain what excites you about the job opportunity. If they ask why they should hire you, have a short but pre-considered answer ready. —Rob, age 43
- If you research the person who is interviewing you through the internet, don't drop too many things you learned during the interview. Especially not personal details. It can come across as creepy. —Michael, age 41
- Do a little bit of reading before the job interview. Be familiar with the mission statement/vision statement of the company. Where are their other offices?
  Know the answer to the question, "Why do you want *this* job?" Be yourself and be honest. Don't try to give the answer you think they want—go with your gut.
  Be confident that *you* are the right person for this job, and therefore your thoughts and opinions are valuable. Get a professional-sounding email for all work correspondence, like Your Name@gmail.com. Save your monikers and avatars (HermioneDoppelganger99@myspace.com) for your friends.—Kris, 33

Keeping a Job

Again, I asked my friends for their advice for you, and I was pleased to see how universally true it was.

Office Relations

Find ways to make your workplace fun and interesting even when the work itself isn't. Invite people to get together for lunch-and-learn (offer to lead a book talk, teach a skill, or share a hobby while you eat). Organize a holiday charity event (silent auction, book/toy/clothing/food drive, adopt a family). Play together (softball, Cranium, charades, poker) in the conference room at 5:00 and call it Happy Hour, with or without booze. —Gair, age 44

My workplace for the past 22 years has been the wild and woolly world of the music business. When we first started out, we lived in Williamstown, where our guitarist was an intern for the famous theater festival. The theater world is warm, incestuous, and rather like a giant Italian family where everyone knows everyone and people kiss a lot. Actor George was in a play five years ago with Actor Jane and now they're reunited in the new production of *1776* (George plays Ben Franklin and Jane does the cameo as Abigail Adams). Getting to know this community, I grew quickly envious, figuring that there could not possibly be an equivalent in the music world.

I was wrong. Though we played plenty of lonesome solo shows, the circles we traveled in grew ever more interconnected as the years went by. We came up through the Boston/New England folk/pop/rock scene, and along the way met hundreds of musicians, promoters, fans, reporters, photographers, record company people, radio people and craftspeople, most of whom we ran into over and over again at various times and places. There were open mic nights to begin with, then split-bills, festivals, benefits, conferences, etc. Like the theater world I'd idolized, the music world too came to feel like a big family.

Office Hierarchy

Someone once told me "to get ahead, look up," meaning always keep your boss happy. Of course that assumes I wanted to "get ahead." --Mike, age 49

And as in any workplace, there's a hierarchy in the music business. Not a consistent hierarchy, but a hierarchy all the same. For example, one might think musicians would occupy the top of the heap, given that people pay to see them and then applaud at the end of the workday. Not necessarily so. Promoters are the ones with the real power; they hire and fire. Ditto the record company A&R and presidents (known collectively as "industry"), and to a certain extent, the radio and press. So adopting a diva attitude, we quickly discovered, did not get a person very far. (Until she drew huge numbers. Then she could act like a diva all she wanted, as anyone who reads *Us* magazine can see.)

The lower people are on the office pay scale, the more respect they deserve. They rarely get any glory for a job well done, they only get yelled at when something goes wrong. Befriend the ones who make the office run —when crunch times happen, the administrative assistant who had been treated with the respect she deserves will be the one who will save the day.

—Lee, age 38

The other bizarre fact about the world of the music business is that the ones with the real economic power—the fans—are often not treated like the VIPs they actually are. They get forced to wait in long lines, are frequently denied access to the artists' inner sanctums, and are sometimes forced to endure their favorite artist's latest projects, which may include albums of blank verse poetry about the new Shih Tsu puppy who has transformed the artist's complicated world and made it finally palatable.

Yet the fans, we realized quickly, were the real bosses. They hired and fired us in tiny ways, by buying our CD or not, by coming to the concert and shelling out the $17.50—or not. A band is ultimately a success or failure according to its fans—not to the critics, and not to the vicissitudes of the marketplace, which one year can garner the artist a top-selling CD, and the next leave it with such embarrassing sales that the artist is declared "finished." (Note: the artist is really only finished when she decides she's finished, but that's another story.) A strong and loyal fan base is the single most important factor in the longevity of a band. Country and folk artists have the longest and strongest careers, even if they never become super-famous. This is because the fans in those genres are true-blue loyal. I know in the folk world in particular, the fans are loyal not so much to individual artists, but to the genre as a whole, to the very existence of a "folk world." When we're seventy years old, God willing, we can expect to still be playing in church basement coffeehouse series to an audience of octa- and nonagenarians.

Conflicts

Keep your promises: follow through how and when expected. Your word is as important as your skills. —Karen, age 58

Be humble. It gets lonely up on your pedestal. And, contrary to what you might believe at first, you need your colleagues.

—Ashley, age 28

Take a solution-centered approach when things go wrong. When you or others make mistakes, try to avoid blaming. "Okay, that project didn't go so well. How can we do better next time?" Do it. If you do make a mistake, don't be afraid to say it. Taking responsibility for your place in the world and how your actions affect those around you is a big part of being an adult. It's okay to make mistakes and it's even more okay to admit it. Taking responsibility for your actions will gain you much more respect than trying to prove yourself always right.

—Gayle, age 28

"Always be nice to people on the way up, because you'll meet the same people on the way down"[41] goes the famous show business adage. We were offered a deal with Rounder Records in 1994, which we turned down because we thought we'd get a better deal from a major label. It turns out we were correct, if by "better deal" you mean a much bigger advance, a lot of postcards of taxis, green canvas high tops for all the members of the band, a near heart-attack when we heard that not only was the major label folding but that they would keep all our CDs in perpetuity and allow us neither to buy nor sell them—and then finally the benevolent gift of said CDs, plus the eternal cachet of getting to say we were on the same label as the Beatles. However, once that label folded, we were exceedingly grateful that our refusal of Rounder four years earlier had been done politely. Shortly after the news of our label's demise hit the airwaves, Rounder's president phoned us up and gave us a fresh offer.

Don't be a whiner. We've all got our complaints, but if your boss sees you as a whiner, she'll never want to pick you when they're handing out perks, extra money, or other good stuff. When you have a legitimate complaint or protest, pick your moments and be very professional. Never do it in a big meeting—you'll humiliate your boss and she'll hate you for it. Discuss it one on one and don't be emotional about it. Also, every office has its little nest of whiners and negative-energy producers—try to avoid becoming part of it. They'll try to draw you in. Just smile and nod and leave as soon as possible. Life will be better that way. — Debra, age 42

Even if you don't get paid to do exactly what you love to do, remember this: up until the late nineteenth century, masters used to routinely beat their apprentices. I try to remember this when I'm angry that the promoter failed to send out publicity for our show or hung up a poster of us that's over five years old. I say, "At least I'm not getting a beating."

You're All in This Together

Be a team player—if your colleagues need help on a project, pitch in and they will probably return the favor when you are in a jam. You are going to come across people who need to take your ideas and pass them off as their own to feel good about themselves. Let it go—those who matter will notice.

—Kris, age 26

In the music business, as in any corporate, medical, retail, or educational setting, we're all in this together. We all have a role to play, and it's helpful to think of the team analogy. If a show does well, it's a combination of factors, which includes our draw, our sensitivity in how often we come to a market (it's bad to oversaturate—remember the law of diminishing returns from Econ. 101?), how hard the promoter worked to get the word out, how helpful the local press and radio were, and most importantly, how motivated the fans were to get off their couches and abandon their widescreen TVs to brave the traffic, and finally on plain old Lady Luck. Playing the blame game doesn't help anyone. It just creates feelings of hostility. If a show doesn't do well, I always apologize to the promoter (after the guarantee is safely in my pocket) and say, "We'll do better next time. Maybe next time we'll come in early and do the rush hour show on WXPN."

The quality that has been key in every job I've ever had is flexibility. Whether you're a teacher, journalist, accountant, salesperson, marketing specialist, bank teller or administrative assistant, things will never go as planned—projects pop up, crises come in by phone call or email, computers crash. It happens, and it's to be expected. Roll with the punches; be willing to stray from your list for the day. The ability to be flexible and go with the flow will save you a lot of frustration and probably your sanity too.

—Kris, age 26

It's good to be flexible. Once we did a show at our local club, the Iron Horse, in early December. There was a huge snowstorm, and after the first of two sets, the electricity went out. We lit candles and did the second show all acoustic, no mics or amps, the drummer playing with sticks on his knees. It was one of the best shows we ever did, and remains *the* legendary show among our fans.

Exit Strategies

Overall: have fun! Most office jobs don't deal with life-or-death things. At the end of the day, work is just a means to an end (money). If you're not having fun with what you do, you're

*going to have a hard time getting along with the folks trapped
down there in the foxhole with you. If you can't find a way to
make your job fun, then look for another one.*

—Meredith, age 34

*Never stay too long in a job you hate, or with a boss you hate.
As soon as you realize you hate your current situation, start
making plans for your next step. Just making those plans can
help you stick it out in your current situation, and soon enough
you'll have your next job lined up (or your plan to start your
own business, or whatever).—Debra, age 42*

If you have a bad vibe at the club, or at the record company, or
at a radio station, or on the phone with a reporter, be polite and get
through the experience, but don't repeat it. There isn't enough time
in your life to waste it on work situations that suck your soul out.

Gossip

*If you have an "issue" with someone, talk to them, not about
them. This includes colleagues, bosses, subordinates, everyone. If you need to grouse about someone, do it outside of
work, and use it to help you blow off enough steam to approach
that person directly and fairly. Own your part of the problem
up front. —Gair, age 44*

*Avoid gossip at all costs: you never know who may end up
being your supervisor or project leader. Better to uncomfort-
ably listen, if you have no choice, but keep your two cents to
yourself.—Karen, age 58*

Don't gossip about other musicians, at least not in front of anyone who isn't in your band. Gossip will come back to haunt you,
and not, perhaps, in the way you think. Sure, it's everyone's night-
mare to find themselves gossiping about someone in the women's
room and then recognize the feet under one of the stalls, but the
real long term damage of gossip is in the way it erodes your own
sense of security. After all, if you are always trashing people behind
their backs, surely (your unconscious will deduce) others are doing
the same about you. On the other hand, if you abstain from gossip,

you will soon believe that so do most good, wholesome people. Of course, you will be wrong, but at least you'll be relaxed and trusting and not indulging in a really nasty (though fun) habit.

Office Rules

1. Never have more than two drinks at an office party.
2. Never be tempted to level with the boss, no matter how sincere the invitation, unless you have a job exit strategy.
3. Never trust a boss/colleague who says, "Trust me."
4. Never kiss the boss. Never kiss a subordinate. (By kiss, I mean, "kiss.")
5. It's your job/career. These are not (necessarily) your friends. They're your co-workers.
6. Never work for more than one year at a job you hate.
7. Be true to yourself.
8. Remember that emails live forever.
9. No one really, really ever wants to know what you really think of them.
10. Leave work on time. Don't make your work your life, unless you love your work above anything else in life.
11. Where possible, don't work with jerks.
12. Do your best. Work hard. Help those around you. Say "please" and "thank you." Praise good work.
13. Enjoy yourself. There isn't anything, except sleep, that you'll spend this much time doing.
14. Be ruthless in your tasks, not in your relations with people.
15. The person who cleans your office has a name.

—Ed, age 53

Rein yourself in. All of our personalities have weird out-growths—we're paranoid, or we love to hear ourselves talk, or we laugh really loud, or we're totally tactless and blurt out the first thing that comes into our minds. But in an office, you have to rein those parts of yourself in as much as possible, smooth down the rough edges, and just be as normal and chilled-out as possible. It's close quarters, you spend a lot of time together,

*and flaunting your major personality tics is a fast way to make
your boss and colleagues do anything they can to get rid of
you. I've seen it happen lots of times—people who are competent but are either fired or "frozen out" (where your boss makes
your life so awful that she drives you to quit) because their
personalities were just unbearable in large doses. Save your
freaky stuff for your out-of-office time. —Debra, age 42*

To this I would add only: wash your hands with soap and water
for seventeen seconds after you use the bathroom.[42]

My friend Ed's office rules apply to us musicians too: don't get
drunk on the job, do compliment others on their hard work, thank
the sound engineers and the volunteers and remember their names,
tip the bartender and wait staff generously (especially if you are eating for free at a local restaurant that has a deal with the promoter).
Spread good karma. Work hard and don't be ashamed to demonstrate your hard work. Ask for help if you need it, but carry your
own amp when you can. And if someone wants an autograph or a
photograph, be gracious. Just think about how cool you would have
thought that was when you were fifteen.

Failure

The bad news is, you have to fail. It's part of the deal. Just as one-year-olds fall down a lot when they're learning to walk, so adults fail a lot when they're learning who and what they want to be. Didn't you try out a lot of identities as a teenager? Change your fashions? Get a really bad perm or a regrettable tattoo? I rest my case.

The first thing a downhill skier learns how to do is to fall properly. The same is true in karate. If you look back on your life so far, I bet you can come up with at least three examples of times when you "failed" where the failure brought you essential wisdom, self-knowledge or perhaps rescue from a dangerous path or person. I have failed at marriage, being mistaken for a Vogue model, and becoming the next Beatles. But when I look back at each of these failures, I see a huge gift in each of them. I am in a better marriage now; I know how to dress so that I look like the most authentic and joyful (and comfortable) version of myself; I have a fabulous career that also allows me to be a present and participatory wife and mother; and because I am refused to accept the rules of show business, I am not a washed-up has-been at the age of 45. (At least not in my own eyes.)

Do you know who this colossal failure was?

Lost job, 1832
Defeated for legislature, 1832
Failed in business, 1833
Elected to legislature, 1834
Sweetheart (Ann Rutledge) died, 1835
Had nervous breakdown, 1836
Defeated for Speaker, 1838
Defeated for nomination for Congress, 1843
Elected to Congress, 1846
Lost re-nomination, 1848
Rejected for Land Officer, 1849
Defeated for Senate, 1854
Defeated for nomination for Vice-President, 1856
Again defeated for Senate, 1858
Elected President, 1860[43]

Of course this is Abraham Lincoln, arguably the greatest president ever. As a kid who totally failed at figuring out how to be popular or how to do long division, when my fifth grade teacher Mrs. Edelson first read me this litany, it gave me great hope.

When I was in high school, our wonderful headmaster Charlie Saltzman, a gray-haired character who read us the King James Version of the Bible and drove a bright red Harley motorcycle around campus, opened assembly one April with ee cummings' "In Just-spring."[44] I was taken to a place I'd never visited before, and later that day in English class Mrs. Thomas read us the poem again, this time all of us following along on the page. I got to see the way the poem was laid out, how unusual the "bettyandisabel," how delightful the "lame balloonman." The language literally pulled at my heart and I understood in a three-dimensional way what poetry actually was, what poetry can do. I felt it with my ears, I played with it in my mind, and it flooded me with memories of my own spring days and weeks, internal and external. I felt sad and happy and excited and wistful all at once. I *felt*.

At the time, I was divorced from my own poetry, the songs I'd been writing. I'd traded in my guitar for a set of color-coordinated composition books, one for each subject. I'd stopped trusting poetry, or at least I'd stopped trusting that I could dare to believe I was a poet. Poetry was hard. Poetry demanded a connection to something otherworldly, a muse outside of myself and, for the moment, I was in the process of fleeing all that. I was hungering for letters I could subjugate, sentences I could diagram and verbs I could conjugate. I wanted numbers that added up, proofs I could brandish, equations that would balance. I wanted something outside of myself to tell me I was good, like a big red A on a paper, or an acceptance letter from an Ivy League college. I didn't have any faith in the murky, marshy world of music-making, the topsy-turvy world of fiction—unless of course it involved my writing a five-page essay describing the theme of livestock in *As I Lay Dying* or the color white in *Portrait of the Artist as a Young Man*.

"I am not a very good artist," my friend Avery confided to my reflection one day as we were washing our hands at the girl's room sink. "But I am a fantastic critic."

Lucky, I thought. *I want to be a critic. Much safer.*

By the time I got through college, the role of student, theme-chaser, and critic had lost its appeal, and I once again felt confident enough to write my own material. Either that, or my brief foray into the working world convinced me that I was not cut out to wake up at 6 a.m. and work for anyone else, and being somewhat unemployable anyway, I dove headfirst into a career in music, with the desire to do what ee cummings had done for me that day in April in the assembly meeting. I wanted to write something that would make someone think in three dimensions. So I started a rock band.

Fast-forward four years to five musicians, one sound engineer and an enthusiastic tour manager driving around the belly of the United States in a fifteen-passenger van. The enthusiastic tour manager turned around in her seat and asked all of us this question.

"Which would you rather be," she said, "rich or famous?"

"Rich," said the guitar player and the drummer.

"Famous," said the singer and the bass player.

"Neither," I said. "I don't care about money at all. And it's not that I want to be famous. I want to have *influence*. I want to make a difference. I want people to know my work. They don't need to know me, just my work. I'll be fine as a great unknown, but after I'm dead I want to be discovered."

This might seem a worthy goal—arguably more morally acceptable than wanting fame or money. Wanting influence is a kind of side-stepping around the issue of ego, or so it seems. But wanting to be influential is still a way of trying to boss around What Is. To paraphrase Martha Graham, do your thing, and do it with all your heart. Then let go of the results because it's none of your damn business what people think of your work.

Recently, Tom and I were walking along the river in just-spring. The ground was still brown and the forest floor covered with leaves, and if I had closed my eyes and listened to the sound they made, I might have been tricked into thinking it was fall, except my sense of smell wouldn't let me. It was simply too rich at that moment to be anything other than the most potent, life-giving of seasons. And strange plants whose names I may never know were poking up from the ground, strong stem-green scrolls that looked like they meant business.

Tom pointed to the scrolls. "That," he said, "is influence."

This is what I learned from my years in the van, the years of trying to simultaneously play critic and artist. I learned that artists do not get paid for their work but for their effort, and even then they frequently don't get paid. To be paid is nice—it's gravy—but if that's why you are doing what you are doing as an artist, you might want to think about another line of work. I also learned that some people make it and others don't, and if you line up the artists in terms of talent, it makes no sense at all. I learned that the very best part of the whole experience is the moment you get to put pen to paper, fingers to strings, voice to air, feet to stage. No one can put a price tag on that experience in either direction—what you paid, what you get paid—and we certainly ended up paying more than we were paid.

And I'd pay it again.

At one point in our career we hit a wall, a critical junction where it looked for a time that we would lose our record company, our van, our booking agent, lose in short all the trappings that made us feel successful—lose the big red A on the paper, the letter of acceptance from the Ivy League college.

This really was serious. What I was most afraid of losing was our catalog of CDs. The story often went, in the music business, that if an artist got "dropped" or a label folded, the parent label would warehouse the artists' CDs. They would live in a vault somewhere, never to be heard again. I was pretty upset contemplating this fate for my CDs, not to mention the end of my dream of being discovered posthumously. My stomach roiled, my brow furrowed, and answering my email stopped being fun. I went to bed and wrote angry letters I would never send. Then I began to laugh and pretty soon I'd stopped caring about the record company or the records. We'd make more. I picked up *War and Peace*, which I would be reading for the next seven years, and soon I was back in the world of the War of 1812 and sleigh rides and wolf hunts and Pierre and Natasha. I felt so grateful that Tolstoy had taken all that time to write such an amazingly vital story, and I had no interest in either criticizing it or trying to write a better book myself. I just felt happy.

And so the next morning, I turned to the bass player and said, "We can still play. We can *always* still play. No one can stop us." And from that point on, I was free.

Like those plants by the river, those scroll-like bottom-feeders poking up like river crocuses, intrepid and resilient, the point is not the statement, nor is it the product. Maybe the point is just the action, the beautiful action, the poking up, the assertion, the first one to celebrate spring. And once that message is delivered, to relax and unfurl and watch the rest of the parade go by.

As it happened, I wrote the record company president, saying we were a scrappy little band trying to make a living and we would really appreciate having our CDs back. Three months later, as I was writing a new song, he called me at home. At first I thought it was a prank (he had a distinguished British accent, the kind people like to put on). He assured me he was himself, and told me he was sorry that our label had folded and he would give us back not only the rights to our CDs, but also a deal on the actual CDs. One of many in a long line of lessons whose theme is "don't panic."

Work to Live/Live to Work Revisited

Early in our career, while loading in to a gig on the streets of New York, we ran into a friend who was about twenty years older than we were. He'd been in a band all his life, and from my point of view his band had done (and was doing) pretty well.

"What's new?" we asked.

"I got a job!" he exclaimed. "I'm working at Discmakers! It's 9 to 5! I have my weekends off! I have health insurance! I haven't been this happy in twenty years!"

Whoa! Was he telling me he was going to work to live? He was done with living to work? How could this be okay?

I am a nosy person, and so I am always asking people if they like their jobs.

"This is not what I meant to be doing," said my dental hygienist the other day as she was cleaning my teeth. "I was a potter. But then I got married, Bethany came along, and you know the rest."

"But don't you like what you do?" She shrugged. I persisted. "I mean, isn't it satisfying to have a specific task to do in a specific period of time and actually get it done? Every hour you make someone's mouth go from gross to glistening."

She nodded. She was at the point where she was polishing my teeth with that tasty gritty toothpaste. "That's true. It is pretty sat-

isfying. But I think we're going to install a potter's wheel in the
basement for Bethany. And then maybe I'll get to throw some pots
again too."

When Katryna told my father that she wanted to be a singer,
he was concerned, and not for the obvious reasons. "I'm worried,"
he said, "that if you make music your career path, you won't enjoy
sitting around the campfire and singing anymore."

I loved the craziness of my twenties when we single-mindedly
pursued the Rock and Roll dream. I traveled all over North America
with people I adored, I performed in nearly every major city and ex-
plored all the interstates and rest stops, I met lots of famous people
and had some very satisfying critical successes. But when my band
broke up and my marriage fell apart, I looked across the fence at
the Melindas and the Priscilla-and-Richards of the world—those
friends who worked to live—and felt a little confused. Should I have
let my avocation remain an avocation? Maybe having a calling was
overrated.

I have built a whole life that feels of a piece, and I see everything I do as grist for my own artistic and personal mill. This is a
wonderfully integrative way to live, but as I said earlier, there have
been times when I've wanted to check out, to close an office door
for the weekend and not think about my work. But when my work
is about creating, everything presents itself to me as potential material. This makes "working" somewhat irresistible, not to mention
unavoidable.

Working to live, living to work—these are not diametric oppo-
sites as we thought in our twenties, but rather a spectrum. As I have
gotten older, and after I became a mother, working to live began to
appeal a bit more.

When the publicist for our label interviewed me, his last question was, "What are your hobbies?"

"Hobbies?" I was stumped. "Well, I run," I said lamely. "I . .
I...hike mountains. I read a lot of books."

"But what do you do for fun?"

"Watch movies?"

I knew this was pathetic. Everything I did had to do with being a musician: listening to music, playing the guitar, taking voice

lessons, even watching films and TV—this all got folded neatly into my career. I couldn't untwine any of it from work, even my exercising.

Don't get me wrong, I am very grateful to have such a wonderful career, and I don't think I would be happier any other way. I merely offer this perspective to those who find themselves in the "work to live" situation, who look over the edge of their cubicles to the window outside the office park and sigh, thinking, "If only I'd gone to New York and tried to be a hoofer, I'd be on my way to stardom right now. My face would be in *Playbill* and I'd be donning my tux for the Tony parties." There have been many Sunday mornings when I've looked out the windshield of my car on my way home from a gig and sighed and thought, "If only I had a real job, I'd be on my way to church right now with Tom." In other words, even those who have found their dream jobs can bitch and gripe on Monday morning. Happiness is an inside job.

> *Live the questions now. Perhaps you will then gradually, without noticing it, live along some distant day into the answer.*
>
> —*Rainer Maria Rilke*[45]

You're supposed to be confused in your twenties. It's totally developmental. If you are completely clear, beware the looming midlife crisis! The more you wrestle with your confusion now, the better you will be able to handle the bigger waves that inevitably come. Think of all this as a training ground.

We evolve and change. That's part of becoming an adult. We also get more conservative as we age; Churchill famously said, "The young man who is not a liberal has no heart. The old man who is not a conservative has no brain." One reason for this is the increased sense of vulnerability we feel as we age. Conservatism—the desire to protect and conserve what we have—comes primarily from fear. Fear comes from vulnerability. When we are young, we feel invincible and invulnerable. There have been many times when I've wanted to take the safer path, the more comfortable path, and some days it's only the memory of my twenty-year-old self vowing to keep recycling, keep working as an artist, keep voting to preserve the income tax, that allows me to stay true to my values. Do I reassess my values? Constantly. And even though I sometimes grumble at the choices I made and continue to make, when I sit still and think about it, I choose them again.

If you don't know what your vocation is yet, don't worry. It will come. Try to get a job that's somewhere in the ballpark, but know that if you don't, whatever it is that you do will point you in the direction you're supposed to be going anyway, if (and it's an important "if") you keep your eyes open and stay true to your values ("know thyself"). After all, each road we go down takes us somewhere, and if we don't like the destination, that is good and useful information to have.

And anyway, your work may well find you. If you are open to it, it will be better than your wildest imaginings. Maybe not sexier, but better.

Book Three
Bloom Where You Are Planted

Hearth & Home

Tools and Rules:

- Location, location, location
- Renting: read the fine print
- Take care of your trash
- Think well before buying a house
- Think well before acquiring a pet
- Don't live with crazy people
- Clear your clutter
- Eat your veggies
- Baking soda and vinegar clean almost anything
- Raise chickens and eat their eggs
- Avoid rodents at all costs. Unless they are your friends or pets.

Location, Location, Location

In many ways, the place you choose to live after college may be the most significant decision you make. After all, as the poet Joseph Brodsky wrote, geography equals destiny. In whatever town or city you choose, you may make friends, find employment, create social and cultural networks, and even meet the person with whom you will build your family. All that being said, nothing is forever, and the twenties are years of transience, so don't sweat this one too much. Many people who move to a city at the age of 23 are not still living there by the age of 33. From the *New York Times* in a recent Magazine article:

> *The 20s are a black box, and there is a lot of churning in there. One-third of people in their 20s move to a new residence every year. Forty percent move back home with their parents at least once. They go through an average of seven jobs in their 20s, more job changes than in any other stretch. Two-thirds spend at least some time living with a romantic partner without being married. And marriage occurs later than ever. The median age at first marriage in the early 1970s, when the baby boomers were young, was 21 for women and 23 for men; by 2009 it had climbed to 26 for women and 28 for men, five years in a little more than a generation.*[46]

The big question to ask yourself is this: which is more important to you, location or emotional security? Are a whole group of your friends moving to Seattle and sharing a big old house, but you happen to get Seasonal Affective Disorder above the 47th parallel? Is your girlfriend moving to Miami, but the idea that you'd have to live without your wool sweaters feels tantamount to shaving your head and

tattooing "Kenny G Rules" on your skull? Perhaps your boyfriend just got into the University of Pennsylvania Law School but your dream is to busk in Nashville until you get discovered.

Or is your desire to be with friends or lover stronger than any concerns for climate or employment opportunities? Again, your decision now is not written in stone—you could always sing in the local Philly bars and see how things go with the boyfriend; Nashville will still be there in six months.

But this brings up another lesson in the introspective portion of our program; once again, "Know thyself." That is to say, What do you care most about? What are your values? Do you value independence more than community? Do you value living among trees and bushes over convenience of transportation? Rents tend to be cheaper in the suburbs, but if you aren't downtown, you'll have to factor in buying a car. Do you value protecting the environment and believe this means living car-free? Or do you value your *actual* environment and therefore desire to live in the woods away from car pollution, thereby necessitating that you own a vehicle (preferably a biodiesel or hybrid one)? Do you care more about staving off the loneliness than you do about the weather? There's no right or wrong answer here. This whole journey is a process of slowly, sometimes painfully, figuring out who you are.

The two most easy and obvious choices both have drawbacks. One is to go back to your parents' house and live in your old bedroom. Pros: all your old posters from high school may still be up on the wall. Cons: Your mother may have redecorated. With florals.

The second is to stay put, becoming a townie in your college area, which may not be all that different from senior year. Pros: you just have to load your things into plastic shopping bags and convince your friends to move you into your new apartment on the eve of graduation day. Cons: your college town might have a population where cows outnumber humans by a ratio of three to one.

Don't rush to grow up! After college is the best time to explore and experience new things when you are free as a bird and have the tolerance to live out of a backpack. Or the resilience to start new things over and over again and have fun with it.

—Katie, age 34

Go to the big city of your dreams (or the foreign country of your dreams, or the rural outback of your dreams) where you know no one and have no prospects for work or housing. Katie (above) joined the Peace Corps and spent two years in Eritrea. She is cool. Pros: this is definitely a time in your life when new beginnings are encouraged and the spirit of adventure runs high. Cons: you may find yourself co-habitating with large rodents and eating meals by yourself at McDonald's.

Housing

Renting: The Fine Print

Once you've found your dream apartment, or at least the place you can afford, and have chosen your roommates (or to live alone), most landlords will require that you put down a security deposit as well as the rent for that month. A security deposit is usually one month's rent, which the landlord holds in case there ever comes a month when you can't afford to pay. Also, if you damage some aspect of the house—for example, break a window or  set fire to the wall-to-wall carpet—the landlord will kindly take the payment for damages out of your security deposit.

Most landlords actually ask for first, last and security when you move in, at least in my experience. I remember this was a shock to me the first time I moved into an apartment of my own, to have to pay three times one month's rent up front!

—Kate, age 26

 If you move into you apartment halfway through the month, your landlord will usually prorate the rent, which means he or she will figure out what the monthly figure comes out to by the day and charge you for the remaining days of the month.

They are to renting apartments what realtors are to selling houses.

 *I had a horrible experience when I sublet an apartment from someone. I took the renters' word that they had a security deposit with the rental company. In reality, they had skipped a month's rent, and the security deposit went to cover that, so I paid the current tenant the security deposit assuming (ha!) that I would get it back from the rental company at the end of*

the lease. When I realized I wasn't going to be getting my $400 back, which I really needed, I went to court. That was a learning experience. In small claims court, I sued the rental company first, and then realized they weren't at fault, so I sued the original tenants. Long, long story short, I never got my money, and learned the hard lesson, that I should never take the word of some unshaven college boys from Jersey, and that I should have checked with the rental company about whether there was a security deposit there. Ugh, I hate thinking about that experience. —Courtney, age 31

Don't move in to a house or apartment sight unseen, or at least without the witness of someone you trust. If possible, scope out the neighborhood (rodents come out at night!), check the appliances, sniff around for strange odors. You do *not* want to live for a year with the smell of mold. You might think it's sort of charming at first, sort of reminiscent of your childhood YMCA, but believe me, come July, you will deeply regret this oversight.

Other things to check for:

- Water pressure. It is one of life's great disappointments to have to endure a daily shower that feels like someone is languidly spitting on you.
- Do they allow pets?
- When it snows, who pays for the plowing of the driveway or parking lot? Is it your responsibility to shovel the portion of the sidewalk in front of the building, or the landlord's? Some cities have ordinances about keeping your share of the sidewalk shoveled. Is this included in the rent? Ditto the lawn and garden maintenance. Ask about both of these, even if it's the off-season.

- Are heat and utilities included? If not, don't forget: you might be able to bargain.
- Can your landlord enter your home whenever he or she wants? You can negotiate this.

One excellent rule of thumb to follow when apartment seeking is: *you should never pay more than one third of your expected monthly income on housing costs.* This will not be realistic if you live in New York City, Los Angeles, or San Francisco, but in most areas, it's a good rule to follow.

Pay your rent on time; it's usually due the first of the month. If one of your roommates is the designated check-writer, make sure that he or she is actually writing the check. My friend Sally wrote a check to her roommate Ann every month, confident that Ann would in turn put it in her own account and write a check for the full amount of the rent to the landlady. So it came as quite a shock and disappointment, to say the least, when Sally ran into the landlady one afternoon. "I'm going to have to evict you girls if you don't get the checks to me on time!" she shouted. She shouted a lot, and Sally didn't always know if it was because she was angry or because she was deaf. The TV in her apartment was always turned up so high, the entire building got a good hit of *I, Claudius* every Sunday night on PBS.

Trash

Do you have to pay for its removal? This depends on whether you own or rent. Generally speaking, if you rent, it's paid for by your landlord through their property taxes or the city.

If you own your home, in some states you will have to purchase a permit from town hall to enter the dump. Here you may dispose of your trash and your recyclables at your desire. In my first home, I had to pay for garbage pick-up and they also took my recycling (every other week it was either paper or containers). In my current home, I go to the dump and pay a quarter every time I throw a bag of trash away.[47] There's no charge for disposing of recycling.

You might also pay a fixed monthly or yearly bill and have some garbage collector pick it up curbside.

The average American produces about 4.6 pounds of trash per day. That's up from 3.5 in 1992.[48] When you throw out your garbage, the trash goes (eventually) to a landfill. The bad news is the nation's landfills are filling up, if not full. Huge swaths of land in this country have been used as gigantic garbage pits, and there's not a lot of space left. Burning the trash is not a great solution either, as it not only releases toxins into the air, but the burning also contributes to global warming. Global warming, in case you have been living in a cave for the past few decades, or grew up listening only to Fox News, is a rise in the earth's average temperature as a direct result of gases and emissions humans create every year. If we don't take drastic action, the polar ice caps will melt, the southern US will turn to something akin to the Sahara desert, and much of the East and West coasts will be underwater. Florida will be the new Atlantis.

This is why I am urging you to recycle throughout this book; one mark of adulthood is responsibility, and garbage is as good a metaphor as any to start with. As an adult, you must deal with your physical and metaphorical trash. This means not just tossing everything into a can and leaving it on the front walk for someone else to take away. (I know someone who would let her dishes pile up in her sink. On several occasions, rather than wash them, she literally threw them all away.)

Different cities deal with the issue of trash removal in different ways. Boulder and Seattle make you pay, either by the can or through a monthly bill. Trash disposal is not free; trash doesn't just disappear. It's one of those ongoing civic problems that we're all hoping your generation will solve. Good luck!

We Pause Here To Go Over Some General Green Tips So You Can Feel Great About Your Carbon Footprint

- Change your normal (incandescent) bulbs to compact fluorescent or LED bulbs (your local utilities company may give you some to start you off.)
- Never throw out paper. Recycle it.
- Use aluminum foil instead of plastic wrap (and recycle the foil after you've reused it a few times).

Don't use aluminum foil just once; as long as it hasn't touched meat, it should be fine.

- Save rubber bands and keep them in a convenient place. Use them to seal food that already comes in plastic wrap, like cheese or bags of chips
- Recycle your plastic and aluminum cans and bottles (in some states you can get money back from this).
- Insulate your windows with curtains, blinds, or even that sticky cellophane in the winter to keep drafts out.
- Dress warmly in the winter. A certain couple who shall remain nameless set their thermostat to 72 degrees year round and wear tennis attire in January. With bare feet. I judge them. Wear a sweater. Bundle up. You'll get used to it, and it's a great excuse to snuggle with attractive people.
- Plug your electric appliances (especially the big ones like cable box, TV, computer) into a power strip and turn off the whole strip when you're not using them, for instance before you go to bed. You will save a lot of money on your electric bill by doing this.
- Turn off the lights when you leave a room.
- Put a bottle in your toilet tank to use less water per flush (unless you already have a low flush toilet).
- Don't buy disposable things, like razors, cameras, diapers (or at least use some cloth diapers in your baby's changing routine).
- When cleaning your house, use baking soda, vinegar, hydrogen peroxide and hot water. Some people say to use lemon juice, too. There are lots of toxins in modern cleaning products. Use earth-friendly cleaners and minimize products with extra packaging. For instance, buy homemade bars of soap instead of plastic bottles with liquid soap in them.
- Keep a collection of canvas totes in your car and an extra one in your purse or backpack so that when you go shopping you don't need to take a bag from the store.

- Reuse and clean out ziplock bags. Better yet, buy Snack Taxis: reusable bags for snacks and sandwiches made by a woman who lives in Western MA.[49]
- Put a second trash can wherever there is a first. Have one be for the landfill and the other for recyclables (paper, plastic bottles, etc.).
- Wait until you have a lot of clothes to wash before using the washing machine. Don't use the machine for one item just because it's your favorite shirt.
- Take shorter showers. Heating water uses energy.
- Don't leave the water on! Use only what you need. See if you can bathe more efficiently. When you're brushing your teeth, turn the water off after you've wet your toothbrush and until you need to rinse.
- Close the blinds on a hot day if the sun is shining in. Dress more lightly instead of asking for the air conditioning to be turned up, or use a fan. A window box fan, for those of us in the Northeast anyway, can work just as well or even better than AC.
- Keep the air filters on your air conditioner and furnace clean.
- Whenever possible, walk or bike or take mass transit. Give yourself a reward when you do this if you are extra lazy and hate not using your car.
- Plant a tree.
- Call companies that send you catalogs you don't want and ask to be taken off their lists.
- Use old washcloths or torn up old T-shirts instead of paper towels.
- Use actual dish towels instead of paper towels.
- Carry a water bottle with you wherever you go. Your local coffee shop might have excellent filtered water; if so, ask them to fill your bottle up for you when you stop in. Plastic bottles are terrible for the environment. Speaking of coffee shops, get a permanent, carry-along mug so you don't need to use a plastic lid (evil). Or better yet, ask for a ceramic mug, sit down, and enjoy your nice beverage on the premises.

- Buy local and organic food.
- When making choices in the marketplace, pay attention to packaging. Speak up—complain to the store about Styrofoam and plastic wrap packaging. Only use plastic bags for produce when the items are really fragile (like mushrooms). Oranges? Please. You do not need a plastic bag for your oranges!
- Don't buy plastic toys for kids—buy them wooden toys and books, and shop secondhand.
- Wrap presents in newspaper, old T-shirts, or simply with ribbon. If you are artistic, draw on the newsprint.
- Pay attention to which political candidates are "green" and support them (unless they are disgusting in some other way).
- Freecycle or buy used wherever possible. Think about every purchase you make in terms of how much space it is taking up on our planet. Try to give away what you no longer need instead of sending it to a landfill, where it will contribute to the release of tons of greenhouse gases up into the atmosphere.

Do these things and you will attain moral perfection! Not really. But you will go to sleep at night feeling like you did what you could, and that is no small thing.

Forwarding Your Mail to Your New Location

As soon as you know your new address, you can tell all your friends where to send the fan mail. These days it is easy to send out a bulk email letting everyone know of your new digs. But you will also need to alert all credit card companies, subscriptions, cell phone bills, banks, and of course anyone who regularly sends you checks—in short, anything you need to keep getting. This is best done by filling out the change of address forms on the back of your statements. As for all that mail you weren't expecting to get, here are some instructions on how to get it:

a. Get a change of address order form from your post office or at usps.gov.
b. Fill it out.

c. Return it to the post office, or you can just leave it with your outgoing mail. The Postal Service will send you a confirmation letter.
d. Note: they will only forward first-class, priority and express mail for 12 months. Magazines and things like that will be forwarded for 60 days. If you want your third-class mail to keep coming, alert your magazine friends directly.
e. Or, submit it online (usps.gov) for a fee of $1. By the time this book goes to print, this may be the only way to forward your mail!

Finding Landlords and Roommates

Rules:

1. Don't live with anyone you don't know unless you have bona fide references from other people. References don't have to be written—just have a phone call with the potential roommate's responsible friend. If the potential roommate doesn't have a friend, consider that a bad sign.
2. Don't rent an apartment or house with broken windows or signs of rodents.[50]
3. Don't sign a lease without getting your questions answered.

Finding a roommate in the real world is not the same as finding a roommate in college. For one thing, your college, for better and for worse, did some of the screening work for you, even though all of us know at least one story about the roommate from hell who woke at 6 a.m. and went to bed at 10 and complained that your Enya CD was too raucous, or the roommate who in a paranoid fit superglued the door to your dorm room shut, with you inside. Nevertheless, my guess is most of you lived with relatively sane people at college. The same may not hold for the people who put up ads like this in copy shops:

Really nice housemate wanted for
Scented-Product-Free, Vegan household.
Must like Cats, but please don't bring your own.

Or, the informative:

Looking for housemate, non-smokers only.
Call Richard 555-6869

Interview your roommates. The same questions they asked you freshman year in college are still relevant: will you be compatible from a neatness perspective? Do you share at least a tolerance for similar music? What's the etiquette about significant others? My friend Rob lived with another man named Daniel. Six months into their mutual co-habitation, Daniel's girlfriend Mariah began spending every night at the apartment. Though she initially confined herself to Daniel's room, over time she began moving more and more of her things into the apartment, including her widescreen TV (which Rob appreciated) and her large dog named Brutus who was half pitbull, half mastiff and completely untrained (whom Rob did not appreciate). Also, when Brutus felt resentful, he would pee on beds, inevitably Rob's. Soon Rob was running out of patience. Mariah certainly didn't do anything to lessen Rob's rent portion, but she did take up space in the kitchen and bathroom, and her dog was an unwelcome presence to say the least. But because he and Daniel had never discussed what the policy was about squatter girlfriends, and because Daniel's was the name on the lease, Rob felt powerless and pretty pissed off most of the time.

Remember: everything is negotiable. The time for negotiating is as early in the game as possible. If there's something about the deal that leaves you feeling ripped off or uncomfortable, say so. You can complain if a window is cracked. That's what landlords are for. You can say no to pets. Or insist on being able to have yours. You may not get what you want, but you should always ask. (For more about Roommates, see the chapter of the same title in Book Five: Other People.)

Domestic Toolbox and Random Household Know-How

Q: My brother-in-law Dave once dropped a toothbrush down the toilet by accident and then also accidentally flushed. The toilet clogged up and the situation definitely warranted a plumber. But who should have to call the plumber and who should have to pay: Dave or the landlord?

A: Dave

Q: Which way do you turn the screwdriver? And how can you conveniently remember this?

A: Righty Tighty, Lefty Loosey

Q: Eventually all my white tee shirts end up with gross yellow stains under the armpits. How do I get rid of them?

A: Put an aspirin in the wash

Q: What are the uses of WD-40?

A: Myriad! Unsticks anything.

Q: And how about duct tape?

A: What CAN'T it do? I used to use it to hem my performing dresses when I lived in the van.

Q: How do you know when not to eat the eggs?

A: fill a bowl of water. If they float, throw them out! If they sink, they're OK. If they stand on their heads— eat them that day! They're about to become floaters!

Q: Is there a good reason not to reuse the salsa jars as glasses?

A: No.

Q: My kid's red wagon has a rusty bolt. What will loosen it?

A: Coca Cola

Q: I have grass growing up in the cracks of my patio. What to do?
A: Pour vinegar on the weeds.

Q: I am trying to open my window, but it's stuck! What should I do?
A: Rub it with a bar of soap.

Q: What's the very best tool to get rid of a stubborn sticky mess?
A: Your fingernail.

Q: How can I fix scratches on my grandmother's wooden furniture?
A: Break off a piece of walnut meat and rub it into the scratch.

Q: Help! I was fixing my bike and my hands are covered in bike grease!
A: Rub them with vegetable oil and the grease will come right off.

Q: Grease stains on my clothing?
A: Dawn dishwashing liquid. Rub a quarter size amount in and leave overnight. Then wash in the machine.

Q: Is it possible to get the wax off candlesticks?
A: Put the candlestick in the freezer! The wax peels right off! (This works on tablecloths too!)

Home Ownership

Should You Buy or Rent?

At this point, this question is probably academic to you; most college graduates are not in the position to buy their own pads. So renting will most likely be in your future for awhile. The question is, when should you think about buying?

If this were a numbers book, I would have you fill in a graph whose spaces included monthly payment (rent/mortgage), heat, electrical, maintenance, and then tell you that owning a home is something like sitting on a time bomb. Things go wrong. Expensive things. It's Christmas Eve and one of your sewer pipes breaks and the plumber charges you triple, and suddenly you're out $1000. There are many arguments being made today about how renting is actually the wiser fiscal option, especially when you are young.

But this isn't a numbers book, and like a good romantic right-brained person, I'm going to argue for buying as soon as you can. Why? Because there's nothing like the feeling of owning your own place. You can paint the walls whatever color you want! You can papier-mâché them for all anyone cares! You can tape *Xena: Warrior Princess* posters to the walls! Not only that, there *are* some practical (financial) reasons to own. You can get a tax deduction for your mortgage interest, plus the fact that at least in recent times when interest rates were low, housing was a great investment. That is *if* you buy (invest) wisely. First rule of real estate: location, location, location. Why? Most everything else can change. Location cannot. So think twice about buying beachfront property on Martha's Vineyard. A friend of mine sold hers five years ago. That land is now underwater. Along these lines, watch out for radon and other toxic issues on the property. Take the inspection very seriously. Think about what can easily be changed (the carpet, the paint job), what can possibly be changed (for a big chunk of change: the exposure, the siding, the kitchen), and what can't (which state the house is in).

How to Qualify for a Mortgage

Here are the criteria for buying a house:

- Having a down payment, which is no small thing: in these post-2008 years, it must be at least 20% of the price of the home. This percentage will be up to your lender (bank or mortgage company).
- Having a job with a steady paycheck so you can make monthly mortgage payments—remember, housing costs should be no more than 33% of your monthly income.
- Not being an idiot and deciding to get a hunk of junk that will require years of hard labor to make habitable.
- Buying in an area where resale values are good. This you can find out by seeing how quickly the houses in the area sell. If fast, this is good. If slow, shop elsewhere.
- A lender needs to approve you. So be polite and seem like a good solid citizen when talking to your potential lenders.
- Shop for a good rate. If rates are above 10% you may be better off renting.

Advice on Obtaining a Mortgage and Home-Ownership in General:

- Avoid "interest only" loans because they only benefit banks. Sure, your monthly payments may seem less, but you won't be paying off any principal, so you won't build equity in your home unless the market takes a drastic upturn.
- Avoid variable rate loans because they are a huge gamble. An ultra low interest rate for a set period of time may seem attractive, but at the end of that time, you could get locked in to an extremely high interest rate. If you haven't built up home equity during this time, you may find that you're not able to refinance to a lower fixed rate loan.

- When deciding whether or not you can afford to own a house, don't focus solely on the monthly mortgage payments. You will now be paying all utilities, insurance, taxes and home improvement/repairs in addition to your other monthly payments (car loans, student loans, etc.)
- Do your homework if you decide to refinance. In addition to knowing your home's approximate value vs. the outstanding principal balance, you will need to figure out what loan rate and term will save you the most money. My rule of thumb is that for refinancing to be worthwhile, I would have to save at least $10,000 (not including any closing costs) over the life of the loan.—Theresa, age 40

Why Is It Harder For Me to Qualify for a Mortgage than It Was For My Older Sister?[51] *courtesy of Jennifer, age 46*

The cost and availability of home loans has changed dramatically in recent years. If your sister sought financing between 2000 -2006, she did so during a residential housing bubble. As prices rose steeply, lenders loosened up on their underwriting standards. Previously, prudent lenders followed the 3C's -- Capacity, Credit History, and Collateral. This meant that a borrower needed to demonstrate wages sufficient to make monthly payments, on what were traditional 30-year fixed rate loans. Also, the borrower had to have a good credit score showing a record of payment other loans on time. Finally, the collateral—meaning the home—had to be appraised at least 80 percent of the amount borrowed. This meant a healthy 20 percent down payment.

However, with home prices rising in the early to mid '00s, lenders did two things. They innovated, and they abandoned the 3Cs. They allowed for very low down payments and even extended credit without requesting documentation (such as tax returns or W-2 forms) to confirm a borrower's income. Some borrowers were qualified for homes larger than they could afford, because the lender only considered their ability to make initial low "teaser" rate payments. Though the monthly payments were scheduled to recast, sometimes double, in a few years, the lenders would still make the loans even if the borrower would not have the income to pay. The reasoning was that the borrower could refinance into a new loan, assuming the home rose in value (as making the minimal payment made the principal balance grow). Additionally, lenders were not sufficiently concerned about defaults on mortgages because they often sold the mortgages to other bigger banks who then packaged them and turned them into securities for investors.

Meanwhile, new homes were being built on spec by builders taking advantage of this hot market. Then, in 2006, with excess inventory of homes, the housing bubble burst. Prices reversed. Defaults skyrocketed and banks and other investors that owned securities backed by cash flows from these teaser-rate, no-documentation or other high-risk loans began to fail. Since 2006, more than 5 million people have lost their homes, and presently, more than 10 million households are underwater on their mortgages (owing more than the home is worth). The U.S. government had to bail out the banks and other financial institutions that were exposed to high-risk mortgages, both directly through capital infusions and through indirect support, totaling in the trillions of dollars. As a result of that collapse, laws and rules have come into effect that require among other things, lenders to consider a borrower's capacity to make not just an initial teaser payment but the full monthly payment after any reset or recast. As a result of the legal reforms and the poor judgment of lenders in the past, it might be more difficult for you to qualify for a loan, but it may be better for you in the long run.[52]

Refinancing a Mortgage, *courtesy of Theresa age 40*

We got our first mortgage in 2000 when we bought our house. This was when the housing market was booming, and interest rates were relatively high. We took out a 30-year mortgage at a fixed interest rate of 8-3/8%. After 6 years, interest rates were much better, so we refinanced to a 20-year mortgage at 6-3/8%. With the economic crash, interest rates had plummeted by early 2009 to the point where refinancing again actually made sense. Unfortunately, I worked with a mortgage officer with whom I had not previously worked. I made the mistake of submitting the paperwork he requested, but not following up – I assumed he was doing his job, but he was not. Because of his delay, we lost our locked-in rate and the rates went up from 4-1/4% to over 5%, which was too high for us to equitably refinance. Thankfully, after about 9 months, the rates were back down and we were able to successfully refinance at 4-1/4%. In December 2010, we refinanced (for the final time!) at 2-3/4% for 10 years. Remarkably, our loan was approved without our house being re-appraised.

Cooperatives and Co-Housing, *courtesy of Grace, age 29*

Another housing option is living in a non-student cooperative that is unaffiliated with a college or university. Cooperatives are organized around living with many people, eating together, sharing chores, resources and skills, making decisions through consensus, creating community, and cooperating. It is wonderful to come home from work to a hot delicious dinner and not shop for groceries by yourself every week. If people are open and caring, it is a great way to make friends and support each other. The flip side is that people may reenact family dynamics like poor communication, rebellion, petulance, and bossiness, without being aware. Some co-ops have themes like vegetarian food, art, activism, international cultures, families with children, or urban gardening. Traditionally cooperative members co-own their house or apartment building, but many cooperatives are comprised of renters. Certain cities like Madison, Minneapolis, Philadelphia, Berkeley, Davis, and New York have high concentrations of cooperatives, but they can be located or started almost anywhere.

Co-housing is a variation where people own an individual house or apartment within a large complex and intentionally share common spaces, meals, tools, laundry, yard space and child care. Co-housing is popular in western European countries like Denmark, and it is spreading across the United States and Canada.

The North American Students of Cooperation website www.nasco.coop has information on student and non-student co-ops.

Pets

The trouble with a kitten is that
Eventually it becomes a cat.

—*Ogden Nash*

Who can resist the allure of a little tiny kitten, its whiskers tickling your face, its tiny pink nose wet and cool? Or a puppy, the very embodiment of adorableness, enthusiasm and exuberance? The answer is, not a lot of people, and unfortunately, a large number of these adorable puppies and kittens get abandoned by their new owners once they hit the gangly, disorderly adolescent stage, about seven months after arriving at their new homes. About three to four million cats and dogs are euthanized by shelters annually.[53] A sobering statistic.

The good news is that many more dogs and cats are kept and loved and incorporated into households than are abandoned. For me, getting my first pet—one who was actually mine and not the family dog—was a huge milestone. I felt like a regular householder. And like a lot of people, my first pet experience was entirely unpremeditated.

There's also the issue of vet bills. I had a friend who had to take all the money she'd been saving for years for a down payment on a house and spend it on a $3500 vet bill when her beloved Jana, a cockapoo, was diagnosed with cancer. (To save yourself from this kind of grief, consider getting pet insurance.[54])

Now of course she didn't have to make this choice, but then again, this is about love. When it comes to love, all bets, financial and otherwise, are off. Likewise, you may fall in love with a human who happens to be allergic to your beloved cats with whom you've been sharing your life for seven years. For some, this is a traumatic deal-breaker; for others, the cats find new homes to make way for the human partner.

Both cats and dogs require a lot of attention, love, and maintenance, but they more than give it back if you are willing to open up to their funny, fickle gifts and friendships. At one point, I realized that the four pets living in my home were my gurus; that if I lived in perfect obeisance to their whims I might actually evolve to become a more patient and kind person. Dogs and cats live in the present moment in a way that humans can't or won't (at least this human).

From a practical point of view, there are some things you should do to keep your dog or cat healthy and happy. First of all, make sure you have a good vet, one who actually likes animals. (You'd be surprised . . .) Second, if they give you medicine for your dog or cat, make sure you give it to them when they're supposed to receive it. A lot of animals in the Northeast require a monthly heartworm pill or a flea/tick treatment. Some dogs need professional grooming. All dogs need exercise, and if you find your dog is driving you crazy, it's probably because he's not getting out enough.

When your animal gets older, say over eight or nine years old, you should probably forgo the cheap dog- or cat-chow and shell out the bucks for the expensive brands your vet's been telling you to get all along. And unless you are still somehow eight years old yourself and have compulsions to feed the dog all the remnants of your dinner so you can have dessert, do *not* feed the dog human food, especially from the table or from your hand. This encourages begging, which makes your pet annoying to your guests and is just plain wrong. Dogs should never eat chocolate (it is a carcinogen to them) and many of them have other sensitivities which you may not discover until the evidence is on your living room carpet.

Some training is a must. The obvious is housebreaking which, depending on when you got your dog or cat, may or may not be an issue. Cats are quick to use a litter box. Dogs are easy to train if you crate train them. There are many excellent books to read on the raising of dogs, and the more you put into training in the first year, the easier and friendlier your relationship will be for the rest of the dog's life. Some books I'd recommend:

> *How to Be Your Dog's Best Friend*
> by the Monks at New Skete
> *The Art of Raising a Puppy* also
> by the Monks at New Skete
> *What All Good Dogs Should Know*
> by Jack Volhard and Melissa Bartlett

Exotic Pets

Some of you might want something other than the chocolate and
vanilla flavored dog and cat. So a
word about your options.

ferret

Although it might seem as though having an animal in a tank,
cage or Habitrail might be easier than having to walk a dog or deal
with an insane cat who tears your posters off the walls, don't be too
sure.[55] I have done a bit of research via Dave's Soda and Pet Food
City in Hadley, Massachusetts, the premiere wholesaler of exotic
pets. Below is a rundown of the costs of many varieties of exotic
pets and what you can expect in terms of hours spent daily on their
care.

Fish: You want a nice aquarium with some low-maintenance
fish? Fine. But remember: even though some fish (at least all the
ones I kept in a clear glass fishbowl as a kid) only live a few weeks,
if well-cared for, fish can live for 6 to 8 years. They cost between $5
and $50 per fish. The aquarium will run you a minimum of $25, and
the yearly cost of the chemicals will come to $100-$500. To feed a
bunch of fish for a month—about $7.

Rabbits: How about a cute little bunny? They're cheap: $40 at
Dave's (cheaper if you live in Flint Michigan). Expect them to live 9
years. You'll shell out around $75 for a hutch, $14 for litter, $13 for
a month's worth of food. But don't let your bunny loose around your
cat: bunnies kick cats' asses. Also, rabbits can be litter box trained.

Snakes: That boa constrictor you bought on a whim? It can
live around 16 years. $75 is the cost, with $25 for tank, food (remember it's live or frozen mice, one a month) $1.99 per mouse,
which you will have to dangle down to them.

Amphibians: A frog's lifespan is 6 to 16 years, and it will
make you a mere $10 poorer. They eat crickets, which are 10 for
$1.25; they eat 10 to 20 a week.

Dreaded Rodents: Hamsters and other rodents live for 4 to 6
years and cost between $13 to $25. Habitrail costs $20. (To continue
my anti-rodent rant, we had gerbils for years when we were growing up. The worst thing about gerbils is they have this predilection
toward infanticide and cannibalism. I won't say more than that, but
be prepared if you get a pair of the opposite sex.)

Turtles: American Box Turtles live for 123 years! They cost $20 and can dwell in the aquarium with your frog.

Birds: A parrot's lifespan is 80 years. Many people have to bequeath their parrot to a willing recipient upon their deaths. Parrots cost $500. Canaries generally live for 10 years, though that may be greatly reduced if you invite the neighbor's cat over, as we did. Cost per bird is $30. Large cage is $40. Bird food for a month is $20. Sweet little songs they sing—priceless.

Handy Chart For Exotic Pets

Animal	Price at Pet Shop	Housing/Food	Life Expectancy
Fish	Between $5-$50	$25	A few weeks to many years[56]
Cute Little Bunny	$40	$75 + about $30 per month	9 years
Boa Constrictor	$75	$25 for tank; about $10 per week	16 years
Frog	$10 plus aquarium	About $2.50/week	6-16 years
Hamsters and other Rodents	$13-25	$20 Habitrail[57]	4-6 years
American Box Turtles	$20	$25 aquarium	123 years!
Parrot	$500	Unknown. Fire that researcher.	80 years

Housekeeping and Organizing Your Space

I learned a lot from Julie Morgenstern's excellent book *Organizing from the Inside Out*. Beyond the truism that "every object must have a home" is the even more helpful insight that every object  ought to have a home that's convenient to the location where said object will be used. So, if you always wrap presents on the floor of your office, it makes sense to have the tools for wrapping presents grouped together in your office: perhaps in a basket, perhaps in a drawer, as opposed to keeping them in the downstairs hall closet. This concept revolutionized my whole organizational style. I rearranged my kitchen so that spices went into a drawer or cabinet right next to the stove, since that's where I use them most. Instead of alphabetizing my spices (a practice I could never keep up for more than a day or two) I keep the ones I use most handy and hide the Cream of Tartar in the back. Utensils for eating go in a drawer nearest the dishwasher, so that it's easy to put them away when they're clean, whereas other kitchen utensils which I don't use often, such as cookie cutters, go in a drawer in the suburbs of the kitchen. Knives go on a metal knife rack above the sink where I usually do my chopping. This may seem obvious to some of you, but before I read this book, I just kind of randomly assigned different drawers and cabinets to different categories.

I also read Marla Cilley's wonderful *Sink Reflections* and went on a clutter-clearing rampage. Better known as FlyLady[58], Cilley has a whole website that you can visit, join, and be connected to her community via multiple daily emails. Some high points of her program:

- The 27 Fling Boogie—go through any room in your house as fast as you can with a box and remove 27 items you can live without. Then fling them (or give them away).
- Divide your house into five zones and focus on one zone per week. The zones are: entryway/porch; kitchen; living room/dining room; master bedroom; other bedrooms and office.
- Don't be a perfectionist! Just do 15 minutes a day on your zone. Over time, it will get decluttered.

Now, I will never be a stellar housekeeper—it's not really in my Bucket List anyway—but here are some bare minimum suggestions to keep the sanitation department at bay:

How to Keep Your House or Apartment Clean

General suggestions:

- Keep bottles of environmentally-friendly cleaners and rags in every room of your house, neither hidden away where you'll never see them, nor sitting right

on your coffee table. Once a week (or once a day, if
you're a Virgo) spray some stuff onto a cloth and dust
your surfaces. I like that orange natural spray they
have at the health food stores because the smell of
Fantastik makes me want to puke.
- The smaller your space, the easier it will be to keep
clean. Similarly, the less stuff you have, the easier it
will be for you to stay organized.
- Establish an "in" box for papers that don't need immediate attention but also aren't obvious throwaways.
Once a month, file all your random papers which
you've let accumulate in your "in" box.
- You can wash your disgusting sponges in the dishwasher (Katryna says to then zap them in the microwave to sterilize).

Kitchen
- Every day: wipe off the sink, wipe off the stovetop,
wipe off the counters, sweep floor, empty compost jar.
- Twice a week, take out trash and recycling.
- Once every few months, clean out the refrigerator.
Throw anything out that hasn't been touched since the
last time you did this exercise, i.e. old jars of mustard
or salad dressing and anything that looks like it's got
a life of its own.
- Put an open box of baking soda in the fridge. It gets
rid of odors!
- Actually, while we're on the subject, if you are an
environmentalist and/or a cheapskate, you can use
baking soda and hydrogen peroxide or vinegar to
clean almost anything. Really. Try baking soda on
your grimy dishes.

Bathroom
- Wipe out the sink. I do this at night after I've washed
my face—I use the wet washcloth and then toss the
washcloth in the laundry.

- Swoosh toilet bowl with a brush and a mixture of vinegar and baking soda once a day.
- Once a week, empty wastebasket.
- Once a month, clean tub, floor, shower door if you have one. If you have a plastic shower curtain, you can wash it in the machine, but use cold water only! Mine looks like crinoline now because I accidentally stuck it in the hot cycle.
- Clean out your medicine cabinet. Toss anything whose expiration date has come to pass. Before you invite a visitor over, throw out or hide anything incriminating like Jolen bleach. If you think your date won't check out your medicine cabinet, you've got another think coming.

Bedroom

- Make your bed every day. It's amazing what a difference this makes. (Do not be a perfectionist about this: just draw the comforter up over the pillows. No hospital corners.)
- Fold and hang clothes after you've worn them unless dirty, in which case put in laundry basket. (This was always my nemesis—clothes strewn everywhere. I solved this problem by having three laundry baskets placed strategically where I was most likely to dump my clothes—the bathroom, next to my chest of drawers, and my closet.)
- Straighten out top of bedside table.
- Vacuum once a week if you have a pet, once every two weeks otherwise.
- Clean out heating grates once a month—and collect the change!
- Dust surfaces once a week.
- Wash windows once every two months.
- Change your sheets every week or two (or, if you're a committed slob, just change your pillowcase).
- Once a season flip your mattress or futon.

Office

- Have several trash cans near your work space(s). I have two trash cans next to my desk (one for paper, one for everything else).
- Keep a cloth or feather duster handy to dust your computer screen.
- Keep your desk neat! "A neat desk is a sign of a sick mind." I mean . . .
- Have a place for paperclips, stapler, stick pins in one location.
- Have your paper stacked near the printer.
- Have your stationery in your desk drawer, or wherever you like to curl up and write letters.
- Establish and maintain a filing system. Make sure it works for you, so that you will, for example, be able to find your last check register when you need it for tax time.

Clutter

The nemesis of all intentions to keep your living space clean is clutter. What is clutter? As US Supreme Court Justice Potter Stewart said of pornography, "I can't define it, but I know it when I see it."[59] Unfortunately, one person's clutter is another person's carefully compiled stack of Boredom-Relieving Material, laid out in a methodical (though seemingly random) manner on the coffee table. If you live alone, you will be able to conquer your own clutter (at least theoretically). If you live with others, you may have to live with some permanent blinders on.

Get rid of stuff you don't need. You will feel like a million bucks. It's really one of the most liberating, mind-opening practices you can have without using drugs or sex, and a pretty cheap hit.

When possible, give things away. That way you won't be contributing to the nation's overflowing landfills, and also, someone else might really want what you think is junk. My wise friend Elizabeth said to me when I was debating whether or not to go through my closet and send some clothes off to be donated, "It's almost *mean* of you to keep those clothes. Someone else will really want them, while you feel half-hearted about them!" She was right; now, I can't even remember what I gave away.

We need a lot less stuff than we think we need. Try this experiment: pack a box full of things you aren't sure you are ready to give away. Put the box in storage. If after one year you can't remember what's in there, give the box away without looking at the contents.

My friend Kaye (not her real name), who used to be the worst slob I have ever met, recently turned over a major new leaf. Her apartment, once almost impossible to navigate without tripping over various bowls of half-eaten meals, is now completely spotless. I asked her for her secrets, and she said she rigorously follows this plan:

- Make your bed every morning without fail.
- Do your dishes as soon as you've finished your meal. Just *do* them then. Do not let them pile up.
- Put away everything you take out after you're done with it.
- Spend fifteen minutes a day decluttering a space, using a timer. Don't do more than that or you'll get burned out and lose all your enthusiasm.

To this list, I would add:

- Clean your toilet once a week.
- Don't worry too much about the rest. Adopt the mantra: "Dull people have immaculate homes." This mantra, by the way, *both* my husbands' mothers had embroidered and hanging on their kitchen walls.

For me, clutter is a symptom of the materialistic society you will hear me drone on about further in this book. It's a symptom of the "not enough" disease so rampant in our culture. The manifestation of the disease goes like this: we're bored or depressed. We go shopping, thinking that will cheer us up, or perhaps we legitimately need something. While at the mall, we notice something that we absolutely need, only we forgot till now that we really needed it. Perhaps it's a new cappuccino maker ("My old one is okay, but the frothing thing is clogged. This one is so shiny and chrome-like! It'll look so great in the kitchen!"). Maybe it's a new pair of running shoes ("If I had that pair of running shoes, I actually might run. Then

I'd get thin and fit and my problems would be solved!") or a new CD ("I'd forgotten that Wilco had a new CD coming out! It would be unthinkable not to get it! I've been a fan of that band since I was practically in diapers!").

So we make our purchases, and we really do feel better, so much so that we go home and arrange our new cappuccino maker to the left of the old one (it turns out that the old one makes twice as much as the new one, so when we have a party it'll be good to have both, even though the counter is getting kind of crowded now). We put on our new shoes and jog around the park, come home in the best mood and blast the new Wilco CD as we make ourselves a fresh cappuccino. Life is grand!

But two weeks later, we get our VISA bill, which is $457 more than we'd expected it to be. We haven't gone running since that first evening; the Wilco CD was all right, but we've been too busy to listen since the night we got it. The cappuccino machine is great, but honestly, we mostly just have espresso because we've gotten used to not using the frothing thing; we've grown accustomed to it not working for so long, we keep forgetting to buy milk. Nevertheless, we doggedly use the new machine because we feel guilty about the fact that we bought it in the first place, and at least if we use it we can pretend that it was worthwhile to buy. We vaguely plan to sell the old machine on eBay or maybe to a friend. And thus our counter and our closets fill up and spill over.

A great way to get rid of clutter is to have a yard sale. We have these regularly, and while we rarely make a lot of money, we do get rid of a lot of junk. I asked my friend Courtney, famous yard sale maven and garage sale goddess, to compile a list of tips.

Steps to a Fantastic Yard Sale, *courtesy of Courtney, age 29*

1. Prepare, Prepare, Prepare. Have everything clean and displayed on a table or a blanket on the ground. I have dug through way too many boxes because people are "too busy" to take things out of the boxes. Most people aren't willing to do that though. Everything should be priced in advance. Nothing is worse than finding a ton of things you like and then finding out the person wants to charge ridiculous amounts.

2. Be ready for people wanting to negotiate. There is
    nothing wrong with saying you don't want to go any
    lower than the price marked, but know that you will
    be asked to.
3. Be ready for people to show up at least an hour before
    you are scheduled to open. You want to sell your
    things, they want to buy them—let them start shop-
    ping early. If you really don't want to open early, put
    "No Early Birds" in your newspaper ad.
4. Make sure you are really emotionally ready to part
    with these items. When someone is walking away
    with an item, it's a bit too late to realize that no matter
    how much you need to de-clutter, you weren't ready
    to part with that one thing.
5. Advertise in the local paper with a few lines describ-
    ing the type of items you are selling. If you have
    something collectible, mention it specifically (old
    Barbie, baseball card collection, rare Pez dispenser)—
    it will bring in collectors, but also mention "kitchen
    items" or "furniture," "CDs and DVDs" etc. to bring
    in someone not interested in your specific collectible.
6. The night before, put signs out in strategic locations
    (have date and time on them) and secure them so they
    don't get spun around in the night.

Freecycle

There's a fantastic website called www.freecycle.org. These
are community-based groups whose individuals email each other,
offering things they have that they want to get rid of, and asking
for things they want. If you have an old beanbag chair that keeps
migrating to different parts of your house looking for a permanent
home, and your new girlfriend threatens to leave if you don't get rid
of it, post it on Freecycle. Within a few days, someone will come
and take it off your porch. Conversely, you may be able to find that
nice cheap backpack you've been looking for, yours for the picking
up on someone else's stoop. The danger here is that if you are a real
clutter hound, you will end up taking everyone else's excess and
only contributing to your "more is more" approach to life.

How to Fix a Broken Toilet

Plumbers are the most desirable folks in town (in many cities anyway) and in my experience, they are never available when you really need one. So it's well worth your while to find a good plumber and keep his or her name on a piece of paper on your refrigerator door in case of emergencies. One thing that's sure in life, along with death and taxes, is that toilets malfunction. Below are a list of solutions you can try yourself, should the need arise.[60]

1. A Clogged Bowl

You know it's a clogged bowl because the toilet isn't draining, can't flush and/or overflows. Try a plunger. Push the plunger vertically down and hard, covering the opening of the toilet. Make a seal. Then pull up. If it doesn't unclog after several pumps, you'll have to wait for your plumber.

2. Running Toilets

If your toilet seems to keep running long after you flushed it, the problem is most likely a leak, a tangled chain, a damaged handle, or something with the floater ball, which you will see if you open the top of the toilet tank. If you peer inside, you will see a little plunger over a hole. That plunger should be covering the hole. If it's not, stick your hand in and fix it. (The water in the tank is not nasty, though you may want to wash afterwards. In fact, Katryna just found a study done where there was more bacteria in the ice at a fast food restaurant than in the toilet.) If the chain is broken, and you are lazy, you can still use your toilet as long as you cover the hole manually each time after you flush. (Or you can patch the chain with a paperclip, according to my copy editor, Lori. She says, "It works!") With the lid off, you can flush the toilet and watch to see what happens. All the water should drain out and then gradually fill back up again. When the tank is full, you theoretically should be able to flush again. Check on the handle to make sure it isn't stuck or sticking out at a strange angle. Jiggling works wonders. Check the chain to make sure it isn't tangled. Check under the floater ball for debris which might be keeping it from monitoring the water level correctly.

3. Toilet Doesn't Flush

If this is the problem, you probably have some broken hardware in the circuit of handle to chain to lever to floater ball. Open the lid of the tank and check to make sure everything's connected.

4. Toilet Only Flushes Part Way

This is a water level problem. Take off the lid and look at the water level. It ought to be about three quarters of an inch below the top of the overflow tube. If the water's lower than that, bend the float arm of the float ball so that it's higher. (If too high, make the arm lower.)

In General:

You can shut off the water to the toilet by turning the valve in the back, near the floor. If that valve is the problem, there is a main water valve in your basement that can be shut off, if you have access to it. If that valve is the problem, grab an oar and get a boat!

Mail Clutter

Your mail plays many roles in your life as a human. When you were a kid, mail mostly meant friendly postcards from Grandma and your friends who wrote you from sleepaway camp. In college, mail was probably pretty pleasant in general too, excepting those envelopes that contained your grades for the semester.

Now mail takes on a whole new set of trousers. You will find as an adult that the majority of your mail is junk. Even the mail that may not at first *seem* like junk (catalogs you think you might someday want, special offers for free stuff, coupons) probably is. And yet, lurking in that stream of junk mail will be *incredibly important documents* which you really must not lose or your life will become, to put it mildly, unnecessarily complicated. For example, if you toss out your credit card bill, you will pay a fine plus 18% interest on your purchases. If you throw out your DMV registration—woe betide. My friend, Melvin (not his real name) owes tens of thousands of dollars to the IRS just because he neglected to open his mail for three years.

Mail Not to Throw Out Without Inspecting Carefully

- Anything from the IRS
- Anything from the DMV or RMV
- Anything from the town or city you live in
- Any bill
- Anything that says "Important Tax Document Enclosed"
- Anything from your bank, though this will mean opening lots of dreck
- Anything from your insurance companies
- Checks made out to you that are not from car dealerships

Mail to Toss Immediately

- Anything that spells your name incorrectly (Unless it also falls in the above category. Pride has its limits.)
- Offers from Discover for a credit card
- Pottery Barn catalogs. They are evil; they will make you want to change your entire lifestyle so you can afford their ridiculously beautiful and overpriced furniture. Don't even look!
- Checks made out to you from car dealerships

When you pick up your daily mail, sort it carefully. Throw out the obvious dreck and proceed directly with your Not To Throw Out Pile to the neatest, safest place in your apartment. Sort the mail first by owner, then by kind: bills, important, and friendly correspondence (does anyone send postcards anymore?). At a designated time, anytime between that moment but no longer than a week from then, be prepared to sit down and fill out all the important forms, pay all bills, put necessary documentation into addressed envelopes (which may or may not be provided), affix postage, and mail!

I approach my mailbox daily with gritted teeth, as though I am entering the jungle. I throw out almost everything that comes in the mail, like offers to subscribe to magazines at 75% off the list price, "checks" from car dealerships, coupons from Bed, Bath and Beyond, and a ridiculous number of requests for donations to all sorts of causes and institutions I believe in. When I get a bill or statement from my bank, I pick out the relevant sheet of paper and toss the rest—all the offers for their brand of insurance, and "checks" that I can fill out and turn to cash. Once a week—it happens to be Tuesday—I tackle it all.

But if you don't have a couple of hours once a week as I do, here's a good time to reinforce my life-coachy rule of breaking down all activities into bite-sized chunks. I got this tip from writer Anne Lamott, whose cardinal rule of daily writing is to keep the daily assignment the size of a one-inch picture frame. (In other words, just write a little bit every day, and soon you will have an entire novel.) The same holds true for most activities: just clearing a little of your desk every day keeps the clutter demons at bay and allows for the chance that at least some bills will get paid on time and that you won't default on your student loan—this month, anyway.

My filing system is pretty simple; most of the mail goes directly in the recycling can by the front door and doesn't make it to my desk. The rest goes up to my office. If there are bills that I can pay online, I do so right away to avoid late fees and just to get it over with. I save the relevant information from the bill and file it in a drawer marked "bills and receipts." Once a year, in early March, I go through this drawer for tax time (see section called "Taxes"). If you can't or don't want to pay your bills online, follow the above, but instead of paying the bill at your computer, put all bills into one "bill" box. This box should also contain your checkbook, a calculator, envelopes, stamps, pens, and return address stickers. Once a week put on a Decemberists CD and pay bills. Again, once the bill is paid, file it in a file marked "bills" with the year written along the side.

Laundry

Separate whites from darks, or your whites will turn pink. Wash whites in hot or warm water (only if they are stinky—hot uses a lot of energy, and your whites will be fine in cold water). If it's colored laundry it has to be cold. Save money and be kind to the environment by using a combination of baking soda and white vinegar instead of detergent, or use an excellent green detergent like Seventh Generation or Ecos. If you live in a warm climate, set up a clothesline outside and hang your wet laundry up to dry. Or get an indoor drying rack. Or feel guilty and dry your clothes in a dryer (dryers use a ridiculous amount of energy).

Big tip for your Bucket List: if you ever have the change/choice, get a washer/dryer rig near your bedroom. I can't tell you what a difference it makes once you have kids not to have to lug laundry up and down stairs. We toss it all onto our bed (another reason to keep it made!) which also means we are forced to fold it before we can sleep.

Cooking

*Maybe it was because I am a male born in 1955, but I had
virtually no idea how to cook when I was a young adult. In
college I was hanging around some groovy bohemians who fin-
gerpicked guitars and drank wine, and as dinner was coming
together, they gave me the assignment of making garlic bread.
They gave me a loaf of bread, stick of butter and a clove of
garlic and I was baffled. We had garlic powder growing up but
what gives with the cloves? Just getting the skin off of it was
insanely difficult. I didn't want to admit that I didn't know how
to make something as simple as garlic bread, but eventually I
pleaded for assistance. —John, 51*

Of the many things that frightened me as a child, near the top
was the fear that one day I would have to stick my hand into the
body of a raw chicken and pull out the heart and livers and terrifying
innards. Watching my mother do this I experienced so much nausea
and trepidation, I decided to avoid the problem by becoming a vegetarian. I did not particularly love animals, and it was certainly not
for health reasons. I was just grossed out by raw meat (particularly
the aforementioned chicken innards). Plus, all the cool people were
vegetarian; I was a burgeoning radical, and it just felt like the right
thing to do. At the age of 22, I was not sure of many things. Labeling
myself a vegetarian was convenient; it gave me an instant identity
and some built-in limits.

For the first few years post-college, I became an enthusiastic
vegetarian cook, scanning recipes in the various Moosewood cook-
books and spin-offs, trolling the grocery stores, my lists of ingredients in my fists, throwing huge dinner parties with international
themes around my tiny coffee table in my two-room apartment.

As I said earlier, the job I got after college—Assistant Dean of
Students at an all-girls boarding school—was perfect in that it fell
into my lap and allowed me to return to my hometown where my
fiancé David lived. It was not so perfect in that it had nothing to do
with what I wanted to do with my life, which was to be a famous
rock star. Instead of riffing on power chords and wearing five-inch
high-heeled boots, I ran social activities, sat on a discipline com-

mittee, assisted the Dean of Students in all matters, particularly in trying to keep track of the boarders during the weekends, and single-handedly ran a 40-student dorm. I had an apartment in that dorm on the first floor which consisted of two dorm rooms connected by a small bathroom and an even smaller kitchen. The kitchen was really just the entryway into the apartment; when I opened the door from the dorm, I was literally a foot away from my stove/countertop/sink situation. A half-size refrigerator sat under the countertop portion of this one unit super-appliance. Needless to say, I quickly became adept at creative ways to use counter space.

I was terrible as far as the actual job went. I hid in my apartment and lived in terror of the girls—many of whom were only four years younger than I was. I hated planning social activities and blew my budget hiring obscure indie bands to play at the spring formal dance. I was bored at disciplinary meetings, anxious about the students' welfare over the weekend, and generally a lot more interested in planning my wedding and playing my guitar. But I did learn how to cook, a direct result of my hatred for my job. Because my main survival technique was to hide as much as possible from the students, I would leave work as soon as I could (usually 5 p.m.) and drive directly to the Safeway. There I'd buy ingredients for dinner, then come home, put on some Indigo Girls or Neville Brothers (it was the early 90s) and cook up a vegetarian feast. (Actually, the vegetarian phase ended when I got married because someone gave us a "fajita maker" for a wedding gift, which is really just a small oval shaped cast iron skillet and a clay dish with a lid. I used this as an excuse to start cooking meat, but only meat that came in Styrofoam and plastic-wrapped packages.) I learned that if you follow the directions in a cookbook, generally things turn out pretty well. I learned that cast iron skillets make all food taste better, ditto wooden spoons. I learned that onions form the base of almost anything delicious, and that garlic is easily peeled when you press down on the "backs" of the cloves firmly but gently with the flat side of a knife handle.

David came over every night around 10 p.m. and I tried to replicate the meals we'd enjoyed at the local Washington DC restaurants, usually ethnic cuisines like Chinese, Indian and Salvadoran. Our favorite was Ethiopian, whose base is a flat spongy bread which takes three days to rise. Somehow, I felt it absolutely essential to learn *exactly* how a meal should be prepared—down to making my own ghee (the liquefied butter Indians cook with instead of oil) when I cooked Indian food, or my own berbere, the Ethiopian spice for wa'ats (stews).

I also liked learning to cook because it gave me an excuse to call my four aunts, all of whom I secretly admired but was too afraid to just call and chat with. When I was in the middle of a recipe, and I didn't know for example if you could substitute salted for unsalted butter, or white sugar for brown, I could call one of my aunts and ask. Inevitably, she would be glad to help and we would end up talking for a half hour, me with the phone wedged between ear and shoulder, measuring out flour or chopping vegetables.

A word from our Eco-Preacher: Don't buy nonstick pans. The pans may be bad for you. They can give off potentially harmful fumes at medium to high temperatures, and a chemical crucial to the manufacture of nonstick surfaces—but not found in the finished surfaces—is prevalent in the environment, including most Americans' blood.

> *"We recommend that people phase out the use of Teflon cookware in their home," says Lauren Sucher of the Environmental Working Group, a Washington, D.C. organization that compiles data on toxicology."*[61]

Instructions for Seasoning and Cleaning a Cast Iron Skillet[62]

The surfaces of a new cast-iron pan are porous and have microscopic jagged peaks. You season a pan by rubbing it with oil, heating it for 30 to 60 minutes in a 300-degree oven, then letting it cool to room temperature.

The oil fills the cavities and becomes entrenched in them, as well as rounding off the peaks. By seasoning a new pan, the cooking surface develops a nonstick quality because the formerly jagged and pitted surface becomes smooth. Also, because the pores are permeated with oil, water cannot seep in and create rust, which would give food an off-flavor.

Preparing a Cast Iron Skillet For the First Time:

1. Rinse with hot water (do not use soap) and dry thoroughly.
2. Before cooking, prepare the cooking surface by oiling and rubbing the oil into the pan with a paper towel (made from recycled paper) or clean dishtowel (you can designate one oily rag for the job; we keep ours in an empty yogurt container with the cleaning supplies). Avoid putting a cold skillet onto a very hot burner.
3. After cooking, clean skillet with a stiff brush (but not the kind you use to clean a grill! A gentle stiff brush) and hot water. Using soap is not recommended, and harsh detergents should never be used. Avoid putting hot skillet into cold water. Thermal shock can cause metal to warp or crack.
4. Towel dry immediately and apply a light coat of non-stick spray or vegetable oil while skillet is still warm.
5. Store in a cool, dry place.
6. *Never* wash in the dishwasher.

Take care with metal utensils, as you would with any pan you want to stay nonstick. If I have cooked something that isn't sticky (like eggs or a grilled cheese sandwich or other easy-to-clean-up-after thing), I simply scrape anything that comes up with a wooden spoon while the pan is still hot. Once the pan cools, I rub it down with vegetable oil and Kosher salt to get up anything that is still sticky, and wipe it out with a clean towel. Does amazing things for the seasoning, and salt cleans far more effectively than you would expect. If I've cooked something extremely greasy/sticky/gross, I take the pan off the heat and deglaze while it is still hot, usually with hot water, and scrape scrape scrape with the wooden spoon, then pour it out instead of making sauce with it. I'm frequently scared I'll lose an eye when I add water to grease, but I still have both and it

does the trick. I actually picked this idea up from a soup recipe.
Also, prior to the soup recipe I had no idea what 'deglaze'
means. —Meredith, age 28

Your Trip to the Grocery Store

* organic bananas

Here are some general tips about grocery shopping: if you're into nutrition, an easy rule is to stick to the perimeter of the supermarket. That's where most of the whole foods are. The junk food is up and down the aisles.

Another thing about shopping: you don't need to wrap all your produce in individual plastic bags. Save petroleum. Take just one or two plastic bags, and leave the rest of your fruits and veggies loose. When you get home, mix the salad greens and anything that might wilt in one bag and the fruits and veggies in danger of rotting in the other. You will notice that your fridge probably has two produce drawers with little levers. Put the salad greens in the drawer set for high humidity and the fruits and veggies that might rot in the drawer set for low humidity. Plastic does keep the produce fresher for longer. And be honest with yourself: if your vegetables end up rotting week after week in the vegetable drawer, buy frozen. That will stave off your guilt and keep your refrigerator from smelling like Union City, New Jersey. (Fruits and avocados keep very well in a bowl on the counter, too.)

I can't resist doing a little eco-preaching here too. There are very good reasons to spend a little more and shop organic. Why? Because agribusiness is destroying the country from an economic and ecological and sociological point of view. Also, non-organic foods are covered in pesticides, many of which cause cancers and other horrible diseases. Commercially farmed animals, raised to be eaten, are often given antibiotics (which reduces the effectiveness of antibiotics on human disease), added hormones (which is considered one of the reasons why American girls now begin menstruating much earlier) and other drugs. Usually, organically raised animals are treated better, allowed to roam and graze at will. Organic farmers have their eye on the global or at least local environment and don't make decisions to save money at the expense of the land or air or water. Commercial farms produce excess manure, which they don't recycle as fertilizer and instead dump in the nearest river, thereby contaminating the ground water with nasty bacteria such as E. coli and other pathogens. Finally, industrial farms use a lot more fossil fuel, which is of course, a limited resource. Organic farms spend a lot more psychic energy figuring out ecological management techniques to solve pest problems, transportation issues and crop rotation. Also, organic tastes better. Don't you think we should pay for these virtuous qualities?

If you buy locally, you're obviously not contributing to the glut of gas-burning trucks clogging the interstates, not to mention the planes flying your mangoes in from Mexico. Local farmers often use organic techniques, but because it's costly and takes a long time to gain organic certification, the produce might not be marked as such. See Barbara Kingsolver's wonderful book *Animal, Vegetable, Miracle* to learn more about the joys of eating locally.[63]

Whenever possible, buy organic or, failing that, support your local farms and dairies. You are voting with your pocketbook, which is at least as effective as going to the polls. (See "Being an Adult in a Democracy.") If you can't afford to *always* choose organic, check out the Environmental Working Group's "dirty dozen" and "clean fifteen" lists for produce.[64] For example, apples are sprayed with much more terrible pesticides than bananas (plus of course one usually eats the apple skins, but not the banana peels), and so if you are counting your pennies, spend extra on organic apples and go ahead and buy non-organic bananas. (Although I swear I can taste the difference, and so choose organic bananas.)

One of the coolest new movements in this country is the CSA, which stands for Community Supported Agriculture. For $400-$800 a year, you can "buy in" to a farm and get yourself all the fresh fruits and veggies you can eat. Small farms are using this model to great effect. They harvest their produce and once a week (or more frequently, for bigger farms) they put it in a shed for "pick up" by farm shareholders, who show up with their canvas bags at the ready to gather their weekly share of vegetables. Many farms even have "pick your own." It's been the great pleasure of my life to stroll through the sugar snap pea vines in June and pick pea pods to my heart's content (better yet to watch my kids do this). When shareholders support farms in this manner, farms are able to survive when the inevitable bad weather years hit. In 2011 our farm almost went down after Hurricane Irene swept through, drowning several fields of produce. But because our community had "bought in," though they lost part of their crop, they did not lose all. Not only that, neighboring farms donated bushels of what we'd lost (winter squash) while our farm traded their surplus of onions to another farm who'd lost that crop. Isn't this the way the world ought to work?

My great aunt Sally introduced us to our first CSA in Williamstown in 1991: Caretaker Farm. Today we are proud members of Crimson & Clover Farm in Florence, MA. Find a CSA near you.[65] P.S. Farms are a great place to meet new people in your town. And if you are looking for romance, I mean, please. What is more romantic than a farm?

Essentials Tools for the *How to Be an Adult* Kitchen

I've lived in five different kitchens since college, and I've inherited, bought or been given many tools. Here's what I'd give my daughter or son for their first kitchen:

- 1 cast iron skillet
- 1 small pot for heating up soup and cooking rice
- 1 larger pot for cooking spaghetti and making chilis and soups
- 1 roasting pan
- 1 flat pan (cookie sheet)

- 1 coffee maker
- 1 tea kettle
- 2 wooden spoons
- 1 really really sharp, excellent knife (invest!!)
- measuring spoons
- measuring cups
- flatware, plates, glasses, mugs and bowls for 4 (if you have more people over for dinner, you can ask them to bring extra plates, flatware, bowls, etc. They will think you are charming.)
- can opener
- combination bottle opener/corkscrew
- carrot peeler

Advanced:

- Toaster
- Vegetable steamer
- Food processor and/or blender
- Garlic press
- Colander
- Rolling pin
- Pizza stone

General Nutrition

For optimal nutrition, as a general rule, put equal parts vegetables, protein and whole grains on your plate, maybe leaning a little heavier on the veggies. Commit to having a salad or some kind of additional vegetable every evening, at least. Eat three fruits a day. If you are a woman who is not lactose intolerant, try to eat three servings of lowfat dairy per day. You will be glad later when your hips don't break. Try not to snack, but if you are going to, eat real food (like fruit, nuts, carrots, small amounts of cheese) instead of junk. Here's  why: although you may not have a problem with your metabolism now, if you are like most Americans, you burn a lot fewer calories than you take in. As you get older, your body needs good nutrition more than it did when you were young and invincible and able to eat Red Hot for breakfast. Katryna used to eat Red Hot for breakfast. She claims she put it on very healthy food, but it must be stated that the other staple of her breakfast was a can of Coca-Cola. By senior year, she had to go to the hospital to find out what was wrong with her stomach.

You want every calorie to count. If you remember your mom talking about "empty calories," here's what she meant: some calories are packed with nutrients. Say, spinach, for example. Chock full. Vanilla frosting, on the other hand, not so many. Actually, none. If a person needs 2000 calories to get through the day, and specific amounts of vitamin C, protein, iron, calcium, and all those other numbers listed on food boxes by the FDA, it stands to reason that you're going to have to eat a certain number of calories that contain these nutrients. But if you're spreading vanilla frosting on everything, that's a whopping 118 calories per tablespoon. And let's face it, no one eats just one tablespoon of vanilla frosting. You can see how the calories add up fast, and there's virtually no nutritional value to vanilla frosting (though if you eat a whole can, for 2000 calories, you will get 4% of your daily requirement of iron). It's actually possible to become severely malnourished *and* be grossly obese at the same time.

Honestly, there is nothing essentially wrong about eating a bowl of cereal and milk every night; while somewhat pathetic from a culinary point of view, it's actually not a bad nutritional option (although you may want to draw a distinction between Crunchberries and that Uncle Sam's flaxseed and sawdust cereal). Still, you can definitely make some improvements.

Breakfast should include a protein, a whole grain (also known as a starch), and a fruit or vegetable. Of course, there are variations galore, but if you think about it, the classic breakfasts follow this general rule, such as:

- Cereal (grain) and Milk (protein) and banana (fruit)
- Eggs (protein) on toast (grain) with orange juice (fruit)
- In Japan, they eat fish (protein) and rice (grain) with some seaweed (vegetable)

- Egg McMuffin. Biscuit (vaguely grainish), egg, Canadian bacon and cheese (vaguely proteinish, though mostly fat) and, if you add ketchup, you will have a bona fide vegetable, according to our 40th president.

Lunch should also include equal parts starch and protein, plus some vegetable. Sandwiches are an easy and ever-popular option. Whole grain breads are best. Rye is yummy, as is any hearty seven-grain. Put a couple of slices of turkey with lettuce and tomato, or a mound of tuna fish (mix one can of tuna with a tablespoon of mayo plus a chopped up stick of celery or dill pickle) on the bread and you're good to go. Soup is also nice if you're home and own a can opener. Choose soups with vegetables. Part of being an adult, unfortunately, is eating your vegetables. Ignore me at your peril.

Top 10 Reasons You Should Eat Your (Organic) Vegetables

1. They are loaded with nutrients you can't get any other way
2. They fill you up and don't have a lot of calories
3. People will judge you if you don't and be so impressed if you do
4. They make a plate of food look much prettier
5. They actually taste good once you get used to them, especially if you put dressings and butter on them
6. They are full of water and will keep you hydrated

7.   They are real food, as opposed to things like Cheez Whiz and Bugles.

8.   If you're ever compelled to give up sugar, you will find that there is nothing more delicious in the whole world than a Sweet Dumpling Squash in late September

9.   You can grow them yourself and feel like a million dollars

10. Your mom will be proud of you

How to Make All Vegetables Delicious

Roast them. That's the secret. Roasting slowly releases all the natural sugar and flavor in vegetables. You will never say yuck again!

Preheat your oven to 400. Put the veggies in a roasting pan. Drizzle them with olive oil and a little salt. Roast them until they are very well-cooked. Best veggies for roasting are:

-Brussel sprouts. Cut these in half and broil them, or better yet, fry them! They should be crispy and very dark.

-Asparagus. Sprinkle with salt and spray with oil. Broil till almost blackened.

-All root veggies, especially parsnips, beets, winter squash, sweet potatoes, and rutabagas.

-Cauliflower! Toss with some Indian spices and roast till brown and crispy.

-Kale! Spray with oil and sprinkle salt, then broil till crispy. They turn into potato chip-like crisps, but with more nutrients.

-Eggplant! Bake whole until completely soft and liquefied in the middle. Then mix with salt, oil, spices. Or cut first into rounds, spray with oil and season. Bake till soft.

-Summer squash is best grilled or panfried. Try patty pan squashes in July and August.

The Dinner Party

Informal:

Pour a box of
pasta into salted, boil-
ing water. Watch it
(casually) as it boils,
about seven minutes
(consult the box).
Meanwhile, pour a jar
of marinara sauce into
a small pot and heat
on low to medium.
When the pasta starts
to get soft, observe it

carefully. Pull out a strand. Taste it. If it's only slightly hard in the
middle, it's done. You can also use the old throw-a-strand-against-
the-wall technique, but I don't recommend it. If it sticks, it's more
than ready, and you will have to wipe down the wall before your
guests arrive.

Pour the pasta and the water into a colander. If you don't care
about calories, swish a couple of tablespoons of olive oil around in
it to keep it from sticking (or, alternatively, put the oil directly into
the boiling water *before* you put the dry pasta in). If you are serving
people you want to impress, put a mound of spaghetti on each plate
and top it with a smaller mound of red sauce. Put some Parmesan
cheese into a small serving bowl with a teaspoon and place on the
table so guests can add what they like. If you're just having your
sister over, you can go ahead and mix the sauce and cheese in right
away with the pasta and let her serve herself.

Formal:

Find a recipe that looks good in a book or online, or if you have
a friend who's recently served something you love, ask her to give
you the recipe. Read it carefully first. Do you have time to follow all
the steps? For beginning cooks, don't attempt shortcuts right away.

Or try my foolproof chicken recipe.[66] Yes, I know, chicken. This involves removing innards. At some point I just, well, grew up and did it.

I am on a mission to teach people how to roast a chicken. I have been shocked and appalled by what most people think is an acceptable roast chicken. There is nothing more disgusting than a chicken with that pale, yellowish rubbery skin which looks like, well, chicken fat. There is simply no need for this. So make this bird, perfect it, show it off to your guests and then for God's sake, evangelize! Pass these instructions on!

Foolproof Chicken Recipe:

Buy a whole chicken. Preheat the oven to 400 degrees. Over the sink, take off the plastic wrap and wash the bird. Then, say a prayer and stick your hand into the cavity of the bird. Remove the innards, which are, these days, often conveniently packaged so the yuck factor is minimized. Salt a roasting pan. This means, pour a lot of salt on the bottom of a roasting pan. Put the bird back-side down in the pan (if the back is down, the wing tips are sticking up). Pour a lot of salt all over the bird, inside and out, making sure that every inch is nice and salty. This keeps moisture in and creates an incredibly delicious crispy skin. Stick the pan in the oven and let cook for at least two hours (I prefer 3 to 3 1/2). The skin should be puckered and obviously crispy and golden brown. There is practically no such thing as overcooking, contrary to what your mother might tell you (if the bird is properly salted, it really won't dry out).

After the chicken's been in the oven for an hour, wash some small potatoes and cut them into quarters. Toss them around the chicken and let roast. The salty chicken juices will surround them and give them a rich, buttery taste. Katryna puts sweet potatoes in with the chicken for the whole two hours. Yum!

When the chicken's been cooking for an hour and forty minutes, cut up an onion. Put some olive oil on the bottom of your cast iron skillet and heat to medium high. When the oil is hot (test by flicking a couple of drops of water into it—if it's hot, it sizzles) toss the chopped onion in. Take a clove of garlic and crack it with the handle of a knife. It will peel easily. Mince it. Toss it into the pan. Chop up some other vegetables—anything you want, including eggplant, zucchini, broccoli, green beans, spinach, okra (bags of frozen vegetables work really well here, if you don't feel like chopping). Season with salt and pepper as the frozen veggies thaw in the hot pan. Experiment with spices, but not all at the same time. Most spices work best if you put them in after the hot oil and before the onion.

Note: The chicken may not be fully cooked to its crispiest falling-off-the-bone potential after two hours. Be patient and wait until the bird is truly brown and tender. The drumsticks should feel loose in their sockets. You will learn by trial and error how long to cook a bird based on your oven and the size of the bird (the bigger the bird, the longer it takes to cook).

When the chicken is truly cooked, it will be easy to carve; it should be practically falling off the bone. Cut off the drumsticks first, then the second joint (the thighs), then the wings. Now begin to slice the meat off the body of the bird. Put all the nice pieces of chicken onto a platter, in the center. Make a circle around the chicken with the potatoes. Last, put the vegetables on the outer ring. Put three serving utensils (a big fork and a big spoon and another spoon) in sight, and serve your meal!

Dessert and Ambiance

Here's the secret for the insecure chef: if you want your guests to love your food, don't skimp on the three ingredients Americans love most: flour, sugar, and fat. These three horsemen of the apocalypse constitute 90% of what we think of as dessert. That being said, dessert does not need to be a big production. A nice option is fresh fruit and good quality dark chocolate. These days, I just go to the Qwik Mart and get a couple of pints of Ben & Jerry's and some fresh strawberries.

Splurge for candles if you are having special guests. Pick some appropriate dinner music. Clean the bathroom. And don't forget to enjoy yourself.

More Recipes

Pesto and Goat Cheese "Pizzas"
Flour tortillas
Commercial or homemade pesto (recipe follows)
Goat cheese

Put the tortillas on a cookie sheet. Smear some pesto on them, as if you were making a pizza and the pesto is the tomato sauce. Then sprinkle some goat cheese on top. Set the oven to 450 and cook till the cheese is melty, about 7 minutes.

Variations on the above pizza:
* Use just gorgonzola and sprinkle with rosemary
* Tex/Mex pizzas: salsa for tomato sauce and Monterey Jack for cheese
* Good old fashioned tomato sauce and mozzarella, plus parmesan.

Pesto

A huge bunch of basil so you yield 4 cups of leaves
3 tablespoons pignoli nuts (if you are a snob) or walnuts (if you are a plebian)
3/4 cup Parmesan cheese
3/4 cup olive oil
1 clove crushed garlic
1/4 teaspoon salt
(Unfortunately, you really need a food processor, or at least a blender, for this one.)

Follow these directions carefully! Clean the basil leaves with a damp paper towel. Trim the stems off the basil so that you're working with the leaves only. Put all the ingredients but the leaves in the bowl of the food processor. With the machine running, add the leaves by the handful. Process so that your pesto (which means "paste") comes out pretty rough, not like baby food. You want it to have some texture.

Put it into plastic containers and freeze any that you won't be using in the next week. Pesto can be successfully frozen and thawed and tastes nearly as good in March as it does in August.

Sesame Noodles
8 oz spaghetti or other noodles
Sauce:
2 garlic cloves, minced
minced ginger, about a tablespoon
2 tablespoons Chinese sesame paste
    (you can substitute tahini or even peanut butter)
1 tablespoon dark sesame oil
2 tablespoon rice vinegar
optional:
1/2 teaspoon fresh cilantro, chopped
1 tablespoon honey
pinch of 5 spice powder
and you can toss with:
1 scallion
roasted peanuts

Cook noodles until tender and drain immediately, rinsing with cold water. While you're waiting for the noodles to cook, make the sauce. In a blender or food processor (or with a fork) blend all the sauce ingredients until free of lumps. As soon as the noodles are drained, toss them in the sauce. You can serve immediately, although I think they taste better after they've soaked up the sauce for a few hours.

Once when I was cooking these noodles, the phone rang, and as usual, it was one of those people trying to sell you something. In this case, it was a studio that specializes in family photography, Katryna answered the phone politely and said, "No, I'm sorry, because of the policies of the Bush administration, we're unemployed and can't afford a family portrait." The salesperson tried to prevail upon her ("But that's exactly why I'm calling—this is a discount"), but Katryna managed to extricate herself from the situation.

Not ten minutes later, the same salesperson called back, and not realizing that he'd called the same number twice, entreated me to have my family sit for a nice family picture. I figured we needed a better excuse, so I said, "Sorry, it's just that we're really ugly and don't want to be reminded."

We were congratulating ourselves on our cleverness when the phone rang again for the third time. This time, he said, "You know, my girlfriend runs a top notch cosmetic service. Maybe I should send her over so she can show you folks what she can do. And I'll bring my camera and we'll take a look-see. Whaddaya say?"

Chicken with Balsamic and Mustard
2 to 4 boneless skinless chicken breasts
1/4 cup Balsamic vinegar
1/4 cup mustard, spicy or Dijon
1 teaspoon dried rosemary (or 1 tablespoon fresh)
1/4 cup tamari (or soy sauce)
1/4 cup olive oil (or less if you want to save calories)

Set oven at 375. In a small bowl, mix together the vinegar, oil, mustard, and rosemary. Put the chicken pieces in a baking dish, then cover them with the mixture. Bake for 45 minutes, then add the tamari. Bake another 10 or until the chicken is done. Here's how you know chicken is done: it is no longer pink when you cut into it. Unlike beef, fish or lamb (but like pork) you really should never eat undercooked chicken or you might get massively sick. (Note: Handle raw chicken as if it were kryptonite. Clean everything it touches, including your hands aggressively with scalding hot water and soap.)

Black Bean Chili
1 onion
2 garlic cloves, minced
1 carrot, chopped
1 green bell pepper, 1 red bell pepper, chopped
¼ cup olive oil
1 tablespoon cumin
1 teaspoon coriander
1 teaspoon chili powder
1 teaspoon cayenne pepper
1 tablespoon dried basil
1 tablespoon dried oregano

salt and pepper to taste (about 1 teaspoon each)
2 15-ounce cans black beans
1 large 28-ounce can tomatoes
grated Monterey Jack or cheddar cheese.
tortilla chips
salsa
guacamole (recipe follows)

Heat the oil (about 1/4 cup) in your deepest cast iron skillet to
medium high. Chop the onion up and throw it in. Put in the herbs
and spices. Stir. Add the chopped carrot. When the onion is translucent, add the chopped red and green peppers, then the garlic. When
all the veggies are soft, add the tomatoes and the black beans. Lower
the heat to simmer and let sit at that temperature for about 10 to 15
minutes. Grate some cheese and put in a bowl. Place the salsa in a
bowl, too. Make the guacamole and put the chips in a bigger bowl.
Let guests top their own chili. This chili tastes even better the next
day, so be sure to save leftovers!

Guacamole
2 ripe avocados
1 or 2 cloves garlic, minced
Juice of 1 lemon or lime
salt and pepper to taste
optional: a few leaves fresh cilantro
salsa to taste

Mash all the ingredients together and serve immediately with
tortilla chips.

Pasta Fagioli
1/4 cup olive oil
1 large onion, chopped
1 tablespoon dried basil
1 tablespoon dried oregano
1 teaspoon salt
2 teaspoons black pepper
3 cloves minced garlic
2 carrots

1 zucchini
1 28-ounce can plum tomatoes
1 15-ounce can of cannellini beans
 (or any white bean, like Northern)
1 pound box of chunky pasta
 (ziti, rigatoni, anything but long noodles)
Parmesan cheese as a garnish

In your cast iron skillet, on medium high, heat the olive oil. Add the chopped onion. Then add the herbs, garlic, and salt and pepper. When it's translucent, add the other chopped veggies (carrots and zucchini should be cut in half moon shapes) and cook till the veggies are limp. Add the canned tomatoes and beans. Taste the mixture and add more salt and pepper if you want.

Boil some water. When it's bubbling, put in the contents of the box of pasta. Let cook for about four minutes; drain and add the pasta to the soup, letting the pasta finish cooking in the mixture. Serve when the pasta's done; add Parmesan cheese to taste.

This also tastes even better the next day, microwaved or re-heated on the stove.

Leg of Lamb

Get a good cut from your butcher. Put it in a roasting pan. Shake a *lot* of salt on it (the way you would a chicken). Also, if you feel adventurous, add a ton of crushed garlic and fresh rosemary. Roast at 375 for about 3 hours if you like lamb well done, less if you like it rare. An hour and a half before you take it out, put cut potatoes around the lamb so they cook in the juices.

Garlic Bread (In Honor of John)

1 loaf of French bread
A lot of butter (one stick)
A lot of garlic. If you can't find fresh, use garlic powder. Or
 better yet, both.

Preheat the oven to 350. Make diagonal slices in the loaf of bread. Put slices of butter in the slots you just made in the loaf. Then, sprinkle garlic powder into the slots. Or, mash up the garlic cloves by gently pressing the handle of a knife down onto them and peeling off the skin, then either mincing them or using a garlic press, and put half a teaspoon or so of mashed garlic into the slots. Bake for ten or twenty minutes, until butter is melted and the bread is slightly toasted.

Trader Joe's Slow Cooker Meals

I got a slow cooker a few years ago. This affordable little appliance is fantastic for making good nutritious meals, and even better, you can prepare them in the morning and come home at night to a hot meal. I am lucky enough to live near a Trader Joe's, which has healthy, affordable, ready-made ingredients for great meals.

Chicken with Olives and Artichoke Hearts
1 package TJ's frozen chicken breasts
1 package TJ's frozen artichoke hearts
1 carton chicken broth
1 jar Kalamata olives
2 heaping tablespoons of TJ's jarred minced garlic
salt and pepper to taste
some nice herb like rosemary, thyme, basil, oregano
dash of red wine
TJ's 10-minute farro or barley

Put all ingredients into the slow cooker except for the farro. Cook on low all day. When you get home, add the farro. In 10 minutes, eat your meal! You will have a lot of leftovers. For more veggies, add a bag of frozen spinach, and/or a bag of frozen peppers and onions.

This recipe also works well with TJ's frozen fish.

Yam cookies
3 yams
oil spray
apple pie seasoning or cinnamon (optional)
salt

Slice the yams into ¼ inch-sized rounds. Place on a baking sheet that's been oiled lightly. Spray more oil on top of the rounds. Season with a bit of cinnamon or apple-pie seasoning and a tiny bit of salt. Bake at 400 for 20-30 minutes until slightly crispy (or you might prefer them soft, in which case, cook for less time). This works well with regular potatoes too; just skip the cinnamon and use salt and pepper.

Green Smoothie Recipes

If you have a blender, this can be a great, healthy meal for those who are on-the-go. Here are a few ideas. Obviously, you can add, subtract, substitute. The basic idea is to drink your greens with some protein (yogurt, milk, soy, peanut butter, etc.) and some fruit or honey to sweeten it all. Since I am new to the smoothie business, I asked my friends for some advice.

"Nerissa's Ridiculously Healthy Green Smoothie"
½ cup unsweetened almond milk
6 oz (about half a bag) of frozen chopped spinach
8 oz (about four large) carrots
4 oz banana (I peel a bunch of bananas and cut into chunks, for this purpose, and I keep them in a zip lock bag in the freezer)

Blend till smooth. If you haven't time to freeze the bananas, add a couple of ice cubes to make the smoothie have that great smoothie/Slurpee texture. You can add a teaspoon of spirulina to this if you want it to taste like pond scum.

"Basic Green"
courtesy of Lori Shine, writer,
this book's copyeditor and mother of two.

1/2 cup milk (almond milk works great here)
1/2 cup plain yogurt
1 frozen banana in chunks
Either 1 T peanut butter or 1/2 cup frozen mango chunks (Trader Joe's)

Cram the rest of the blender full of baby spinach (about 4 cups), whirr. This is for people who don't like to taste a lot of the green, just a little.

"High Octane Green"
courtesy of Jennifer Eremeeva, author, blogger (the Moscovore), homemaker extraordinaire:

1 bunch of kale with the stems removed
5 ribs of celery
1 apple, peeled and cored
1 lime
1 fennel bulb
large bunch of parsley
1 frozen shot of wheatgrass
1/2 avocado
1 tablespoon of spirulina powder
1.5 cups of nonfat yogurt
1-1/2 cups ice

Juice all but the last 4 ingredients. Pour juice with the last four ingredients into a blender with an ice-crushing function. Pulse the ice-crusher button until the ice is worked into the juice. Then hit BLEND or SMOOTHIE until velvety smooth. Do not serve in a metal container as the wheatgrass reacts badly with that. Serve immediately.

And for a very different take on green smoothies, try this, courtesy of Michael Mercurio and Larry Ely:

"Green Smoothie"
Pistachio ice cream
Dumante (Pistachio ice cream liqueur)

Blend. Drink.

Marinated Tofu
One pound tofu (that's how it's generally sold—one tub)
½ cup low sodium tamari, or soy sauce
¼ cup sesame oil
½ cup rice vinegar,
sesame seeds

Drain the tofu and cut into large dice-sized bits. Toss in a zip-top bag and freeze, at least overnight (frozen tofu seems to keep indefinitely). Take out and marinate in the other ingredients for an hour or more. Put all of this into a cast iron skillet and cook until liquid is evaporated. Will result in a fantastic, crispy tofu!

Pesto-Lentil Stuffed Spaghetti Squash
Spaghetti squash
2 cups lentils
1 bay leaf
1 batch of pesto, or a 7 oz tub of storebought
3 potatoes
goat cheese
black truffle oil

Preheat oven to 350. While it's preheating, boil the potatoes (about ½ hour in boiling water—keep checking the water to make sure it doesn't all evaporate.) Cut squash in half and scoop out seeds. Bake for 30 minutes. Meanwhile, boil lentils with the bay leaf. Remove and drain any remaining liquid. Mix pesto with lentils. When potatoes are cooked, mash them and then mix into lentil/pesto mix. Take squash out of oven and with a fork, loosen the "spaghetti" part of the squash so it resembles…spaghetti. Create a bird's nest effect with a space in the middle. Mound the lentil mixture into the center, top with goat cheese and return to oven for an additional 20-30 minutes. Drizzle with black truffle oil and serve.

Tom's Crack Brownies

These brownies, served faithfully on Saturday nights at every one of my writing retreats, are so named because of their addictive qualities. Note: There is not actually any crack in the ingredients.

- 1 lb dark brown sugar
- 1.5 sticks unsalted butter
- 2 tablespoon instant espresso (any strong instant coffee will do, though)
- 2 eggs, room temperature if possible
- 2 tablespoon vanilla
- 2 cups flour
- 2 teaspoon baking powder
- ½ teaspoon salt
- 1 cup of chocolate chips, or 5 squares of semisweet baking chocolate

Preheat oven to 350 degrees. Butter an 8 x 10 pan.

Dissolve instant espresso in 1 tablespoon hot water.

Heat brown sugar, butter, and chocolate in a large saucepan over medium low heat until butter, and chocolate have melted. Stir in coffee mixture. Let cool to room temperature. When cool, beat in eggs and vanilla. Sift flour, baking powder and salt together and stir into the butter/chocolate mixture with a wooden spoon. Spread evenly in pan. Sprinkle with some extra chocolate chips. Bake until lightly browned, 25-30 minutes (don't over bake!). Cool completely before cutting. Makes 20 brownies.

Eggs

Eggs are amazing. I could wax poetic about them for pages. In fact, I think I will.

As a food source, eggs are cheap, and if you wanted you could raise some chickens and have fresh eggs every day. In fact, I am going to ask my friend Tricia to write about how easy and fun it is to raise chickens in your backyard. Barring that, keep a dozen in your fridge. You know that the eggs have gone bad by putting them in a pot of cold water. If they float to the top, do not eat them! They're bad! If they stay on the bottom they're fine. But if there is an egg or two that stays on the bottom but is sitting up vertically, that egg is about to float, so eat that one first.

Raising Chickens in Your Backyard,
courtesy of Tricia, age 38

Raising a few chickens in your backyard is rewarding and fairly easy to do, once you have the structures in place. Backyard eggs are far superior in flavor, nutrition and freshness. Also, you can feel good knowing the hens that laid them were treated humanely.[67]

1) Check local ordinances. There may be rules about roosters and how many chickens you can keep.
2) Build or buy a sturdy coop. The coop must be strong enough to keep out predators. Hens will need a nesting box, a roost to sleep on, and at least four square feet per bird (more if they can't access the outside world). Ventilation provided by windows (covered with sturdy wire) and small holes at the top of the walls are necessary to allow for airflow.
3) Provide outdoor space whenever possible. Some backyard hens are allowed to range freely. If not fenced in, however, they can roam too far or dig up gardens, grass and flower beds. A chicken yard offers them room to scratch for nutritious bugs and take dust baths while protecting the rest of your outdoor space.
4) Find your birds. Farmer supply stores, newspaper listings or people raising their own backyard hens can be good sources. Look for healthy, young birds with plenty of laying left in them. While chicks are cute, raising them requires a lot of extra equipment, expertise, and care.
5) Take good care of your hens. Provide fresh water at all times and good quality feed. The best nutrition will result in healthier birds and higher egg production. Clean the coop regularly to remove litter and keep the air clean.
6) Build good relationships with your neighbors by offering them fresh eggs.

Egg Recipes

Scrambled: Heat a cast iron skillet with some butter or oil spray, on medium or even low. Crack two eggs into a bowl. Add a tablespoon of milk, a dash of salt and pepper. Whisk the eggs till the yolks are broken up. Pour the mixture into the pan and start stirring. They will cook up in about two or three minutes. Don't stop stirring or they'll burn! Serve immediately, with or without ketchup. You can add almost anything you want to scrambled eggs: bits of veggie, bits of protein, bits of cooked rice, or any leftovers. Or put the eggs on toast.

Hard-boiled: In a small pan, boil water—enough to cover eggs. With slotted spoon, place two eggs in pan. Turn off water and let sit for 13 minutes. Take the eggs out of the water with a slotted spoon. Cool them off by running them under cold water or immersing them in a bowl of cold water. Gently tap them on the counter to crack the shell, then peel off the shell. You can then slice your eggs or just eat whole, dipped in a little salt and pepper. These are portable and will keep for a week if refrigerated.

Soft-boiled eggs: Much yummier, in my opinion, than hard boiled, but you have to eat them right away. Boil water. With slotted spoon, lower your eggs into the water, and remove after 7 minutes. Cool under cold water for a minute, then place in an egg cup (you can substitute an espresso mug or a shot glass.) Peel the tip of the shell off and scoop out the egg with a spoon. This is good with toast for dipping into the gooey yolk.

Fried: My favorite! Heat the skillet to high. Add butter or oil spray. Crack two eggs into the pan when the skillet is hot hot hot. Add salt and pepper and any other spices you like. Cook until the edges are crispy, but try not to let the yolk cook through. This is what Lila calls a "Mama egg." I like to pop the yolk and let it run over the white.

Japanese omelet: I don't know if this is really something some-one in Japan would make, but here's my version. Heat the pan to medium high. Spray with oil spray. Crack two eggs into a bowl. Add a quarter teaspoon of dry wasabi powder and a teaspoon of tamari.

Whisk till yolks are broken and mixed with whites. Pour into pan. Cut up some scallions and sprinkle on top. Watch closely: as soon as edges seem firm, gently fold the circle of eggs in half. Cook a bit longer (when the eggs stop running from the sides) and serve immediately.

Other omelets: Again, anything can go into your omelet. Add ingredients at the stage where you've got the raw eggs in the bowl. Try:
-goat cheese and pesto
-feta cheese and spinach
-cheddar cheese and black beans
-brie and finely minced kale
-cooked bacon bits

Frittata

I got this recipe online at http://www.thekitchn.com. A frittata is an omelet in formal wear. Here's your chance to bring the humble egg to the dinner table.

Ingredients
-6 eggs
-1/2 cup to 1 cup cheese
-1 onion, chopped
-any other veggies you want: peppers, garlic, broccoli—you name it
-any meats or tofu
-really any leftover in the fridge that isn't growing a beard
-seasonings like salt and pepper, garlic powder, paprika, basil, oregano—experiment!

Heat oven to 400. Sauté any uncooked veggies with the seasonings you choose (sauté means cook in a skillet with a little oil). Flatten the veggies with a spatula. Cover with cheese until it just starts to melt. Whisk eggs in a bowl. Pour them over veggies and cheese. Make sure they are covering the veggies and cheese. Cook for one minute or until you see the edges of the eggs beginning to set, then put the pan into the oven and bake for 8-10 minutes. If you like things crispy, turn on the broiler for the last minute.

Serve like a pie. This will keep for several days in the fridge.

Book Four
Money, Insurance, Cars, and a Bunch of Other Boring Stuff

It's because I find this stuff so baffling that I might be the perfect person to explain it to you. What you find here is how I rightbrainedly found my way to some clarity about these most adult (or at least necessary) topics.

Money

Tools and Rules

- Bank local
- Don't debt
- Make a spending plan, not a budget
- Pay your taxes joyfully
- Get health insurance, auto insurance, but not life insurance
- Take care of the vehicle that is your car

As a college student, I was dangerous with a credit card, or a charge home account, or even with cash. I could not hold on to it. I knew what people meant when they uttered the phrase "burning a hole in my pocket." I racked up over $2500 of credit card debt, which hung out collecting interest for four years until David sold a life insurance policy to pay it off when I was 24 years old. My checking account was not much better. I kept about a $75 balance and bounced my fair share of checks at the local convenience store (Wall Foods) across from my college. (I think at one point there was a little sign hung up next to the cash register saying, "Do not accept checks from this person" with my name underneath.)

During the years of my first marriage, David and I shared a joint checking account and he paid all the bills, balanced the accounts, and generally acted as the emissary between me and the world of commerce.

After six years of not taking an income, of buying clothes with an official band clothing allowance and snacks with my per diem, I started teaching guitar lessons. For the first time since my detested Assistant Dean of Students job, I earned my own money, one $30 check at a time. With that money, I opened my own checking account again. This time around, I was extremely careful. I wrote down all transactions. I found this so helpful and fascinating that soon I was using my checking account register to record all transactions, even if they were cash or credit purchases. By the end of that year, I had a complete record of every purchase I'd made, greatly helping David when it came time to figure out our taxes.

I mostly paid cash for groceries, writing the amounts in my checkbook register. I shared a credit card with David and he paid the bills, but by this time I had learned my lesson and didn't spend money on what I knew I couldn't pay for myself.

Today, I continue to write down everything I purchase. This is a helpful exercise from a practical point of view for two reasons. First of all, I know where my money is going, and when I sit down to "do my numbers" I can see exactly where I have spent. Second, the Hawthorne effect[68] comes into play. Because I know I have to write it down, I am less likely to buy that fourth package of Zebra pens or that bargain slightly-too-large T-shirt. Recording my actions adds a layer of mindfulness that's extremely helpful; a sort of benign watchdog. If I were hipper and more trusting, I would use Mint.com, a convenient website with a free app for iPhones that connects directly to your bank account. But my old check registers and scrawly handwriting work pretty well too.

Setting Up a Checking Account

Unless you are completely paranoid or need to protest what the US government and the financial institutions of this land are doing to the globe at large, you will want to set up a checking account with a bank.

My friend Patty said she was absolutely clueless about how to open a checking account and that I should give very specific instructions, so here goes.

Enter the bank. Find one of those people at a desk. Say "I would like to open a checking account with a low minimum balance and low fees." They will help you. Listen to them, but don't necessarily trust them. Bankers are in the category of people who are out to get your money and it's in their interest (ha ha, no pun intended) to get you to store as much of it as possible in their clutches. (Eventually, they will try to get you to take high interest loans, but you don't have to worry about that now.) They will give you a choice of colors for your checks and little plastic folders. Don't get distracted by this, and don't spend any extra to have hearts and unicorns and flowers on your checks. You will still be self-actualized if you have plain old boring Bank Green checks.

Give them some money to deposit, at least the minimum amount needed to avoid charges. Write that number down at the top of the check register. Now: every time you write a check, write down the number of the check, the date you wrote it, to whom it's made out (in the top line) and what you got for it (in the line right below) and (most important) how much the check is for. Then, subtract that number from the total number. Voila! You have successfully balanced your checkbook. It's an easy thing to do if you do it every single time you write a check. It's a pain in the neck to do if you procrastinate and wait for some lovely, relaxed time later on in your life. Remember Life Lesson #157: Do It Now? (I do this on Tuesdays when I pay my bills and listen to the Decemberists.)

Also, once a month when you get your bank statement, make sure the numbers "add up." If the bank has charged you a service fee, put that in your register and subtract it. And when you use the ATM, be sure to note in your check register the money you took out, as well as the fee charged (if applicable). And of course, when you deposit your paycheck and/or all those royalty checks and all that prize money, be sure to add that!

Why Bank Local?

Here's what my friends say.

[Why one would choose a local bank is] no different from [why one would choose] any other local business. Doing business with neighbors de-incentivizes being an a-hole. Doing business with anonymous and remote customers does the opposite. Also small organizations vs huge corporate structures has same effect on management-employee relations.—Anand, age 38

There are community reinvestment requirements in the chartering or governance of banks that require civic engagement, and banks with local boards can be (they aren't always) more responsive to local issues and needs in the application of those resources. –Alan, age 49

Also, if you ever have a problem, it's nice to be able to go in and talk with someone who is in a position to be able to actually deal with the issue at hand. —Hosie, age 44

Our local bank supports local businesses by displaying their business info on a regular basis. Also in light of the tragedy in our town [Newtown, CT] on Dec. 14, our bank was instrumental in organizing, with the town offices, a place to donate money that we knew would be safe and used wisely.—Cady, age 39

Getting a mortgage locally allows you to find a place that won't sell your loan. Then if you need to work with the bank on payment options, they can actually work with you.—Anne Marie, age 39

I'd say the biggest reason [to bank locally] is that more of the money is invested in local projects. This is a micro finance effect, not macro. Easier access to capital locally means more small businesses overall. The whole is strengthened, but via the parts. Local banks are less speculative, and many being community-owned by its members rather than shareholder-owned (by people not living in your region!) means they will act for the good of the local owners. And finally yes, like any other local business many hire people. Decent jobs, many women - so they hire your neighbors to work.—Michael, age 56

In the first edition of this book, I said that I'd chosen to bank at the gigantic conglomerate Bank of America because it happened to have a tiny branch in my Stop & Shop. (Actually it was a Fleet Bank when I opened my account. BoA bought it out and closed the branch.) I wrote that I suspected I would eventually switch and report back to you in a future edition. That time is nigh. A couple of years ago, I made the switch from BoA to our local, lovable Florence Savings Bank. Here are some of the reasons why:

Does the bank have:	Bank of America	Florence Savings Bank
ATM fees?	Yes! In any branch that isn't BoA.	NO! They refund your fees even if you use your card in Alaska!
Free checking?	NO!	Yes!
Free gifts when you open a checking account	NO!	Why, yes! A great abundance! All of which are sitting unused in my attic, but still. Something for (almost) nothing!
Interest Rates on Checking accounts (with <$10,000)	0.01%	0.87%
Fees for using debit cards?	That was the rumor	No!
Monthly service fee	Depends on balance	Never
Friendly flexible service?	Depends on whom you get that day. In my experience, they were very friendly in person but when I'd call, I'd inevitably get someone in Texas who had no clue where Northampton was.	They all know me by name, and I've only been banking there a year. They always try to accommodate my needs, and when you call on the phone, you actually get to talk to the person you were dealing with in the branch.

Budgeting

Note: "Budget" has a restrictive connotation, akin to the word "diet." I much prefer the term "Spending Plan" which I use throughout this book.

Most of my artist friends, upon receiving their utility bills, stuff them on their desks underneath the rough print-outs of their novels and leave them to molder with the idea that they will pay them later, at some more convenient time. Right now, what's really important is to finish the chapter they're in the middle of. And they're right—that chapter *is* a lot more important than the utility bill. But one still would prefer not to get hit with late fees and penalties. Or have the electricity turned off.

I got a little worksheet once as part of my Day Planner. I decided on a whim to figure out a monthly spending plan—how much I made in one box, and each of my expenses on another. This required a bit of research. Re-enter those bills I'd filed in my yearly accordion file. I pulled out the credit card bill and my checkbook register. Doing a bit of addition gave me the amount I spent that month on food, clothes, books, telephone, doctor visits, going to the movies, etc. I got to see what were my fixed expenses (my ISP, my mortgage, my Netflix account) and what were variable (clothing, postage, books, CDs, going out to shows. And food, though over time I saw that food came out to about the same amount every month, as long as I only went out to eat once every week or so). After about six months of doing a monthly spending plan, I got a pretty clear sense of what my monthly expenses were, and I was horrified to see how close the margin was to my monthly income. What to do? I felt betrayed. Why didn't anyone tell me I was poor and had no spending money? (For a Sample Spending Plan Worksheet, please see Appendix C.)

I highly recommend software like Quicken. I use a simple Excel spreadsheet. By keeping track of what I spend each month, within my designated categories, I experience a huge amount of freedom, decreased anxiety, and pure gratitude about what I *do* have, and am consequently way less concerned about what I *don't* have. I can see, month by month, the savings accrue within the "vacation" category. I can make sure that the "heating" category is always stocked. I know how much is in my "books" category and whether it's time to make a trip to my favorite local independent store, Broadside

Books. I allocate enough for two books a month, which for me, is about the max I can read. If I magically read more than two books, I make a trip to the library.

Spending

By spending your money, you are entering into a relationship with the corporate world; you are voting with your dollars. You might be supporting a family in Guatemala, or your kid's friend's parents. Or you may be perpetuating a regime of sweatshop laborers, environmental plunderers and homophobes.

Sorry. End of radical rant. Spending is good clean fun. We all know the pleasure of taking an afternoon off and moseying downtown to buy a new book, CD, scarf, sweater, electronic device, cup of coffee, lamp, food processor, cure for baldness, whatever. It's the American way. It's our civic duty to contribute to raising the GNP. I regularly give in and buy the latest iPhone.

Spending is necessary and unavoidable. We need clothes to keep us warm and to keep us looking relatively normal in the workplace; some would say we need clothes of a certain style to maintain a competitive edge in the workplace. We certainly need to eat, to pay for our shelter, our transportation. And for me anyway, as I confront the reality of my monthly budget, I count reading, listening to music, and watching good movies an essential component of my personal happiness, as well as my vocation, (which is also my avocation—see Book 2) so I put these in my spending plan.

On good days, I try to resist the huge societal forces which con-

spire to compel me to buy things I do not need. Even so, my house is full to the brim, and I need at least a yearly trip to Goodwill and frequent postings on Freecycle to dump my excess and hope that someone else will derive pleasure from my purchases. Being a political person, I understand that I vote every day with my dollar. If I buy a Diet Coke, I have to acknowledge that I am supporting a company who served the Nazi regime, contributes to the erosion of dental hygiene, and abuses its workers in international plants. But hey, it's calorie-free and sometimes it's the pause that refreshes. I try to make informed decisions and when possible, support companies whose policies I agree with and minimize my purchases of those who don't. I try to buy few articles of clothing, but those I do buy I will wear frequently and hopefully will love.

This is the goal. It is not always the reality. And to quote my favorite anonymous source, it's about batting averages. To keep from supporting regimes of sweatshop labor, planet pirates and homophobes, check out this app at buycott.com[69] that can tell you who your dollars are supporting by scanning the products in the store with your phone! Such an awesome idea.

Debt

I hope you are dedicating a whole chapter to credit and credit cards. If you are over 18 it is fairly easy to start a line of credit whether from Sears or Target. And after that you will get credit card offers from company after company. I had a friend in high school who got her first Sears card and spent a mere $200 on clothes and decided not to pay it back and moved out of state. I saw her ten years later and she joked that she and her family of five could not rent an apartment (and was living with her mother-in-law) because she had ruined her credit in 1993 with Sears. No one ever talks about credit. And what APR means. [Annual Percentage Rate: what you pay annually on your credit cards if you maintain a balance.] And if you miss a payment how your APR can go up and they never tell you. I know more than one person my age who's over $10,000 in credit card debt. We are taught to consume but not taught to curb our consumption. —Ellen, age 31

I racked up a big bill (I think it was $1,000, which was huge at the time) and had to eat 39-cent cans of tuna fish for lunch for a year to save money so I could pay it off. —Joan, age 38

Somewhere my early twenties I discovered mail order, and the utter joy of having a package with some wonderful item I didn't really need waiting for me when I got home from my dismal day at the office. My goodness, did those charges ever add up fast!—Elizabeth, age 42

The American dream is a wonderful thing. It gives each of us the hope that no matter who we are and where we were born, no matter how poor or disadvantaged we might be, any one of us might "make it." By "make it," I mean become rich, though "become famous" could just as easily be substituted here. We all know the Horatio Alger success stories touted in the media. And these stories are true, and they're wonderful, and this is a truly remarkable country. I love it, and I wouldn't choose to live anywhere else.

That being said, I believe some of us choose to wear a pretty powerful pair of rose-colored glasses. We cling so strongly to the hope that we, too, will one day become rich that it blinds us to reality. We go along, for example, with tax cuts for the very very wealthy with the idea that one day we might also become wealthy, and if and when that day comes, we certainly don't want to give a huge percentage of that wealth to the government! We watch *Lifestyles of the Rich and Famous* and lose ourselves in fantasies about "when our ship comes in," and we're willing to go to absurd measures to protect that fantasy—like vote for politicians who aren't helping our own economic situation in the least. It's the lottery ticket mentality; even though the odds of winning the lottery are about one in a hundred million, (that's 1 in 100,000,000 to give you a graphic), we hear the stories of those who do win, and we imagine ourselves in that position, even though the odds of us getting in a car crash are a whole lot better (1 in 18,000).

I don't mean to sound like a total paranoid, but the fact is, the system is against you here. Every financial institution, credit card company and car dealership will try their smilingest best to get you to owe them money. Other than nags like me and other people who write How to Handle Your Money books (and perhaps your parents), most of the messages you get will be aimed at getting and keeping you in debt. This came as a shock to me—having grown-up (mostly) around adults who were looking out for my best interest, I naturally assumed the corporate authorities would do the same.

My best advice is to stay out of debt and avoid it at all costs. As I said earlier, in my early 20s, I accrued about $2500 worth of credit card debt, which my then-husband paid off. After that, I swore I'd never be in debt again. This was greatly aided by the fact that I stopped earning *any* money for a number of years and that my then-husband paid all bills. But the other truth in this case was that I was plunging into my music career, and my attitude was akin to one who is part of a crusade, a team of people who are fighting for their lives, for a cause that is far bigger than any one individual. For many years, we lived on a $10 a day per diem. Because we were a rock band, we'd often get fed by the clubs at which we played. We had what's called a rider to our contract, which specified what kinds of foods we'd like to have once we finished sound check. Most groups have expensive bottles of red wine and fancy chocolate (or the green M&Ms of Van Halen fame). But we opted for peanut butter and jelly, rice cakes, fruit, a bag of baby carrots, chips and salsa. We'd take all the leftovers and hoard the food in the van. We ate a lot of peanut butter and jelly, which I really don't ever need to see or smell, let alone eat, again in this lifetime.

This experience had a lasting and profound impact on me. When things became a little easier financially with the band, I had inadvertently developed some pretty good financial habits. I learned to have one—and only one—credit card for myself, and keep a second one for band expenses, and to never mix them up. I pay off my credit card each month, so when choosing a credit card, I went for one with a frequent flyer option, which means that for every dollar I spent, I got a mile. And this in turn meant that when Tom and I went on our honeymoon, we flew to California for free. (Although, in the spirit of truth telling, I must confess that it was his credit card frequent flyer miles we spent, not mine.)

But—if you have some credit card debt, you should ignore my previous instruction and go rifling through your garbage can looking for one of those 0% credit card offers and transfer all your money to that card. Most of these 0% cards say in the fine print that it's only 0% for a year. That's okay. I know several people who have just jumped from 0% card to 0% card for years on end. It's kind of a stressful way to manage debt, but it's better than paying 18%.

You have probably heard this before, but it bears repeating: *the absolute stupidest financial thing you can do is keep a balance on a credit card with an interest rate higher than 5%.* If you do just one thing, switch to a lower interest rate credit card.

Good Debt?

There is good debt and bad debt. Most people will not be able to live completely debt-free, paying for everything in cash. That's fine—in fact, there is an excellent argument to be made for building up your credit history, having "good credit." So, if you get a Sears credit card at age 18, just be sure to pay it off. In fact, you might want to do this, just to begin to establish good credit.

It's considered good debt to have a mortgage on your house. Why? Because the interest on the loan for your mortgage is tax-deductible. This adds up, trust me. In fact, a lot of people who have the money to pay off their mortgages choose not to (if they have a good rate that is, and good rates these days are anything below 4.5%) because they believe the savings on their taxes will ultimately be more beneficial than the long-term savings of not having to pay the yearly interest on their mortgage. Not only that, but owning a home (even if the bank technically owns it) significantly helps your credit rating and standing in the eyes of financial institutions. This can help if you ever really need to borrow a lot of money.

We can put student loans in the "good debt" category because theoretically, having a college degree will put you in a higher-paying job bracket. In general, college graduates earn more than high-school graduates (73% more, according to the University of Wisconsin Credit Union's website; they also say "advanced degree holders earn two to three times more than those with a high-school diploma.")[70] You can defer your interest on your student loans for 6 months after graduation, and you can deduct this interest from your taxes, too.

Bad debt is everything else. And financial wizards (of which I must remind you, I am not one) say don't let your monthly debt add up to more than 36% of your monthly income or banks won't like you. So if you are currently carrying a lot of debt, try to get rid of it as soon as possible. Make a monthly plan by which you pay off a little at a time, but make consistent payments. Whenever I have debt, I pay it off as fast as I can. I feel like a slave when I am in debt. And as this country was founded on freedom in 1776 and rejected slavery in 1865, I regard it as my patriotic duty as well as my personal duty to my one and only self to stay debt free. It is one of my top priorities.

If you are paying off your debt, treat this period of your life as a special adventure. Rather than focusing on deprivation, focus on the many ways the universe conspires to help you. If you have a need, rather than whip our your credit card to get what you want, write down five other possible ways you could achieve your goal without incurring debt. Make it playful. Check your local freecycle.org or craigslist. Let your friends know what you are looking for. (See "follow your bliss" quote—the universe will bend over backwards to help you if you are sincere.)

Here are some time-worn steps people have taken to recover from debt:

- Figure out how much you owe, total. Then play triage: what absolutely needs to be paid first? The loan with the highest interest rate (though for some people who have taken loans from friends, it might feel more right to pay those off first, even though the interest rate is sure to be lower).
- Curtail spending, but don't completely deprive yourself. Make it a game to see how little you can get by on. Set aside a portion of income to pay off debt, and within what's left over, allocate reasonably.
- Pay your bills on time.
- Consolidate your debt (to a creditor with the lowest interest rate you can find).
- Keep track of *every penny you spend.* Write it down in a little notebook or blank check register, be it a cash, credit, or check expenditure.
- Have only one credit card and cut the other ones up— after you've paid off your bills, of course. Better still, just use a debit card.
- Create a spending plan and adhere to it. The loose rule is to spend no more than 35% on housing, 15% on transportation, 10% on savings, 15% on debt repayment and 25% on everything else. Be sure to create categories that feel nurturing. As with a diet, if you deprive yourself too much, your Willful Child will rebel.
- Ask for a raise or look for a higher-paying job.

- Think about selling some of your assets (do you really need three cars? Or five guitars?).
- Start investing your savings.

Saving

If you start investing and saving when you're 20 you could actually consider retiring at age 40 or 50! Imagine that. Ha! I definitely wish I knew more about investing when I was younger. It would have been nice to be aware of the choices I was making in terms of money. —Katie, age 34

I got through grad school financially okay just by following general frugal maxims, particularly Spend Less Than You Earn. (It helped to not have prior debts, to live with roommates, to use cash wherever possible instead of credit, and to defer owning a car.) Looking back, if I had also known how to financially plan in grad school as the books outline, I could have also had a decent start to a retirement fund built up (and well-nourished by the 90s run-up in stocks) instead of having to start a nest egg after 30. (But at least I got to buy on the dip.) Now, it's harder to be frugal, but I at least do decently with the Save Automatically maxim I've picked up since then (e.g. get your employer to skim off your retirement fund saving, and your bank to skim off your short-term saving, at each paycheck, before you ever see it). Much more effective in practice than having to consciously budget and move a contribution any time you want to save. At least for me. — John, age 39

Saving is really hard. But make it a priority. My life changed in this department when I began to bank online. I set up a savings account, and with the click of a mouse, I can transfer money from my checking to my savings and vice versa. I even opened an IRA on my own. An IRA, by the way, is an Individual Retirement Account (as opposed to a 401K which is the equivalent if you work for a business; see "The Difference Between a 401K and an IRA" later) in which you can make yearly contributions (of up to $4000) and deduct these contributions from your taxes that year. However, like

John, I was in my thirties when I finally opened an IRA. I wish I had acted sooner, like my friend Kate:

> *I was hesitant to start an IRA with [my company] because I didn't know how they worked, and I didn't know when or how I'd ever be able to access that money. I did decide to do it, though, and now that I've left, I've realized that the account is completely independent of [my company]. It sounds silly, but I didn't know that would be the case; I thought that money would be tied up with [the company] somehow. So it was a relief to realize that my leaving the company didn't have an impact on that money or my ability to monitor it.* —Kate, age 26

Remember that $1200 paycheck I got when I was living rent-free and having access to free meals three times a day? Did I take advantage of the school's retirement plans? Did I open a 401K when my employer offered? Noooo. So learn from my mistakes. If you save a ridiculously small amount of your paycheck ($50) starting when you are 25, you can retire a millionaire at the age of 65. If you don't start saving until you are 40, you will not even come close. Why? Because of compound interest. And that's as much as I knew, so I called my friend, Melissa, to get more information.

Compound Interest, *courtesy of my friend Melissa, age 38, Wheaton School Graduate, Financial Business Consultant, and Full Time Mother of Two*

It's so important to save money, for immediate emergencies, for retirement, etc. People in their twenties just don't think about this. Most large companies these days offer 401K plans, and the participation of younger workers is really low. This is one of the best, easiest ways you can save for retirement. The money comes right out of your paycheck before you even see it, and is often matched to some degree by your company (free money!). If you look at the numbers, starting this type of savings in your twenties and continuing it throughout your career can virtually guarantee you'll be a millionaire by the time you retire.

One principle behind why saving early makes such a difference is called "compound interest." We all know when we save money (like in a bank savings account or CD) we earn interest. Interest is the amount of money our money "earns" when it is deposited at a financial institution.

"Simple interest" is when interest is only calculated on the amount of money you put in. Deposit $100 in an account that earns 5%, and make $5. Leave the money there for another year, make another $5. Third year, another $5. Pretty simple.

"Compound interest" is different. With compound interest, interest is paid on both the principal and also on any interest from past years. So your $100 investment at 5% earns $5 in the first year. No difference so far. But in the second year, the 5% interest is paid on $105 (the $100 you started with plus the $5 you earned in interest). And the third year it is paid on $110.25 (the $105 from last year plus the $5.25 you earned in interest)—get it? Each year the amount of money you earn on your original $100 goes up. Over time, your $100 will earn much more than the same amount at simple interest—and this is the magic of compound interest.

Just to show you how the benefits of compounding add up, if you put $10,000 into an account earning 5% simple interest for 10 years, you would have $15,000 at the end of that time. But if you put that same $10,000 into an account earning 5% compounded interest, you would have $16,288.95 at the end of the 10 years. Almost $1,290 more just by changing the way the interest is calculated.

Pretty cool, you say. But why does this mean I should start saving now? It won't make much difference if I wait a few years. Wrong again. A general rule of financial planning is that for every ten years that you wait, you approximately double the amount you need to save for your retirement. Double it.

And you don't have to have $10,000 to invest in order to make compound interest work for you. Let's say you want to take advantage of compound interest, but you don't have a lot of extra cash. If you put $50 per week into an investment account earning 10% compound interest, at the end of 5 years you will have saved $16,850.54. Don't stop and after 10 years you will have $44,632,38. After 20 years? $165,955.78. After 30 years? $495,746.97. Really. About half a million dollars by putting $50 away every week. Don't have $50 a week? How about $50 per month? Put this in a retirement account earning 10% interest for 40 years and come out with about

$265,000, Yes, over a quarter of a million dollars just for saving $50 a month.

As you can see, there really is a reason to start saving now. Even small amounts can grow into substantial savings. Compound interest and regular savings are just about the only sure fire way to become a millionaire these days. Sure you could start an internet company or win the lottery. But for most of us, it won't take a miracle; regular savings over the course of your lifetime is all you need.

So…if you work for a company that allows you to put some of your salary automatically into a 401K plan, do so. Open an IRA and contribute the maximum every year. Go visit an old folks home if you need a kick in the pants. Do you want to end up in a place like this? I thought not. Open that IRA.

The Difference Between a 401K and an IRA, *Also Courtesy of Melissa*

The basic difference between an IRA and a 401K is who sets it up, where the money comes from and how it is treated from a tax standpoint.

A 401K is an employer sponsored plan. That means it is a benefit provided to you by your employer. You cannot set up a 401K unless you are employed by a company that offers one. With a 401K, you are able to have some of your salary put into the 401K before you are given your paycheck, and this money is not counted as taxable income—you do not pay income tax on it until you take it out. This is why it is called a pre-tax, or tax-deferred, contribution. Money in a 401K can be invested in many ways; a common option is mutual funds. Your company will tell you what investment choices are open to you. As an added benefit of a 401K, many employers provide a matching contribution to your 401K account (often your contribution up to a certain percent). But not every company does this.

An IRA (which stands for Individual Retirement Account) is a personal retirement savings account, and has nothing to do with your job. You set it up, you decide how much to put in it, and how to invest it. The tax benefits here differ depending on the type of IRA you have (i.e., traditional, Roth, rollover). The traditional IRA is what is called a tax-deferred account. This means money you put in your IRA this year (up to a certain limit), can be deducted from what you have to pay taxes on this year. But when you take the money out to use in your retirement, you pay taxes then—at whatever the rate is at that time. It is sort of a don't pay taxes now, pay them later approach. In a Roth IRA the money you put in is taxed just like your other income this year (assuming you earned it somewhere and did not rob a bank to get it), but you won't have to pay any taxes when you take the money out to use in your retirement—a pay taxes now but don't pay them later approach. Either way, you get tax incentives from the IRS to use this type of retirement savings plan—the government wants you to save for retirement. And believe me, you do. This is one place where you and the government see eye to eye.

More Q&A with Melissa

Nerissa: How do you open a savings account that will give you compound interest instead of simple interest? How can you tell the difference?

Melissa: Most savings accounts give compound interest. It is unusual to find too many simple interest accounts these days. Just ask whatever bank you are opening the account with and they will tell you. (And if they say simple interest, run away as fast as you can. You might as well put your money under your mattress.)

Nerissa: Do most CDs use compound interest?

Melissa: With CDs most do offer some type of compounding. The thing to ask here is how often the interest is compounded. It's common to find that interest is declared daily, monthly, quarterly or yearly—depending on the life of the CD. Of course, it's better to have the interest paid more often. If you have two CDs that both pay 6%, the one that's compounded daily will earn more for you than the one that's compounded yearly. A good way to compare CDs is to look not at the stated interest rate, but at the "yield." This is the amount that you actually get, based on compounding. A higher yield usually means more frequent compounding.

Nerissa: Do IRAs use compound interest?

Melissa: IRAs can be invested in any way you choose; an interest bearing account is one choice. See above for answer on that. But most financial experts will tell you not to put too much of your IRA in a basic interest-bearing bank account.

Nerissa: Why?

Melissa: Interest-bearing savings accounts are a very safe investment. They are generally with a bank, and your money is often actually insured through the government (heard the term "FDIC insured"? This is what it means—the government insures your savings at a legitimate bank up to a certain amount of money. If the bank goes under or has a major Enron-like scandal, you still get your money). Great if you think this country is on the verge of financial collapse or a major military coup. But your "rate of return" (the amount of money you make from your money) is generally quite low.

There is another common rule of thumb in the investment world: the greater the risk, the greater the potential for return (also the greater the risk for loss, but I will get to that). Historically, the stock market yields well over 9% annually over periods of 10 or more years. Compare that to 3 to 4% for savings or money market accounts. And the fact that retirement money is invested for many years before you need it means many people are comfortable taking a slightly higher risk (stocks as opposed to savings accounts) for a greater return. Why?

Another general investing rule of thumb is that the longer your time horizon (meaning the longer you can keep your money invested without having to use it) the more risk you can afford to take. Here's an example of what I mean. Let's say you have $10,000 you just received from the death of your long-lost great aunt Millie. You want to use it to buy a new car. You know it will take you a few months to check out the different models you are interested in to make your choice. You want to invest that money while you are looking for your car, so it will keep making more money for you. You decide to buy some shares of stock with it, in a nice stable company. Sounds okay, right? Well, the day before you go to sell your shares of stock and get your money (you have finally decided just what car you are going to buy, and negotiated a great price with a dealer who is holding your dream car for you for 24 hours) the stock market takes a nose dive (as it does every once in a while) and the Dow Jones tumbles. Your nice safe stock tumbles along with it. Now your $10,000 is only worth $8,500. You need you money now, the dealer only has the one car in stock; what do you do? Take the $8,500 and try to finance the difference? Give up your dream car? Neither option looks good. See what I mean about short time horizons not being good times to take a risk?

Now let's say you have that same $10,000 but want to save it for a down payment on a house. You figure you will be ready to buy in 5 to 7 years. You decide to put your money in that same stable company by buying some stock. Now when the market takes a nosedive 3 months later and you see your investment value go down to $8,500, you are a little worried, but since you don't need the money for several more years, it really doesn't hurt you today. You figure that the stock market does this from time to time, and that it usually goes back up, and you know the company you invested in is a really stable solid one. So you don't worry too much. Sure enough, over the next several years your $10,000 does go up. Every once in a while you see a decline, but it always seems to be followed by some kind of increase, and the overall trend is up. About a year before you are ready to buy that house, you notice the market is going down a bit again and so you decide to move your money into a CD. Your investment horizon is only one year now (meaning you will need to use that money in a year) and you don't want to risk losing the profit you have made.

See where I am going with this? Generally IRA savings is for retirement, which for most of us is many years away. With such a long time horizon (20, 30, even 40 years), you can afford more risk. But keep in mind, I am not telling you to go out and put all your money in something stupid and risky!

Nerissa: What do you have in your retirement account?

Melissa: Isn't that a rather personal question? But in the interest of "putting your money where your mouth is" (literally) most of my retirement investments are in index funds. An index fund is a mutual fund of stocks that is intended to mimic the performance of a stock index, like the Dow Jones or the S&P 500, which are made up of a group of stocks. Because the index is broad-based and diversified, that generally means lower risk than an investment in one or a few stocks. Even investment experts have a hard time beating the stock market over time. So, unless you *know* that a company is going to be the next Microsoft or Google—and few of us will ever know that for sure—choose a fund of several stocks over just one or a few.

Of course, everyone's personal risk tolerance level is different, and the most important part of this whole decision is to do what is right for you. No matter how many times I explain this whole concept to my mother, she cannot handle any volatility. If her retirement account statement next month is worth less than this month, I practically have to sedate her. No matter that she will not need the money for many years. So she chooses very safe investments—ones where there is no risk to her that she can lose even a penny. And while her return is lower than what she might be able to make otherwise, there is no doubt this is the right decision for her. She is willing to accept a smaller return for the safety of this type of investment. So really think long and hard about your own level of tolerance before making any decisions.

Nerissa: While we are on the subject of "financial topics I don't understand," what are capital gains?

Melissa: A capital gain is the amount of money you make when you sell an investment: the difference between what you bought it for and what you sold it for. According to the IRS, "Almost everything you own and use for personal purposes, pleasure or investment is a capital asset. When you sell a capital asset, the difference between the amounts you sell it for and your basis, which is usually what you paid for it, is a capital gain or a capital loss." Capital gains are declared on your income taxes and paid at the prevailing capital gains tax rate, which can change over time as the tax code changes. Generally capital gains rates are lower than income tax rates. A capital loss (in recent tax years up to a maximum amount of $3,000) can often be counted against your income, meaning you reduce your income by this amount and thus pay less overall taxes.

How much is the capital gains tax? It varies and is determined by a number of things, including when you bought the asset, when you sold the asset, your income and any tax-code changes. Generally, assets owned for less than a year are considered short-term gains /losses, and those over one year are considered long-term. But *please* always check the most current IRS tax codes as capital gain and loss rules do change.

Nerissa: Thanks. How's Tallisen?

Melissa: She's great! She just started pre-kindergarten. Unfortunately, she also just learned how to put jellybeans up her nose, too.

Nerissa: My condolences.

Stuff You Gotta Know About Money, *courtesy of Anne, age 49*

1) Consumer Reports, US News and World Report and Money magazine all regularly run articles with their recommendations for best mutual funds. You may find the most current article online, or ask a librarian for help.

2) If you feel a little queasy about the whole robber baron capitalism thing anyway, most investment firms offer a few mutual funds that are intended to promote more community-oriented or sustainable values. They are called "socially conscious" or "socially responsible" mutual funds. Such a fund might invest in organic farming and workplace daycare centers, but not put money into fracking or armaments. Every fund is a bit different so ask questions to find out if you're comfortable with the values the fund supports.

3) One of the biggest advantages of the employer 401K is that if you have money automatically deducted from your paycheck to go in the 401K, it goes in as "pretax dollars." That means if your tax rate is 15 percent, you can have $100 put into your 401K that would only be $85 if you took it directly in your paycheck. If you're hoping to save money at all, this is a huge advantage, because you

literally get to keep more of your own money by saving it automatically. You will pay taxes when you retire but usually it's better to pay taxes later rather than now.

4) If your employer offers to match your retirement contribution at all, that is free money for you! Don't pass it up! Even if you can only put in $10 a week, and they match that $10, that is the best return on your investment ever. Your money doubles immediately, even before the investments go to work. When I was in my twenties, I did not participate in the matching plan my employer offered because I suspiciously thought they wouldn't offer me the incentive unless it was more to their advantage than mine. Boy, was I wrong. Big companies can do good things sometimes and this is one that you shouldn't miss out on.

Why We're So Bad at Saving

Our enormously productive economy...demands that we make consumption our way of life, that we convert the buying and use of goods into rituals, that we seek our spiritual satisfaction, our ego satisfaction, in consumption...We need things consumed, burned up, worn out, replaced, and discarded at an ever-increasing rate.—Victor Lebow, 1955[71]

There is not a lot of encouragement for saving in this country anymore. It used to be a kind of civic responsibility, almost a patriotic duty, but the Depression Era generation is dying off, and the economists and politicians and corporations—the Powers That Be— have figured out that saving is bad for the short-term economy. (They want us thinking about the next car to buy rather than our retirement.) So don't beat yourself up too much if saving money doesn't come naturally—we are barraged from all sides by messages telling us to spend, inundated with offers from credit card companies. Banks encourage us to buy houses and then take home equity lines to pay for improvements and furniture. (Banks do not give very good incentives for saving money. As of today, the average rate for a Money Market account (MMA) was 0.47%—again, you can check out what it is today at bankrate.com. It changes on a daily basis.)

If you are bank phobic (My friend Phillip says, "My mattress charges no fees") try this experiment: take out an envelope and mark it "secret savings" or "fun money" or "trust fund." Every week, put in $10 cash. (That's two days worth of cafe lattes, or one night's worth of beers, or one cheapo paperback book, or one download-able CD.) Don't count the money. Just do it. Set a reminder for a year from when you start. Open the envelope a year from now and be amazed.

For reasonable saving for your future/retirement/kids college fund, nine out of ten grown-ups say, "Invest in the stock market."

Diversify Your Savings

These are my friend Lora's notes taken while listening to finan-cial advisor Jane Bryant Quinn.[72] Lora (age 47) says, "Jane's general advice is to have a thoughtful plan and then leave it alone and get on with your life."

Try to Save 10% of your gross income.
Allocate the savings in thirds:
* Short term (to keep safe for 5 years or less), use mu-tual funds, money market funds, have this money for any expenses you know will arise
* Medium term (for 5-15 years), use bond investments to stabilize planning
* Long term (for longer than 15 years), use the stock market/mutual funds and diversify within that

About Stocks:
No single stock is "safe." That's why you should diversify.
* The longer a stock is held, the greater the risk
* The longer in mutual funds the better the reward
* "Best" stocks are the most likely to drop in value in under 10 years—but they will ultimately gain in value, so hang in there with them
* Individual stocks aren't worth the risk due to ultimate lack of knowledge (experts spend years getting to know a single industry and have more inside access to knowledge); that's why you should use mutual funds

Diversify: Invest in a good mutual fund. Jane recommends in-dex funds or Vanguard Trader Fund. It's good to have some stocks in international funds. Have a mix of high-risk (for long term growth) and low-risk stocks in your portfolio. And of course, set up that IRA and/or 401K.

What About Investing in Real Estate?

As I said earlier, real estate is generally a good investment as property values tend to go up. When the first edition of this book came out in the spring of 2008, we had just finished a boom cycle for the real estate market, and many people bragged about how much the value of their house or condo had gone up, or how they bought it for $34,000 and sold it for $295,000. (That was pretty amazing.) However, at the time this book went to print, the tide was already turning, the market was "flat" and houses that would have been snatched up in days the year before were sitting with For Sale signs month after month. And three months later, the bottom fell out. People were "under water" with their mortgages—meaning that the value of their homes was now less than what they owed the bank! Meaning people who bought their homes at $364,000 might sell them for $264,000. (This is why you might hear people say, "I took a bath on that one."). But things are looking up, and if I were someone who actually knew something about these things, I would cautiously encourage you to revisit the real estate market in the coming years.

The real estate market is subject to inflation, and a general rule of thumb is that when stock prices go up, real estate comes down, and vice versa. (Also when interest rates are low this is good for obtaining mortgages but bad for saving money, and vice versa.) Nevertheless, as I said, as a general rule, real estate is a good investment, although owning more than one house (being a landlord) is usually not a great idea, especially when you are in your twenties and have, ahem, a life. The last thing you need is to be answering the phone at 2 a.m. and having to call a plumber to fix your tenant's toilet. Remember the section on plumbers? They are hard to find, and that tenant will be on *your* case until the plumber shows up. Also, rent does not always (or even usually) cover all the expenses you'll accrue as a landlord. So after you put the down payment on your first home, sock away the rest of your money in a diversified savings plan (short term, medium term, long term).

The last thing I know about investing: buy low; sell high.

Alternative Lifestyles

There's a wonderful book called *Your Money or Your Life* by Joe Dominguez and Vicki Robin. One of the points this book makes is that you sometimes end up spending more money than you need to by taking a job you don't really want, to support a certain level of lifestyle. Not only that, there are all sorts of "hidden" costs to being employed in high-powered, high-salaried jobs: day care for kids, the price for commuting, travel, even the clothes you will need to look presentable at your job. Not to mention pantyhose, if you're a woman. And this brings us back to vocation, avocation, and doing what you love with your life.

Money is currency. Its purpose is to act as an exchange for goods and services; a means to an end. It is not meant to be an end in itself. Neither are goods and services, for that matter. What we all really want is a quality of life that makes us happy. So it bears merit to sit down and really ask yourself, in the words of the poet Mary Oliver, how you'd like to spend "your one wild and precious life?" Do you really need the kind of house you think you need, or the number of books you think you have time to read? Studies show that greater happiness comes from spending our money on experiences rather than possessions.[73] Again, this is helpful when choosing that job you'll be doing every day. Is it worth making $50,000 more a year? You might get to buy the flat screen TV, and four new pairs of shoes, and even take that two-week trip to the Caribbean once a year. But I, for one, would prefer a job I look forward to going to day in and day out.

Life is short and filled with sweetness, and you are uniquely qualified to do something to make the world a better place, to stamp it with your presence, your gift. To leave behind a legacy of something. Do you really want it to be a regular contribution to the GNP via Gap clothes or a succession of ever-evolving cell phones? Studies show that spending our money on experiences makes us happier in the long run than spending our money on possessions. This is helpful when thinking about choosing a low-paying job you know you will love doing every day versus a high-paying job that you might hate. Sure, the higher paycheck means you can take a vacation to the Caribbean every year. But you might prefer to be happy on a daily basis rather than ecstatic for two weeks of the year and miserable for the other 50.

Taxes

Ah, taxes, The motherlode of adulthood. Nothing in life (other than death) is more certain. And from some points of view, more troubling. Why do we pay taxes anyway? It's the debt we owe the government, I answer myself. But sometimes I hate the government! I say. Not all aspects of it, I remind me. Even when I unilaterally detested both the White House and Congress, I still liked that school was free, even though our public school system is imperfect. I liked the fact that if there were a fire in the neighborhood a fire truck would come and put it out. (Just seventy years ago, you had to pay the fire company ahead of time to put out your fire, and to prove you'd done so, they put a little plaque on your house. If you were plaque-less and your house was burning down, the fire truck would just drive on past. You have FDR and the New Deal Democrats to thank for the way we do things now.)

Though taxes have never been historically popular, we are just coming out of a particularly harsh climate of anti-tax sentiment. Income tax rates have been declining since Reagan's Tax Reform act of 1981, and we've seen the effects across the board, but notably and tragically in our public schools. Now that I am the mother of two school-aged children, I have a huge stake in where my tax dollars go: I want them to pay for my kids' education. And recently I have learned the hard way about the consequences of the past battles for lower revenue. In our town, property tax increases are capped at 2.5%, which means that in many years 2.5% is lower than the inflation rate, meaning the cost of everything goes up, but our taxes do not reflect that. Which would be fine, except that our teachers, for example, will need to pay more for milk and bread and rent (which all go up with inflation) but their salaries will be stuck because their salaries are set (in part) by what the property tax "catch" is. So every few years, our mayor has to call for an override of the property tax, meaning she says something like, "Please come to a special election to vote on whether or not I should raise your property taxes to $_____ in order to pay for _____." (Fill in the blank has been, in recent years, the school budget, and once, for a new police station.) We've had two overrides since I moved here 10 years ago, and we are about to have a third. The first lost by one vote (more on that in Book 5—guess who was responsible for the one vote?). The second passed by 60%. I wonder if we aren't entering a new phase where towns like ours consistently vote to raise their own taxes because it's become so obvious that our shared resources need, well, more resources.

Even so, my taxes in Northampton are significantly higher than they would be if I lived in the town just across the river. That town (Hadley), while lovely, is home to the area's biggest strip malls. The fact that Wal-Mart, Dick's, Target, Barnes & Noble, Pier One Imports and Best Buy, to name a few, pay their taxes in Hadley means the residents pay a lot less. They also have to contend with insane amounts of traffic, not to mention have to drive by the hideousness of Wal-Mart every day. Meanwhile, in Northampton, we protect our historic buildings and wetlands and vast acres of non-developable land. The high price in real estate taxes is a trade off, as is everything.

I like the fact that we have tons of roads to drive on and that they are mostly kept up. I don't always adore the police department, but there have been many times I've been grateful to them. Same with the Army, Navy, Air Force and Marines. I see my taxes as my gift to our town, my state and my country, and I also think I'm incredibly lucky to have as much as I do have, so I don't mind (most of the time) giving some back. The more positive an attitude I can maintain about the government, the better I tolerate having to write that check on April 15th.

That being said, when I got my first paycheck at the age of 16 and noticed that the check was for much less than I had been promised, I felt betrayed. Attached to the check was a stub with an explanation of sorts, rife with strange initials and acronyms. The long and the short of it was that I was being forced to donate a portion of my wages to the federal and state governments. The fact that I might see some of this money later in life, via Social Security (according to my optimistic parents) did not impress me.

Today, being self-employed, my troubles are the opposite. I keep every penny I earn. Until January, that is, when I send in a quarterly estimate. And then again in April, June and September.

More about estimated taxes ahead. (By the way, ignore everything I say about estimated taxes if you have a real job. Estimated taxes are strictly for the self-employed.)

As I noted earlier, David dealt with all the taxes from the time I hit adulthood until we divorced in 2001. In the last couple years of our marriage, he took over the band's taxes, as well. These were too complicated for him to figure out alone, so he did what many Americans do: went to H&R Block, probably the most famous, affordable, and omnipresent service for help with taxes. He worked with a woman there whose name was Lilly Bette Biegner, but we always referred to her as "Li'l Bit Bigger." Lil was a battle axe and a chain smoker who called us frequently during tax season and sounded like one of Marge Simpson's sisters. Lil cleared up our tax problems pronto, but the next year when David asked for her again, he was told that she had died.

So when I was on my own for the first year, I too called H&R Block. I got a fellow named Les Walker. He too chain-smoked. He was a great help with my taxes but messed them up so that I ended up having to pay a penalty. When I called in July to complain about this, I was informed that he too had died. I declined the offer to work with another employee. (And as I discovered on researching this book, tax officials are often held accountable if their clients owe taxes. No wonder so many of them "die" each year.)

State vs. Federal vs. Local

You will pay each of these as a separate bill. Your Federal portion will be the largest. State and Local taxes vary widely, as I insinuated before when talking about Northampton's local taxes versus Hadley's.

> *When I started working, I was in Connecticut. I had no idea that the state tax being withheld from my paycheck would be much lower than the Massachusetts state tax that I eventually had to pay. And this came as a nasty shock when I did my taxes the following March; I owed Massachusetts several hundred dollars that I had not been prepared to pay. —Kate, age 26.*[74]

Some states have no income tax! Yahoo! They also have crappy roads and schools. Some states have flat rates (meaning everyone pays 5%, or 7% or whatever no matter what they make). Some have graduated rates (for example, in California, you could pay 1.25% or up to 9.55% depending on your income).

1040 Forms

The 1040 is the bottom-line form the IRS needs you to fill out. You can get 1040 forms from the Post Office, local library, or on-line.[75] If your taxes are simple and straightforward—if you are not self-employed or married and have no children, and no complicated extra earnings (like money in the stock market)—you can get the 1040 EZ forms.

If you are good at reading directions, this process will truly be EZ. If you are like me, you will need all your friends gathered together to help you decipher it. Eventually, I hired an amazing woman in Texas who cheerfully helps me with my taxes. And my part of tax season goes like this: I collect 1099s (these are forms that come

 to self-employed people in the mail. Do not lose them. They are proof of what you earned. And you should not "lose" them or lie about them, because the IRS has been sent a copy.) I also collect all medical bills, mortgage interest report, and the real estate tax bills, car registration—all of which is tax deductible, meaning you can deduct what you spent from the amount you send the IRS, and all evidence of charitable giving. (Note: giving to a politician or political party does not count as charitable giving.)

Because I work for myself and am a verifiable musician and writer (meaning I have published CDs and books), I collect my credit card bills, my check register, my telephone and utility bills, and everything else that I've been diligently saving for the past year, and I add up everything I spent on CDs, music lessons, equipment and books. I get to deduct all this from my gross income. This almost makes tax time worth it. I feel so proud of myself for making a living doing what I love that I look forward to seeing those numbers. Even though it's technically not true that this means I get all my books and

CDs for free, during the month of March when I am slaving away at
these numbers, I do get the fleeting sense that it is.

As a self-employed person, I need to budget for my taxes. Every month, I need to set aside a good portion of my income (about
15% of what I make) and not touch it with a ten foot pole. Four
times a year, I send payments to the IRS and the state of Massachusetts. Property taxes are paid by my bank via my mortgage (If you
ask, usually the bank will include property taxes and sometimes ho-
meowner's insurance in your monthly payments. They will put this
money in "escrow" and effectively help you budget for these expen-
ditures.). So you will have to figure that in and allocate for that, too.
Property taxes vary depending on where your house or condo is, and
how much its value is. If you are a renter, no property taxes! Though
you may have to pay an excise tax on your car. (No car = no excise
tax. You can see how less can be more.)

Tax Brackets

Note that I said 15%. This number may vary for you. There's
this thing called "Adjusted Gross Income," which is what the IRS
thinks of as your actual take-home pay, after deductions like the
ones I listed above (medical stuff, charitable giving, and for the self-
employed, expenses that are necessary for running one's business).
When I heard that the top tax bracket in the 1950s was 90% I was
shocked. So rich people had to give away 90% of what they made?
Even I thought that was unfair!

It's also not true. We don't pay taxes at our assigned rate on
the entire amount of our income. We have what's called a "terraced"
system, meaning we are taxed at 10% for the first approximately
$10,000 we make, and then at 15% for the next $28,000 we make
above the first $10,000, and then 25% for the next bunch of money
up to $85,000 (roughly) and so on, up to a top percentage of 39.6%
(and then, only on amounts above $400,000).

For the Self-Employed: Estimated Tax Schedule:

For the period	The due date is
January 1 through March 31	April 15
April 1 through May 31	June 15
June 1 through August 31	September 15
September 1 through December 31	January 15 of the next year

Note: If an estimate would be due on a holiday, Saturday, or Sunday, it is due on the next business day. Estimated taxes are based on what you made last year. A general rule of thumb is to take your last year's form and see what you ended up paying, total, and then estimating by dividing that number by four, for both state and federal taxes. So if you paid $1000 last year in federal taxes, pay $250 per quarter to the Treasury Department. If you paid $200 last year to your state, pay $50 per quarter. You can download these forms online.[76]

So Now What Do I Do?

For your very first time filing taxes, I would go to H&R Block, even given my bad experience. Your first visit is free. Have them walk you through the 1040 form. Bring all your documents and the bills and bank statements from that year. If you figure out that you owe more to the IRS than you have to spend, write a letter to the IRS and they will help you work out a payment plan. And then, plan better. You might also want to invest in some software like Turbo Tax, which I have never used, but some of my friends swear by it.

I was totally skittish about using software or doing my taxes online, but then a techie friend of J's recommended taxact. com[77] and it is terrific. They update all the rules etc. every year, and they ask you questions about your spending in human language, but it can still handle complicated situations (we have two separate self-employment worksheets, a home office worksheet, medical expenses, and still it's easy). I've used it the past three years. It costs about $20 to use it and e-file your state and federal returns. We were paying an accountant $375 a year.—Lori, 38

Refund?!?

You may well be due a refund, especially if you have overpaid (as a self-employed person) or if the business you work for has been paying your taxes for you. Don't count on the refund, but if it comes, squirrel it away, or apply it to next year's tax bill. And say thank you.

One more vital piece of information: in some towns, the Post Office throws midnight Tax Parties on April 15. Check it out.

Last Words on Taxes

A few more things about taxes before we leave the topic. My friend Rick, a professional clown, keeps every receipt in a file in his car. Why? Because he's been audited three times. What, you ask, is being audited? I hope you are quaking in your boots! Being audited is what all adults (perhaps especially the self-employed) try to avoid, which is why we all become psychotic around April 15. Being audited is when someone from the IRS comes to your house and demands proof for all those little numbers you (or your accountant) scribbled into those 1040 forms. My aunt Elizabeth, a potter, keeps all receipts in a shoe-box. She marks each shoebox by the year, and figures when the IRS comes knocking, they'll have to go through her shoe boxes. They would, too. What happens if they find errors in your tax documentation? They make you pay the difference! Or they pay you the difference if you've overpaid. So really, it's not that big a deal to be audited; no more unpleasant than going to the dentist, as long as you've been honest. Those adults quaking in their boots don't need to fret—unless they have something to hide.

And finally, keep reminding yourself that your taxes are akin to paying rent or mortgage on your citizenship. The USA is a fantastic place to live, even if we are the greediest most arrogant folks on earth. If you don't like the government, imagine your tax money going to preserve your favorite mountain or river, or to keep the roads paved in your street, or to replace the tires on a school bus in Kentucky, or to pay the salary of a really lovely government worker in the District of Columbia, or to keep Public Radio and PBS going.

Insurance

Q: What is insurance?

A: Insurance is something you buy yearly or monthly to protect yourself in case something goes wrong. Live without it at your peril. Also, just *try* sleeping at night.

Tools and Rules

- Ask people what they know about insurance and whether or not they've had reason to use theirs.
- Life Insurance: Don't need it yet.
- Health insurance: Do need it. This is one of the reasons people get real jobs instead of being rock stars.
- Auto Insurance: Do need it. You can't legally own a car without it. Or drive one.

Life Insurance

Do not buy life insurance until you have your first child or you turn 35 and have a spouse. It's not worth it. The only reason you need it is to provide for the people you leave behind. The fewer dependents you have (dependents are people you live with and love: partners and children) the lower your premium should be. Therefore, if you are currently unattached, there's really not a lot of point in socking money away for a future which may not exist. Not to be a downer . . .

Health Insurance

I was paying $160 per month for a very lame [catastrophic] plan. Getting the fine print out of them about why anything was covered was only slightly harder than finding Jim Morrison alive in South America. —Tom, age 43

In 1991, singer/songwriter Victoria Williams was diagnosed with multiple sclerosis. Like most musicians, she did not have health insurance, and her medical bills were overwhelming. Fortunately, she had a lot of famous friends who banded together and made a

CD of her songs, which Sony Music released as *Sweet Relief*. It was a huge radio hit; she got the proceeds and was able to pay for her treatment.

But most of us aren't so lucky and have to buy our own health insurance without an all-star fundraiser. A policy for someone in her mid-twenties runs anywhere from $350 to $1000 a month, depending on where you are located in the country. That's around what most people pay for their rent or mortgage. Do you need it? In a word, yes. The average uninsured person spends an average of $934 a year on health care, which isn't that much if you compare it to what you'd have to pay per month.[78] But keep in mind: that average person might not go to the doctor when he or she needs to. A typical doctor's visit can cost up to $500, and that doesn't count the prescription drugs doled out. My friend Verna (not her real name) in Portland, Oregon (not where she's from) has to pay $175 just to walk into a doctor's office every time she wants to make sure her lingering cold isn't strep throat, or a bronchial infection, or a sinus infection. If it does turn out to be bacterial, she pays upward of $100 for the antibiotics to get rid of it. She could save money and go to a clinic, but the wait there can be a month long. And what if you get hit by the proverbial bus? A night at the hospital can be $3000. A typical hospital stay can cost you $29,000.[79]

Then there's the argument about preventative care; if you go to a doctor regularly, theoretically, the doctor can be checking out those weird moles on your back that may or may not turn into melanomas. If you ignore the doctor for ten years, you might be dealing with something significantly more expensive, not to mention fatal. Not to scare you or anything.

I am sure your parents or other concerned adults have mentioned health insurance to you before now. As in, "be sure to get a job with." Here's why. "The leading cause of personal bankruptcy in the United States is unpaid medical bills...the death rate in any given year for someone without health insurance is twenty-five per cent higher than for someone with insurance."[80]

If you are a full-time student, you can be covered until the age of 26 by your parents' insurance, thanks to Obamacare (see "What is Obamacare and How Will It Change My Life?"). Check this out before you start spending your own hard-earned money.

There are four kinds of health insurance plans. Fee for Service (FFS) or Major Medical means you can pick any doctor or hospital you want. This plan costs the most, *and* you will have to pay a deductible before your insurance company pays a dime. Also, if you can get a high deductible policy ($5000-$10,000) this might be a good way to save money on your premium.

Then there are the notorious HMOs—Health Maintenance Organizations. They tend to be cheap—as cheap as $200 a month, which is still a chunk of change. Also, you will be required to pick one Primary Care physician who will act as the General Manager of your health plan and won't let you see any other doctor without his or her permission. For example, if you are a runner and suspect you've twisted your knee, you will need to make an appointment with your PCP (Primary Care Physician in insurance parlance) to be seen before you can go see the orthopedist. Annoying. Not only that, your PCP will only let you see a doctor who is within that HMO's network of doctors. So suppose your sister Suzie broke her leg last year. She had a fantastic orthopedist named Dr. Fixitwell. She says, "You must see him, he is *marvelous*! And cute." But Dr. Fixitwell is not on your HMO plan. So unless you want to pay him $500 a visit, you have to go see Dr. Kindofblind instead, because he's the one your PCP referred you to. Ask your potential HMO if they offer the option to pay a portion of your fee for seeing out-of-network doctors; some may. (If it's a true emergency, and you have to go to the Emergency Room and don't have time to call your primary care physician, you will most likely still be reimbursed by your HMO. But don't forget to notify them!)

POS (Point of Service) plans are sort of in between: you still have a primary care physician to refer you to other doctors, but you may be eligible for "out of network" benefits (this means checks come to you in the mail rather than bills). Still, then you have to make a case to your insurance company. This involves writing a letter, finding a stamp, and sticking it in your mailbox, which you may or may not ever get around to doing if you are an incredibly busy artist with your priorities in the right place. Some POS plans have "co-insurance" possibilities where you share the out-of-network costs; usually 80% (they pay) and 20% (which you pay).

PPOs (Preferred Provider Organizations) are organizations of doctors who bill the insurance company directly. You will have to pay a co-pay (anywhere from $5 to $50 per visit, and usually about $25 for prescriptions) but you don't need a referral to see a specialist if the specialist is within the network.

One important thing: do not lie when filling out applications for health insurance. Don't say you don't smoke if you do, or that you consume only a glass of wine a week if you are a daily drinker. Health insurance companies are like Big Brother, and they will bust you and make your life miserable if you lie to them. If you get denied for health insurance from one company, it will be hard to get it from another company. They're like a pack of wolves. Or the Borg.

Once when I was without health insurance I developed a bad earache which I was pretty sure was bacterial. I went to a local hospital emergency room. The doctor was an old New England liberal with white tufts growing out of his ears. He was very kind and, after checking my intake papers, gave me some free samples of basically everything within arm's reach. Then he put his hand on my shoulder and said, "You know, you can save a lot of money by clipping coupons in the Sunday paper."

Q&A With Mark Boardman, Insurance Professional

Nerissa: What is a premium?

Mark: The amount you pay monthly for you health insurance coverage. If you are employed, your employer will probably pay a portion and the rest will be taken out of your paycheck. An HMO plan (Health Maintenance Plan) is usually the least expensive, then POS (Point of Service), followed by a full-blown PPO plan (Preferred Provider Organization), which is the most expensive and offers the broadest list of providers usually on a nationwide network. A Major Medical plan, or HDHP (High Deductible Health Plan) depending on where your deductible lies ($1,000 to $5,000), can be the most expensive or the least expensive. I recommend purchasing a higher deductible health plan and "self funding" the smaller claims to keep your monthly premiums low.

Nerissa: What is a co-payment?

Mark: What you are charged for and pay at the time you go to the doctor's office, usually a minimal fee between $10 and $40.

Nerissa: What is a deductible?

Mark: Paid per year, it is the amount you are responsible for under the health plan before the insurance company will begin to pay. Many insurance companies are covering routine exams not subject to the upfront deductible. These exams include routine, age-based exams along with the necessary lab tests, pap smears, mammograms, colonoscopies etc. So, if you are being treated for a broken arm, for example, you would be required to satisfy your upfront deductible ($1,000 to $5,000) before the insurance company payments begin. Depending on your plan, hospital co-pays may still apply for either inpatient or outpatient services.

Nerissa: What is co-insurance?

Mark: Not all insurance plans have co-insurance. Co-insurance is a split (usually 80%/20%) in which you pay part of the claim after a deductible usually associated with POS or PPO plans. The insurance company pays the bigger share.

Nerissa: What is "in network" and "out of network?"

Mark: "In network" are those providers (doctors, labs, hospitals, etc.) who accept a discounted payment from your insurance company because you're in their HMO provider network. In other words, you're going to have lower co-payments & deductibles if you stay within the local network of providers. Many HMOs only offer coverage within their network of providers and no coverage is available for "out of network" providers unless it for an emergency. "Out of network" are those providers not listed on the "in network" provider list but their services are covered through your POS and PPO plans to which a higher deductible and co-insurance apply.

How to Pick an Insurance Plan

First of all, figure out what you need. You probably know by
now how often you get sick. You might have a pre-existing condition. You might want to be in therapy. All these things should factor
into your decision. Remember: ask a lot of questions, both of your
employer and your fellow employees. Your best bet will almost certainly be to sign on with whatever health insurance company your
employer uses, but sometimes they give you a choice. If you are
married and/or have children, ask if dependents are covered. Does
the health insurance company have a dental plan? How about birth
control? Fertility plans? This may not matter to you now, but if
you're postponing having children till you are 35, and you think you
might still be with this health plan, make sure they provide generously for fertility plans. Do you already have a doctor you love? Is
she or he covered by this new plan?

Compare and contrast your options. Think about the differ-
ences between monthly premiums and deductibles, co-payments,
prescriptions. Check to see which hospitals are affiliated with each
plan; that could make a difference if you happen to live really near a
good one, but it's not the one covered by your insurance.

If you leave your place of employment, you can be "COBRA'd."
COBRA stands for the Consolidated Omnibus Budget Reconcilia-
tion Act, which gives "workers and their families who lose their
health benefits the right to choose to continue group health benefits
provided by their group health plan for limited periods of time under
certain circumstances such as voluntary or involuntary job loss, re-
duction in the hours worked, transition between jobs, death, divorce,
and other life events."[81]

This is good news; most COBRA plans last for eighteen months
or so, which is usually enough time to find new employment and/or
a new health plan.

The bad news about COBRA is that you have to pay the whole
premium, including the part that your employer used to pay on your
behalf.

If your job doesn't provide health insurance, leave it. Or, stay
and see if there's a professional association that provides its members with the opportunity to join a health plan.

What Is Obamacare and How Will It Change My Life?

The point of Obamacare (not its real name, but everyone, including Obama has adopted it—its real name is Patient Protection and Affordable Care Act (PPACA)) is two-fold: to increase the number of Americans covered by health insurance, and to bring down the costs of health care. To that end, starting in January 2014, no one will be excluded from getting health insurance (due to a pre-existing condition), and everyone *must* get health insurance. You in particular might not like that last part. Many twenty-somethings are extremely healthy and have little need for a doctor. And if they do, they are willing to take the gamble and pay "out of pocket." This makes sense: say you get sick once a year with a sinus infection. Out of pocket, the whole deal might cost you $550 with doctor visits and antibiotics. Buying health insurance will be a good $200 a month (depending on your plan, your premium to deductible ratio, whether or not you smoke, etc.). So clearly you'd be better off (in the short term) with no health insurance—at least for a few years. But part of the idea of Obamacare is that if everyone "buys into" the system, costs will be lower.

But let's go back to that whole "nobody being denied" part. Up until now insurance companies could deny coverage to anyone for any reason, and if they decided you were a bad risk—say you have a history of cancer in your family, or you drink, or you've been in a car accident, or you were born with a congenital ailment—they could charge you more for your insurance. And suppose you were perfectly healthy, but at the age of 30 you got thyroid cancer (a highly treatable cancer, but still—who wants cancer?). Your health plan, under the old laws, would pay for it, but say a few years later your wife changed jobs and you moved with her from Denver to Atlanta. Your wife gets new insurance, and—surprise!—you get denied coverage because you once had cancer. Nice, huh?

Well, this can't happen anymore. Not only that, there are other reasons Obamacare is a good thing. According to Fox News[82] as of 2011, 86 million Americans had already benefited from lower health care costs; 2.5 million young people were able to stay on their parents' insurance plans until they turned 26 (you might like that!); and 2.5 million seniors had already saved money because of caps called for on their medications costs. Adopting Obamacare will save the government an estimated $200 billion over the next 10 years and over a trillion by the end of the second decade.

Auto Insurance

Every state is different, first of all, so you will need to find out from your insurance company what your state's requirements are. Some states have "no fault" insurance which means it doesn't matter who caused the accident; each driver must pay his or her own costs for damages.

When shopping for an insurance plan, you'll want your company to cooperate if you are responsible for an accident. Some are more punitive toward young drivers than others. Ask questions! It's your money, and right now, before you buy, you have all the power. Your state will require you to purchase a minimum of coverage. The more you drive, the more coverage you'll need.

Liability insurance: This covers the damage you do to others. If you are in an accident and it's your fault (and you don't live in a "no fault" state), then this is what will pay for your victim's mangled car and body. It will also pay for your legal bills, doctor's bills and even the wages you will lose by cleaning up this mess. To find out what your state's minimum levels of auto liability insurance are, go to info.insure.com/auto/minimum.html

Collision and Comprehensive Coverage: This covers the damage you do to your own car (again, if you are the one at fault). You know the expression "I totaled my car?" That means the damage was so great that the insurance company would rather replace your car than pay to fix it. Unfortunately, this doesn't mean that if you paid $48,000 for a Beamer your insurance company will hand you $48,000. You'll only get the blue book value of the car (to find out what your car's blue book value is, just for kicks, use their website[83]). This portion of your total yearly auto insurance bill will be the highest, usually. As with health insurance, you will be able to chose a higher deductible to keep your premium costs down, or vice versa.

Comprehensive coverage includes anything bad that happens to your car—not just when you're on the road. If someone vandalizes it, that's covered. If it's stolen, set on fire, or a gigantic redwood tree falls on it when you're out car camping in the Sierras, you're covered. But only after you've chipped in with your deductible!

You know that link I just gave you about finding out the value of your car? The Kelly Blue Book value? You might want to check out what your car's worth; if it's less than what you'd pay for insurance per year, you might not want to keep it around. Even better, ask your insurance company. They might advise you to have only collision, or even to skip insurance altogether.

Medical Payments, Personal Injury Protection (PIP) and No-Fault Coverage: This covers the medical expenses incurred by you and your passengers after an accident. If you buy this, you will be covered no matter who is at fault. Again, each state is different, so talk to your insurance salesperson and ask about this.

Famous Auto Insurance Companies to Get You Started:
GEICO: www.geico.com
State Farm: www.statefarm.com
Allstate: www.allstate.com

Also, following the Golden Rule of *How to Be an Adult*, ask smart-looking older people what they do about car insurance. And when you see a clueless-looking college grad next year, pass on the good information.

Cars: The Vehicle That Is Your Vehicle

Cars Tools and Rules:

- Don't buy from a friend.
- Bring some reading material with you to the DMV—you will wait in line for approximately three weeks.
- Keep your registration in your glove compartment.
- Change your oil every 5000 miles.[84]
- Don't buy a brand new car.
- Get a vehicle that gets over 35 miles to the gallon.

Sometimes I feel that having a car is like having a very high maintenance pet—one in which the state government has an inordinate interest. When I was in my early twenties and owned my first car (an '82 Chevy Chevette with no FM radio, no AC, manual windows, no power steering, a broken back window—but it got great gas mileage!), it seemed as though there was a neverending list of things I did not know I had to do for my car, all of which involved the Department of Motor Vehicles, which in turn meant taking several hours out of my day and waiting in an interminable line with extremely cranky people. I would get to the front of the line and inevitably have to return home with my mission not accomplished because I'd failed to provide some document with someone's signature. The whole thing was baffling. I wish someone had given me a one-page list of things to do. So that's what I will try to do for you.

Annoying Car Details

1. License Expiration: Most of you will have gotten your drivers' licenses by the time you were between the ages of 16 and 18. I'm sorry for those of you who don't have yours yet, but it's outside the province of this book to tell you how to get one. Suffice it to say, the Department of Motor Vehicles (DMV, or RMV in Massachusetts) will tell you how. But for the rest of you, keep an eye on your license expiration date, and be sure to renew it when the time comes. Go to your local DMV, fill the paperwork out thoroughly, and smile pretty for the camera.

2. Registration: www.dmv.org. If you own a car and are moving to a new state, one of the first things you'll want to do is register that vehicle. Nowadays, this can be done online, glory hallelujah! Just go to the link above. Fees for a normal car (as opposed to an 18-wheeler or a school bus) are $50 in Massachusetts. After you've registered once, the DMV will send you a bill/form, which you must open and fill out, and write a check, and then mail it back. This is an example of a piece of mail that is incredibly important to not lose, misplace or throw out by accident.

3. Inspection Dates: In most states, your car will need to be inspected to make sure it is not spewing more nasty emissions than are legally allowed, contributing to the melting of the polar ice caps, etc. There should be a sticker on your windshield with a big number on it and a little number, too. The little number is usually the year (say 2013) and the big number is the month number (4 for April, for example).

Look around when you're driving around town, (or preferably, when being driven) and notice that some gas stations have signs on their garage doors proclaiming that they are official Inspection Stations. Make note. Then, when you have an hour or so, drive up, wait in line (sometimes when the gods are smiling, there are no lines) and get them to inspect your car for you. The cost is around $40 or something. The problems only come if you fail inspection. Not only does this suck in terms of the money you will have to spend to fix whatever's wrong with your car (could be anything from a broken signal light to needing new brakes), but you will also technically be driving an illegal vehicle around, which means the cops can stop you and give you a ticket with a fine. This is why it's often better to get your car inspected *before* the big number marking the month passes. (So if 4 is your number, plan to get your car inspected in February or March. But especially don't go on the last day of the month, when inspection stations are packed with procrastinators.)

4. Making Sure the Auto Insurance Is Paid Up: This is as complicated as paying the bill once it comes in. For some of us, this in and of itself is a grand feat.

5. Oil Changes and Maintenance: You need to get your oil changed every 5000 miles or so. If the oil gets too low, you will destroy your engine. I know this firsthand. Different auto aficionados have different opinions, but I always just went to Jiffy Lube. Tom says go to your friendly neighborhood repair shop (this assumes one has such a relationship) because Jiffy Lube doesn't do a great job with lubrication, ironically. As for maintenance, if you are so inclined, you can study this and become adept at taking great care of your car, changing its own oil and studying what's under the hood. I've found that one can be a passable adult knowing next to nothing about cars at all, especially if one is a friendly person not afraid to ask for help.

Tips on Buying a Car[85]

- Buy the least expensive model from the best automaker. So if you love Volvos, get their cheapest model.
- If buying used, try to get one that's two years old or less.
- Buy through the newspaper and not dealerships (they mark up and are harder to negotiate with).
- Buy from owners who keep their maintenance records.

If you can, buy your car outright. Spending money on your car payments will feel more and more annoying as the months go by and as your car is becoming dingier and older and less valuable. (Unlike a house, a car does not appreciate in value.) By the time you're done paying your car off, you may have spent up to 50% of its original worth and have to turn around and sell it for $3500 to buy a new one. Better to buy a good used car with money you've saved. A car's market value drops significantly (about 30%) as soon as you drive it off the showroom floor. So don't ever buy brand-new. Great deals can be had online (try Craigslist.org if you live near a major urban area) and from classified ads or from friends of friends. If you really love that new car smell, you can get it in a bottle.[86]

My brother-in-law Dave says that it's good to buy from a friend of a friend; but not from a friend. Think about how bad you'd feel if you sold your car to a pal only to watch helplessly as your previously Trusty Toyota turned into the Lemon of the Century.

AAA

At this point, as I sit here in a Starbucks in Saratoga Springs, I'd like to suggest that you might get along fine for a few years without a car. Perhaps I am influenced by the fact that Tom's Subaru sits outside this Starbucks on the street with half a key in its ignition, and it's the Sunday of President's Day weekend, and the only locksmith in town is watching the Daytona 500 and refuses to come help us. (The other half of the key, as you might have guessed, is still on Tom's keychain.)

This might be a good time to mention the benefits of joining AAA. With just one telephone call, we are being helped. (Or we hope we will be helped; I'll let you know.) Membership to AAA costs $87 the first year (with a $10 enrollment fee) and $77 thereafter for the Plus membership; for Basic, it's $61 the first year (plus that $10 enrollment fee) and $51 afterwards.[87] With either, you get four service calls a year. Plus membership also covers 100 free miles per tow. Anything after that is $3 a mile. You're covered up to $100 for a locksmith if you've physically lost the keys to start your car; he will make you a key on the spot. For Basic, you get only 5 miles free on the tow and you pay $50 for the locksmith.

While I'm waiting to see if AAA is worth our Plus membership fees, I think I'll tell you how to do a bunch of common auto tasks.

How to Change Your Oil

Everyone should know how to do this. Not that *I* do this; I'm too prissy. But still. I'm glad I know how.

What you'll need:
- 4 to 5 quarts of API-certified motor oil
- a new oil filter
- a vise grip or adjustable wrench
- a shallow pan to collect the old oil—should be wide enough to hold 4 to 5 quarts of oil
- a filter wrench

You can get these things from an automotive store. Ask the clerk to help you choose the proper filter for your car.[88]

1. Wearing grungy clothes, scoot yourself under your car, near the front. The oil tank is a relatively large tank with a bolt coming out of the bottom or side of it.

2. Put the pan under the bolt of the tank. (This bolt is called the discharge bolt.)

3. Without rounding the edges, remove the bolt using the vise grip.

4. Let the oil drain from the tank into the pan.

5. Tightly screw the bolt back in. *Do not forget this step!*

6. Get up and out from under the car, pop the hood, and look for the oil filter. It is usually somewhere on the side of your engine.

7. Remove the filter with a filter wrench, rotating counter-clockwise.

8. There will be oil in the filter, so try to pour it inside the pan under the car.

9. Screw in the new filter, rotating in a clockwise direction. Don't make it too tight. Once the filter makes contact with the engine, only rotate an additional 3/4 turn.

10. There is a cap located on the top of your engine, usually marked "oil." Pour the new oil into the engine. Consult your owner's manual for the proper amount, normally 4 to 5 quarts.

11. After adding all the new oil, check the dipstick to make sure you got it right.

12. Look under the car for any leaks.

13. Turn on your car and check for leaks again.

14. Take your old oil to your local gas station or auto parts store. Do not *ever* throw used oil in drains or anywhere else where it could come in contact with the water table. You will wreck things, and hurt the environment.

15. Change your oil every 5000 miles.

16. When you see a bunch of cars waiting in line at Jiffy Lube, roll down your window and call, "Suckas!"

How to Jumpstart Your Car

Warning: you *must* hook up the cables in the proper order *or your car could explode!* Also, check out the dead battery. If it's cracked or leaking liquid, don't attempt this. Suck it up and buy a new battery. If you try to jumpstart with a cracked or liquidy battery *your car could explode!* (Also, make sure your jumper cables are not too rusty. Your car won't explode if they are, but neither will your dead battery start.)

Now that you are properly terrified, rest assured, this rarely happens. Still. Do not attempt this maneuver if you are intoxicated or a space case.[89]

You'll need two cars: the dead one and a healthy one.

- Drive the healthy car close enough to the dead car so that the jumper cables will reach from one battery to the other.
- Click open the hoods of both cars
- If your car is manual, put in neutral. If automatic, put in park. Pull up the emergency brake. Turn the engines off.
- Attach the red clip, which is a positive terminal, to the battery of the dead car. Make sure you are attaching it to the battery's positive ("+") terminal.
- Attach the other red clip, which is a positive terminal, to the battery of the source car. Make sure you are attaching them to the battery's positive ("+") terminal.
- Do *not* let the other clips touch each other. *Never* touch the metal on jumper cables.
- Attach the black clip nearest the healthy car to that car's negative or "-" terminal.
- Connect the second black clip to something grounded—either any exposed metal on the dead car's engine or the frame.
- Start the healthy car.

How to Be an Adult

- Try to start the dead car. If nothing happens, make sure all the cables are connected properly, metal to metal. Keep running the healthy car, and try again.
- If the dead car starts, keep it running for several minutes at a high idle, and turn off the healthy car.
- Disconnect the black cables first. Don't let the cables touch each other.
- Disconnect the red cables.

How to Change a Flat Tire

Step 1: Find a Safe Place to Change your Tire!
- Get off the road so that there's no chance you will be hit by the flow of traffic.
- Also, make sure you are visible to the cars coming up on you.
- Make sure the ground is level—you can't jack your car up on an incline.
- Turn on your hazard lights.
- If you have a manual car, put it in gear. If automatic, put it in park.
- Pull on the emergency brake.

Step 2: Assemble your tools
- Spare tire
- Lug nut wrench
- Jack
- If you have blocks, put them under the tire opposite the flat.
- Car owner's manual

Step 3: Loosen the lug nuts
- Remove the hubcap if you have one
- Loosen the lug nuts with the lug nut wrench
- If they are tight, jump on the lug wrench
- Don't actually remove the lug nuts; just loosen them

Step 4: It's Jack Time!
- Your car's owner's manual will tell you where to place the jack.

- There is usually a small plate just in front of the back tires. Or just behind the front tires.
- Put the jack under the car, and raise it up until it makes contact with the frame.
- Make sure the jack is stable.
- Keep raising the jack until the tire is about 6 inches off the ground. The spare needs some wiggle room because it's fully inflated.

Step 5: Get rid of the flat
- Now you can take the lug nuts off the bolts and put them somewhere where you won't lose them.
- Put your hands on the old tire at 9 o'clock and 3 o'clock.
- Pull the tire into you and away from the car.

Step 6: You're almost done!
- Hold the spare tire directly in front of the wheel well
- Make sure the holes in the center of the spare tire are aligned with the bolts on the car
- Thread the spare tire on the bolts
- Push the tire onto the car until it is snug
- Find your lug nuts and replace them on the bolts and tighten them, but not too tight—just enough to keep the tire in place while you lower the car.

Step 7: UnJack
- Crank the jack down until the car is resting on all four tires.
- Tighten the lug nuts, starting with one, then moving to the one opposite it, until all four are tight.

Step 8: Put Your Toys Away
- Put the flat tire where the spare used to be.
- Put the jack and lug wrench where they used to be.
- Idiot-check your area to make sure you didn't forget anything.
- When you get to where you are going, get your flat tire fixed or replaced. Most spares are only good for about 50 miles.

Who Needs a Stinkin' Car?

Many city dwellers, or those who live near public transportation, or those who live in warmer climates and/or own thighs that are bicycle-friendly might consider the freedom and lack of hassle of living auto-free. In addition to not having to do all these annoying yearly and tri-monthly bureaucratic do-si-dos, you will save a lot of money on gas, maintenance, taxes, insurance, yearly registration, and inspection, *and* do your part not to contribute to the greenhouse effect.

If you decide to go carless, you have a number of options. Renting cars is not as expensive as you might think: about $45 a day, plus gas of course. This won't work for your daily commute, but if you only need a car for the occasional trip from the city to Saratoga Springs, this is a lot cheaper than the costs of maintaining a vehicle.

Also, in some cities you can subscribe to Zip Cars. Here's how it works: you pay a monthly membership of $50 (though you can pay less if you opt for an hourly rate). You get an electronic key card. Go to the Zip Car parking lot and wave your card in front of the windshield. With the $50 per month plan, you pay by the hour, after your first 8 free hours. It's a really reasonable hourly rate—around $9 per hour depending on which city you're in. Here's some more information, which I have paraphrased from www.zipcar.com.

Joining Zipcar[90]

To join Zipcar, you need to be over 21 and have a valid driver's license (US or foreign). There's an online application, which you must complete. They run a quick check on your driving record. Then a few days later they'll send you your Zipcard. You can start driving as soon as you get it. You can reserve cars online or by phone. You can choose any car you want: they have Minis, Priuses, BMWs, pickup trucks, etc. When you go to pick up your car, your Zipcard will open it—all you do is wave it in front of the windshield! For the duration of your reservation, only your Zipcard will unlock your car. Gas, satellite radio, and insurance come with the car. Just return the car when you are finished, parking it in the same reserved spot in the Zip Lot.

The locksmith just arrived; apparently he's not so into the Daytona 500. He didn't even eat into our $100 credit; he just pulled the end of the key out. Fortunately, Tom has a spare key on his chain, so as soon as I finish my decaf Americano, we are homeward bound. Moral of the story: we are so glad we had AAA!

Our Vegetable-Sipping Car

As I write this, it's 73 degrees. That's not unusual in and of itself, but I should add that it's January, and we live in Massachusetts. Caught between feeling guilty because our collective consumption of fossil fuel has quite possibly caused this strange unprecedented condition, and our joy at taking a long walk in a T-shirt two weeks after the winter solstice, we greet our neighbors, "Happy Global Warming!" And this seems as good a place as any to discuss alternative fuel sources.

Grease Cars

A grease car runs on vegetable oil. Yep, the kind you can buy at the Stop & Shop. The kind you put in salad dressing or deep-fry your chicken in. Soybean oil, safflower oil, even olive oil will do. In order to do this sleight-of-pump, one must buy and install (or have installed) a second tank; the Grease Tank if you will. This tank rests in the well where the spare tire usually is. Then, a fuel line is run alongside the diesel fuel line, and you have to operate a switch to go between the two. You start your car using the diesel tank, and once the vegetable oil is warmed up (a gauge confirms this) you switch over to the grease tank. How do you get the grease, you might ask. If you want it for free (which is part of the point of the whole grease car culture), simply visit a local restaurant, preferably a Chinese restaurant or clam shack where they do a lot of artery-clogging deep-frying. Ask the owner if you might have the leftover fryolator oil. They will generally be happy to give it to you since it often costs them to have it disposed of. Then, take home the grease and filter it, since there will be pesky bits of leftover tempura and clam. The filtering situation is a whole other problem, requiring yet another kind of tank. Once you've filtered, pour your grease into empty milk jugs. Now, when your grease tank is empty, fill 'er up. You can even take the milk jugs with you on the road, dispensing with the need to stop at Mobil to refuel; in fact, you can have your rest stop at Starbucks or Whole Foods or Aunt Nancy's now. This is our dream.

Biodiesel

This is the route we chose. We bought a 2004 Jetta TDI and run it on biodiesel. This seemed like a good compromise. Though we are not saving any money (as of this writing, biodiesel is about $4.50 a gallon), we are driving with less guilt. We were frightened that if we did the Grease Car conversion, we might void our warranty, and also after buying the car, we were too broke to do the $800 conversion plus buy the $800 18-gallon filtration kit. This is why I don't get to judge my friends who say they don't have it in the budget to buy organic food.

The biodiesel sold commercially must conform to strict industry specifications. Unlike the "grease" you put into a car modified as such, straight vegetable oil doesn't work in a regular diesel car. Many owners of diesel cars now use a mix of pure biodiesel and regular diesel fuel. The mix can be anywhere from B-20 (20% vegetable oil to 80% diesel, commercially available at some pumps) to B-100 (100% vegetable oil—this will only work on newer model diesels—post-2004 I think.)

Hybrids

Hybrids use part gas, part electricity and get great gas mileage. As of this writing, they are the #1 vehicle in our extremely progressive town. They combine internal combustion engines and electric batteries, which power electric motors. The battery is constantly recharged every time you brake. Also, they are smart; when you are "cruising," they somehow sense this and don't use as much fuel.

The electric car, by contrast, needs an external source to charge it. Of course, the fully electric car needs no gasoline or diesel, while the hybrid requires fossil fuels, though as of this writing, some can use ethanol.

Honestly, as of this writing, the world is changing so fast that by the time this book goes to press, much of what I write about "alternate fuels" may well be obsolete. Soon people will be driving cars fueled by morning breath! Hey, a girl can dream, can't she?

Why Not Drive a Hummer?

Like all good liberals who were brought up to question authority, including the authority of other liberals, I notice my passionate authority-busting inner teenager itching to challenge at every turn as I travel this particular vehicular spiritual path. So what if I'm using cloth diapers for my child? So what, in fact, if thousands of us weirdos are using cloth diapers? Landfills are still getting filled at atrocious speeds. So what if I drive on soybeans? If everyone drove on soybeans, we'd run out of arable land in a matter of weeks and the planet would starve to death. And besides, the Chinese are now driving at record numbers which are only climbing; the world's population is going to be nine billion in a few minutes. Rather than invent clever ways to get better gas mileage, it remains best to re-duce, reuse, recycle—to slow down and do less, drive less, use less, take up less space in the landfills as well as on the freeways. In the summer of 2006, *The New York Times* ran a story in their Science Times section called "How to Cool A Planet (Maybe)"[91] about all these crazy ideas of how to stop global warming, including a kind of Star Wars-esque space mirror and a plan to infuse the atmosphere with sulfuric clouds.[92] When are we going to stop overthinking this? When are we going to learn that it's about doing less, not doing more? So what if I could drive for free, getting 50 mpg? It would still be better to walk into town, ride my bike to Amherst and leave the car at home. Consume less. Live simply so that others may sim-ply live, tread lightly on Mother Earth and all that.

When I am angry and/or exhausted, feeling like my two-year-old in melt-down mode, I want to shut myself in the one air-condi-tioned room in our house and read a magazine. (Not the *New Re-public* either; something really trashy like *Shape* or *People*.) I have a kind of "I deserve" mentality that reminds me of the way I used to say "I deserve to eat that sundae since I've had such a hard time" when I was an overeater. It's an adolescent cry of frustration. What I'm really saying is, "Mom, take care of me." Mom is food; mom is Mother Earth. To consume is to consume, whether it be food or our precious natural resources.

After we saw *An Inconvenient Truth*, Tom said, "We can't just do things because they're convenient anymore. That no longer cuts it." In *Walden*, Thoreau says, "To affect the quality of the day—that is the highest of the arts." The reason I've always thought recycling was a spiritual path is largely because it forces me to be mindful in a very quotidian way. I don't put my fruit into plastic bags at the supermarket because I know that if I do, I will eventually have to throw away a piece of plastic, so I'm mindful at the supermarket. When I've eaten the fruit, I compost the skin and the pit. This brings me down from my habitual home way up in my thoughts (where I'm doing any one of the following: writing a song, obsessing about my weight, thinking about a client, wondering when I can get back to the novel I'm reading, or griping about the messiness of the kitchen sink) and connects me to the earth, literally and figuratively. I pour my water into a glass instead of using a plastic bottle because otherwise, I'm going to have to sort that bottle from the trash into the containers bin. It's a wonderful way to live, to live deliberately instead of mindlessly.

Book Five
Other People

Tools and Rules

- We're all interconnected. It might not seem like we are, but we are.
- It's always better to be nice, unless you are a pushover, in which case, it's still better to be nice, but work on asserting yourself, too.
- Vote.
- Stay in touch with your friends.
- Get married if you want.
- Try not to get divorced, but if you do, be nice about it.
- Being a parent will make you finally forgive your own.

Being an Adult in a Democracy

We the people of the United States, in order to form a more perfect union, establish justice, insure domestic tranquility, provide for the common defense, promote the general welfare, and secure the blessings of liberty to ourselves and our posterity, do ordain and establish this Constitution for the United States of America.—Preamble to the US Constitution

If you don't vote, you don't get to complain. It's that simple. This is your country, and part of the deal in a democracy is that if you are unhappy with the way things are going, you get to do something about it, which is not the case in 56% of the countries in the world.[93] People fought hard in the '60s so that citizens between the ages of 18 and 21 could have the right to vote. Not to mention people since the 1600s have died for the right to vote. Ashamed yet? Go register! And then vote in the next primary or local or general election. Reward yourself with a sticker if you need to.

The truth is that since the last printing of this book, young people have totally stepped up to the plate. This book's first edition came out in May 2008, before Barack Obama (arguably) brought out the "youth vote" (18-29 year olds). Turnouts in this category for both 2008 and 2012 were around 49%.[94] But as impressive as the youth turnout has been, it's still less than 50%. So why do the majority of young people sit elections out? When I talk to my friends who are between the ages of 18 and 30, what I most often hear is, "I don't know enough about the issues."

How Do I Know For Whom to Vote and Why?

The answer might be as simple as spending a few minutes a week keeping yourself updated by reading *The New York Times* or Huffington Post, watching the nightly news (though please, not Fox—here's why[95]), or listening to NPR. Any of these is a good way to educate yourself. (More friends than I can count have told me they get their primary update through *The Daily Show.* I'm not endorsing that approach, but it is *something.*) If this gets you juiced up, you might then join the League of Women Voters, the Green Party, or the American Conservative Union. But if you were like me in my twenties, you are busy and might believe that your attention is better spent on your important and interesting life than on your 300-millionth of a share of membership in this country.

While most people know who the president is, it's equally important to educate yourself about local politics. Why does it matter who your state representative is? Because for one thing, the state governments are the ones who vote on redistricting; if one party is in power, shocking and horrible as it might seem, they might try to "gerrymander" the districts in order to maintain their control.[96] This is why it is so difficult to unseat incumbents, and it will become more so if we continue to be busy with things we think are more important than self-government.

Here's the bad news: most people don't vote in the midterm elections. These are the elections in which we elect or re-elect our entire congress and one third of our senators (but not our President). In 1998, turnout was 38% according to CNN. In 2002 everyone was thrilled when it hit 39%. In 2010 it was 41%. That means you can bet less than 41% of our electorate in any given state has anything to do with local politics. *Our Congress is elected by a minority.* All those people complaining about the government and heralding democracy, and we barely have one! Just think how different life could be if we participated! If *all* of us participated! (Also, the fewer people who vote, the more powerful *your* vote is. I neglected to vote in a local election once because I was "too busy." I joked with my husband that the measure, which I was for, would probably lose by one vote. It did. I really hate telling that story.)

"Democracy is not a spectator sport," goes the saying, and you don't want to be a couch potato in this arena. There is nothing more annoying than an uninformed person pontificating about politics. Or the well-informed and opinionated person who doesn't vote.

We are all dependent on one another, every soul of us on earth. —George Bernard Shaw

The point of our form of democracy, when you get right down to it, is that *we* are the government. We are responsible for selecting that government, and that government consists of we, the people. People who say the government is causing all our problems are really saying that *people* are causing all our problems. Which, while probably true, is a pretty self-hating stance to take, wouldn't you say?

We live in a community. People are meant to lean on each other and not be completely isolated from each other, the way many of us are today. In years gone by, we relied on our neighbors. We knew their names, their children's names, the kinds of crops they farmed, and we'd often help each other out—even if we didn't like each other—out of bare necessity. Today, we drive up to our garages, pull the SUV in and close the garage door with a remote. We get our gossip from the television, websites, and social media instead of the front porch or church narthex. When I hear people complain about the government, or even about the opposing party (whichever party they oppose), I think about our country's growing fascination with surgery as a solution. Don't get me wrong: surgery is fantastic when it's called for. A lot of people would be dead today if surgery hadn't removed their cancer or unblocked their valves. But the metaphor of surgery—cutting off the offending part of ourselves—doesn't work so well in either community living or personal mental health. Getting rid of an unpleasant behavior simply cannot be done surgically (or, alas, through hypnosis, teeth-gritting, pulling oneself up by one's bootstraps or, arguably, taking pills). We have parts of ourselves for a reason, and sometimes we don't get to know what those reasons are.

If you are dissatisfied with the government, then vote! Blog! Write letters to the editor. Educate yourself and your friends. You are our best hope! You are our future! And for all of you, for all of us, may we find what connects us rather than what separates us. We have a lot more in common with each other than we think.

In 1978, Harvey Milk said this during a speech called "That's What America Is," on Gay Freedom Day in San Francisco:

> *Gay brothers and sisters,...You must come out. Come out...*
> *to your parents...I know that it is hard and will hurt them but*
> *think about how they will hurt you in the voting booth! Come*
> *out to your relatives...come out to your friends...if indeed they*
> *are your friends. Come out to your neighbors...to your fellow*
> *workers...to the people who work where you eat and shop...*
> *come out only to the people you know, and who know you. Not*
> *to anyone else. But once and for all, break down the myths,*
> *destroy the lies and distortions. For your sake. For their sake.*
> *For the sake of the youngsters who are becoming scared by the*
> *votes from Dade to Eugene.*[97]

Because of the courage of so many gays and lesbians who came out to friends and family, public opinion changed so radically, so quickly, that what was once—in 2008—a powerful wedge issue

(Gay Marriage) is now—in 2013—practically a non-issue; at least it's not where we live. In 1978, my parents did not know a single uncloseted gay person. By the early '90s, I had several friends who had come out, but at that time and place (the northeast), they felt they were taking quite a personal risk. Today, a good third of my kids' friends have two mommies or two daddies. My kids grew up with this and don't even think about it.

When we were in our twenties, this is what Katryna and I did: about ten days before election day, we had a potluck at our house. We invited all our vaguely political friends to come over with a dish to pass and a voter's circular that explained all the referendi scheduled to be voted on in that year's election. These parties were always a blast: no one knew everything about all the issues, but between us, we were able to explain to each other what we did know, and I was able to go to the polls and not feel like an idiot when asked to vote on questions like whether or not I wanted local business to overhaul unemployment taxes.

How to Register to Vote

This is easy.

- Go to www.rockthevote.org, follow the directions and you'll be registered in no time.
- Or go to your local City Hall. They will give you a form to fill out and thereafter keep in touch with you by telephone (you can find your City Hall phone number in the yellow pages or online).
- Or go to your local library.
- Or go to your Department of Motor Vehicles. (Or Registry of Motor Vehicles, if you live in Massachusetts.)
- Or download this form: http://www.eac.gov/register_vote_forms.asp
- You must be a citizen of the US in order to vote.
- You must be 18 years old on or before election day.

There is a field out beyond right and wrong.
I will meet you there. –Rumi

Voting With Your Pocketbook

So throw a tiny wrench in the fiber optic wires
Morals are cheap and you can be the buyers
We can let 'em poison and perish foreign lands
Or we can play the greed right into our hand

—*Dar Williams*

If you feel discouraged about democracy and effecting change, remember that you have another kind of voting power: the power of your very own dollar. So use it wisely and well. I buy organic fruits and vegetables and meats and dairy products not so much for my health but more to support organic farms, because I believe in that paradigm.[98] I buy old houses because I don't want to contribute to the further erosion and sprawl that's rampant in our country; I'd rather recycle. I buy my books from independent book stores whenever possible because I like to support local businesses; I know the names of the employees at my local bookstore and they know me and my reading preferences. I like being able to shop in my friendly downtown and not only online or at a big boxy conglomerate. (If my local bookstore doesn't have the book I want, they can order it for me in about the same time I'd receive it if I had ordered online.)

I go into McDonald's only to use their bathrooms.

I think part of the whole *How to Be an Adult* ethos is about responsibility and recognition that we are all interconnected. One would think the more evolved we become, the more clearly we would see this. I think a lot of children, teens, and young adults really have this innate sense of responsibility, interconnectedness and, to use the proper Biblical term, *stewardship*, but somehow by the time we get into our late twenties, thirties and beyond we develop a convenient case of amnesia.

Every action we take has consequences and ramifications all over the world. The big box retailers known collectively and colloquially as "sprawl marts" are a good example of this. If you are thinking pure short-term savings and convenience, these might seem like a no-brainer of a choice for all your shopping needs. After all, that yellow smiley face just goes around slashing prices all day like a cheerful disembodied Robin Hood. Plus, it's incredibly convenient to go to one store to get your hardware, groceries, toiletries, clothes, kids toys and fine housewares. However, when you look closely at the role these retailers play in local and international economies, how they tend to treat their workers, how they interact with the environment, and even how they handle the safety of their patrons, you get a different picture.

If I buy a T-shirt at a big box store as opposed to a stand-alone local boutique, I would spend $4—an amazingly small amount of money. In fact, a T-shirt probably cost my mother about $4 in the 1960s. How does Big Box keep its prices so amazingly low? By using money as the ultimate bottom line in a kind of ruthless, take-no-prisoners approach to business that, unfortunately, is rampant these days (and probably always has been) in a capitalist economy. The shirt is cheap because the people ("labor") who made the shirt live in tiny un-air-conditioned cubicles in low-income housing in China, in conditions that would be unthinkable for workers in this country. The shirt is cheap because Big Box employees work overtime without being paid overtime because they are not protected by unions, because they are not allowed to *be* in unions and therefore have no recourse when they are asked to work overtime (for free) and are afraid if they say no they will lose their jobs. The shirt is cheap because Big Box's rent is cheap—they tend to build their huge disgustingly ugly warehouses on the outskirts of town. The shirt is cheap because it's made of synthetic materials, which cost very little to make but may cause severe endocrine problems for your children and the next four generations (see Gay Daly's amazing article "Bad Chemistry: A Special Report."[99]). The shirt is cheap because at least one Big Box, up until they were busted for it, employed illegal aliens to work their janitorial jobs in the middle of the night, often locking these helpless people into the stores.

All that being said, good friends of mine shop at Big Box stores, and I still adore them. They make the point that right now in their lives, they just can't afford to shop anywhere else. Period. I can't argue with that, though I want to. The point is that we make decisions with our every move and we make these decisions because of our values. If we are connected to our values, we can make the very best decision in the given moment. For my friends who shop at the sprawl marts of the world, right now the greatest value in their lives is survival, and that trumps everything. At some point, they might be doing better financially and have the freedom to choose differently. (If I could, I would go solar—but right now that's no-where near my budget.)

I don't want to leave you on a negative note here. Rather than tell you where not to shop, I'd like to give you a list of places you *should* shop, but that's problematic.[100] Partly this is because the use of sweatshop labor is rampant in this country, and honestly, most other clothing retailers, while charging you more than $4 a T-shirt, still treat their international workers as badly as Big Box does (al-though they often treat their domestic workers better, and they don't wreak as much havoc on the environment). If we take as our maxim "reduce, reuse, and recycle," the very best thing to do is minimize purchases altogether. Every new item manufactured is now taking up space on our ever-shrinking planet, and will one day certainly find its way to a landfill. Do you really need a new T-shirt? A new radio? Can you make do with what you have?[101] That being said, check out A Better World Shopper[102] for stats on how the companies you know rank. A well-informed shopper is a peaceful shopper.

If you really have a jones for a shopping spree, visit a second-hand store. Buying vintage clothes or used clothes is a earth-friendly choice because the damage has already been done, and in the case of vintage, oftentimes these clothes were made by people being paid a fair wage. You can go completely alternative and wear clothes only from websites that tout pure policies, but perhaps we should make space for occasions for Prada. As in everything, a little moderation is a good thing. As I've said before, this is about batting averages.

Relationships

Tools and Rules

- Communicate.
- Say what you mean, mean what you say, but don't say it mean.
- Don't compare your insides with someone else's outsides.
- Comparisons (in general) are odious.

Relationships are the hardest thing you will face in adulthood. You already know this, because relationships are also the hardest thing we face at any phase of our lives. We've all been in a relationship—an intimate one—since the moment we were conceived. When we are newborns, our relationship with our mother, father, or primary caregiver is characterized as one of dependence. In fact, it's the definition of dependence: a newborn is absolutely at the mercy of its mother's whims and willingness to feed it, clean it, play with it, smile at it, help it to sleep—not to mention that she has hegemony over the sound system and the remote control. We learn how to ask for what we need, first by screaming, later by pointing and finally ("use your words") by asking for it. Then we learn that sometimes even asking for what we need doesn't get the desired results, so we become clever at manipulation. ("All the kids in my class get to have birthday parties at Chuck E Cheese. Why are *you* such a strange, withholding, aging hippie of a mommy?")

We also learn that our parents behave in mysterious ways that often don't make sense, don't follow logic, or even the law in some cases, and at a certain point (for most of us), we stop seeing them as the gods and goddesses they were to us when we were babies.

And so we shift our allegiance from the family unit to our friends, our peers, and begin to take our cues from them. We make friendships and are blown away by how excellent kids our own age really are, how they *get it* in a way our parents just can't; they see us in a light our siblings never will. We begin to get a sense of ourselves that's informed by something outside the little tribe we grew up with.

There's a great Bob Dylan song called "Bob Dylan's Dream."
It's on his second LP, *The Freewheelin'* Bob Dylan, and it's about
that early group of friends so many of us had, in our late teens or
early 20s.

> ...With half-damp eyes I stared to the room
> Where my friends and I spent many an afternoon,
> Where we together weathered many a storm
> Laughin' and singin'till the early hours of the morn.
>
> By the old wooden stove where our hats was hung
> Our words were told our songs were sung
> Where we longed for nothin' and were satisfied
> Talking and a-jokin' about the world outside . . .
>
> I wish, I wish, I wish in vain,
> That we could sit simply in that room again,
> Ten thousand dollars at the drop of a hat
> I'd give it all gladly if our lives could be like that.[103]

When I first heard this song, I was too young to have experienced this kind of deep, communal friendship, though eager to. In
college I had just such a group of friends, and listened to this song
as an ominous warning. We sang together in a folk band called Tangled Up in Blue (twenty singers and two acoustic guitar players: we
were a sort of super-sized Peter, Paul & Mary who were unusually
gifted at cracking codes). We met up at coffee shops and the campus
vegetarian joint, plotted revolution, vowed to recycle and fight the
bourgeois oppressors. We also vowed to keep in touch, and though
we see each other at the occasional wedding, we have mostly scat-
tered all over the world: as Bob said, "...the thought never hit/ That
the one road we traveled would ever shatter or split." After I left
college, this song reduced me to tears so regularly that I had to skip
over it when I played the LP.

Dylan is tapping into what many of us experience when we
move from our late teens to our early twenties. The adults over 25
whom I interviewed say they have stayed in touch with at most two
or three friends from the first 20 years of life. What's different about
relationships in adulthood is that we are expected to maintain them

for longer than a year or two. As children, it's normal to have a different best friend every year. I maintain that as adults, it's normal to have a rotating stable of friends too; friendships are often based on your environment, your workplace, your social activities, your common interests. As you grow and evolve and mature, these interests change. So do your friends. That doesn't mean you don't work to maintain those friendships that matter to you; but I have also seen many young people suffer from frustration because their college friends aren't corresponding as consistently as they'd like. They feel let down. They feel they're the ones who seem to be doing all the communicating. On the other hand, they might find their friend awfully clingy and needy and thus feel guilty if they spend too little time with her; resentful if they spend too much. Sometimes it takes years to figure out a good balance between good friends; to trust that the ebb and flow will just be a part of friendship, and to not freak out if months or even years go by with no communication. Look around and notice all the other friends you have made.

> *One of the most important things to me, especially in my post-college life, has been maintaining, strengthening, and just enjoying my friendships with the people I love, both near and far. I'm not always very good at it, but when I do make the effort, it almost invariably cheers me up. My friends know who I am (and, as the saying goes, like me anyway); in many cases, they've made me who I am. We've got history, a shared language of references, jokes, and memories. They are brilliant, funny, kind, and loving, and my time on this earth would be much poorer without them. So I try not to let them go easily. This means that I write to them, call them, send them emails with links to funny websites, but it also means that I don't get upset when they don't write back right away, or even for years. I don't dismiss them or declare the friendship over. I know high tide is going to come again. —Kate, age 26*

Here are some general tips if you are feeling lonely and friendless, coming out of an all consuming, co-dependent romantic relationship (the one all your friends warned you about, and so you of course, conveniently lost touch with them), or just if your work life has temporarily robbed you of the ability to remember how to be a friend:

- Remember birthdays, of old and new friends, and email or call or best of all, send an old-fashioned card.
- Socialize with people; learn to reach out, and also learn not to catastrophize if you get rejected. The bad news for friendships in the 21st century is that as we get older, friends fall lower and lower down the pyramid of priorities (usually it's self, partner, family, job...then friends. If you're lucky. Sometimes it's self, family, job, the new car, *The Daily Show*, your iPhone, your digital camera, your cell phone... friends.)
- Reach out and ask people what they care about. People are wonderfully self-centered, and generally love to talk about themselves.
- Do kind things for people, but don't over-do. You don't need to bribe people to be your friends.
- If you are shy, ask people to go to the movies with you. That way, during the encounter, you don't have to talk much, and in the aftermath you'll have a ready-made topic.
- Join a group of people. Find a common interest. Join a group of activists if you're into social change, or if you're into sports, a team, or if you're into singing, a church or community choir, or if you're into acting, try out for a play. Dive in. There are so many ways to meet people if you really want to.

I think making and maintaining friendships is the whole point of life. I prioritize keeping in touch with friends because if I don't, I won't. When I catch myself feeling guilty for emailing a friend instead of doing some work, I have to remind myself, "What's the priority here? Do you think on your deathbed you are going to regret not having figured out every possible tax deduction, or the fact that you lost touch with Annie?" Looking back over the years, it's all about the friendships I've continued to maintain. I have photographs of old friends in my office to keep them in mind; I carry on conversations with various friends in my head, and I send out emails, try to arrange for visits when we're in the same city. Friendships do change with time, but that's actually a wonderful reality, if you can go with it rather than resist it. Now (post-college) is a great time to set an intention to maintain the friendships you most care about. That being said, just watch: you may be surprised which people stick with you, and whom you want to stick with, for the long haul.

Family: How to Keep in Touch With Parents

When I was about to graduate from high school, my father said to me, "It's easier to leave home when you are on good terms with your parents than when you're angry with them." I remember thinking that was a strange thing for him to say; why wouldn't it be easier to leave if I was fighting with my parents?

Even though I'd spent an unusually harmonious eighteen years with them, I had been noticing the urge to withdraw, to not go with them to church, to shut the door to my bedroom and blast the radio, to publicly roll my eyes at almost everything my mother did. As in any relationship, isn't it easier to leave when things are ugly and combative? Who wants to leave the party when it's swinging?

At the time, I didn't ask my father about this; I just nodded and went up to my bedroom and shut the door. I packed for college, wrote to my still faceless roommates, bought some cheap white wicker furniture and moved out of my childhood bedroom, not fully comprehending that I'd never return as the same person again. And thus began a ten year period in which I barely said anything of real significance to either of my parents, with the possible exception of "I'm getting married." For me, the separation was so painful, I couldn't address it in any way other than to shut down emotionally and become less and less communicative. I didn't even really know I was doing this at the time; it just sort of happened, and then once it began, it continued—the way once you start off calling your doctor "Dr. Miller" you'd feel too weird if you subsequently wanted to address her as "Beth."

I also called them less. I didn't write much, and this was ten years before anyone besides Al Gore and a bunch of nerds knew about the internet. It wasn't until I was 28 and my father's mother died after a long illness that I woke up and rearranged my priorities and began to reach out to them again. It took another couple of years to journey back to a place where I really felt as though we'd healed the ten-year rift, but once we got there, it felt as though we picked right up and moved forward into something new—a relationship steeped in history and commitment, but also one in which all of us could see each other a little more clearly as actual people. Most parents are pretty much naturals at loving their kids unconditionally. It's taken a lot longer for this child to put down her adolescent reservations and allow myself to love my parents that way.

Today, thanks to the advent of the cell phone, I speak with each of my parents at least weekly. I keep in touch with both of them via the internet, and bombard them with photos and videos from my phone. I send thank-you notes when they come to visit, and it may sound corny, but thank-you notes are always much appreciated. In the Bible, the fourth commandment says, "Honor thy father and thy mother," and I like that. It doesn't say, "Do whatever they do," or "be a lawyer because that's what would make your parents happy." It just says to honor them, and I take "honor" to mean respect their views, be courteous to them, remember the fact that they spent countless sleepless nights feeding you and comforting you while you cried, and not go out of your way to upset them.

Now, I realize that I pretty much hit the jackpot when it came to parents. I know people whose mothers and or fathers are walking nightmares, who make life a living hell for their offspring. I'm not suggesting you bend over backwards in these cases to establish a Biblical-style relationship with the people whom you are fairly certain wrecked your chances of having a happy and productive life. Sometimes no contact really is the right choice, although I've seen some miracles occur when one party takes on the deep and rewarding work of amends-making and forgiveness.

Parents and children often become deeply enmeshed in each others' lives in not-so-healthy ways. I think this comes from some kind of ingrained evolutionary tribalism; perhaps at one point it was necessary for all the cave people in a family to like the same baseball team. We are deeply comforted by the fact that "we all" hate George Bush or Bill Clinton, or "we all" love folk music or "we all" think New York City pizza superior to Chicago deep dish or "we all" like big dogs better than cats or "we all" go to mass on Saturday evening. These are seemingly harmless tribal predilections. It gets more uncomfortable when "we all" marry people of our own race or class, or "we all" make six figure incomes or "we all" have children or "we all" are vegetarians.

And yet, moving outside the tribe, particularly when it's time to start a little tribe of our own, is an essential part of growing up. We'll experience a lot of resistance from family members depending on how strong the particular movement is, and how tight the enmeshment gets. My friend Alma (not her real name) moved from her native New York to Los Angeles. Every time her New Yorker mother would come down to visit her, the drive back to LAX was inevitably marred by loud arguments about which city's crime rate was worse and which city had the better rugelach.

Someday, hopefully a very long time from now, your parents will no longer be here and you won't be able to hash it out with them anymore. At this point, you may want to ask yourself, how important is it all anyway? How important is it for my parents to see me for who I really am? And can I truly fault them for not seeing me the way I see me? Do I really see my parent for who he or she really is? Could I possibly, even if I tried my hardest? Maybe not. After all, the prism of biology is a tough one to get around; the generations are divided the way they are by necessity. You may never be able to see your mother as the incredulous little girl holding her very first box turtle; she may never be able to *not* see you as that same little girl, holding yours.

Siblings

Most people I know have complicated relationships with their siblings. And why wouldn't they? Siblings are our primary model for competition in life. If we are an oldest child, our siblings represent the new generation, the young turks out to take our toys, our food, our attention and almost definitely to out-cute us in the eyes of all adults everywhere. If we are a younger child, our siblings are at best in the way, and at worst bullies and tormentors, ready to roll their eyes at whatever we do, tell us we're singing off key, embarrass us in front of our friends, and cause our teachers to say, "Well, since your older sister was such a brilliant math whiz, this section of algebra should be no problem at all for *you*!"

No wonder that many of us, once we leave home, choose to see our siblings only on holidays. If we have spent our entire childhoods trying to measure up to a perfect older brother, or trying to hide from a dysfunctional younger sister, or just plain fighting over who gets the turkey drumstick, why would we want to go out of our way to cultivate relationships with these people?

The answer is; no one will better be able to understand the insanity that is your mother and/or father better than they. Well, I should qualify this; that's not always the case; in fact, one of the most painful issues is one in which one sibling had a totally different experience of his parents than his sister or brother did. Some parents play favorites, and this wreaks havoc on a person's self-esteem, not to mention makes having a close relationship with the sibling next to impossible.

But in other cases, we come to a lot of realizations when we're young adults, especially in how we begin to see the way we were uniquely parented. We begin to see the roadmaps our parents took us down and the effect that particular route had on us; at this point, it can be phenomenal to contact a sibling and say things like, "How was it for you when Mom drank?" or "Was it just me, or did you always think Dad secretly hated his job?" The twenties and thirties are a terrific time for looking back (because we're still close enough to remember it clearly but far enough away to have some perspective and maybe the ability to lay down our gauntlets a bit).

I also hit the jackpot in the sibling department, although it didn't always seem that way. My sister Katryna was born when I was not even two years old, and I actively resented her for the next thirteen years. I thought she was cuter than I was, smarter, and certainly nicer. While I seethed with competition in her presence, she always played to keep the game going, to the point where if she sensed she might beat me at something (tennis, cards, getting a role in a play) she would purposely lose. Though we played together constantly as we were growing up, I was not what you would call kind. She basically worshipped me and I took her for granted.

Then, in my sophomore year of high school, my best friend Melissa kept talking about her sweet lovable younger sister Stacey and how much she adored spending time with her. Stacey, Stacey, Stacey! I didn't know what I was more jealous of: that Melissa loved Stacey more than me, or that she had such a terrific relationship with her sister while I had nada with mine. I finally decided I wanted what

Melissa had and I purposely set out to make friends with Katryna. I put together a book of sentimental poems and old photographs and presented it to her at Christmas, saying, "From now on, I want us to be friends." And from then on, we were.

It happened sort of gradually; she entered my high school the next year, and slowly we began to hang out with each other. We ended up being in all the same singing groups and began to notice that we loved the way our voices sounded when we sang in two part harmony.

As I got more and more interested in writing songs, I also became more and more convinced that pursuing a career as a professional musician was not something I'd want to do alone, and I began lobbying Katryna to be my singing partner. Although she had plans to be Chief Justice of the Supreme Court, eventually I convinced her and the rest is history.

I am equally lucky in relations with my youngest sister, Abigail (whom I always adored and believed to be my twin, separated somehow by seven years in our mother's womb). She is the mother of three, a gigantic fan of Bruce Springsteen, and one of the most creatively organized inventors of delightful life that I know. The three of us talk several times per week, try to get our kids together as much as possible, and we actually like congregating for holidays. But it takes work: it takes time and energy to keep in touch with anyone, and whenever I think I'm too busy to answer an email from a sister or parent, again, I try to remember what my priorities are: when I die will I care whether I got in that gym workout or whether I got to hear what my 18-month-old nephew said this morning?

Roommates

Roommates can be nirvana. They can be the friend you always wanted to live with, there for you when you get home at night, the person who loves all the same TV shows as you, the one to share a pint of Ben & Jerry's when you've been dumped by your boyfriend. Roommates can serve as a surrogate family; the one you chose rather than the one you were born into, and as such, they might be more likely to share your sense of décor, cuisine, music, extra-curricular activities.

Or not. Remember the story about Brutus the dog? Roommates can also make life a living hell. I have a friend who lived with the owner of the apartment. Every time my friend moved a kitchen chair back, the owner drew in a sharp sigh. "Wood floors!" she'd remind my friend. "They scratch easily!"

Whether or not your roommate is an old friend you have joyfully decided to shack up with or a stranger who answered your ad, or the tenant of the apartment whose ad you answered, it's always good to set up the house rules from the outset (preferably before you agree to live together), and spend the first few weeks working very hard to make sure the system works. Now's the time to draw up the constitution. How do you deal with food, for instance? Do you share a grocery bill, or keep everything separate? Who takes the trash out? Who does the laundry? If you feel friendly in the first weeks of your living-together arrangement, and you do the laundry to be nice, will your roommate come to expect this? Maybe, maybe not. It depends on what kind of slob he or she is. If you share a TV, how do you figure out who gets domination over the remote? What if one of you makes substantially more money than the other one? What if the richer one owns the stereo *and* the TV *and* the "good" computer *and* the cordless phone? Does that mean she or he never shares? Or out of noblesse oblige and guilt does he or she offer access every other Monday? What kinds of boundaries do you set?

Whose living room is it? If one of you has a party, do you have to automatically invite the other one? What's your policy on sharing clothes? Does it extend to underwear? What if you get a crush on your roommate? What if your roommate gets a crush on you? What if you drift apart and stop being best friends?

For some situations, these questions might appear ridiculous and unnecessary, causing more problems if raised than they would solve. But the one thing I know about relationships is that they change. So a situation that worked really well in college might not translate into the working world. And once one of you gets hooked up with a significant other, all bets are off.

Fluidity and flexibility are terrific aspects to bring into all housing relationships. It helps too to remember that just because you're doing your roommate's dishes tonight doesn't mean you will always have to do them; by the same token, if you really are the one who always does the dishes, and you resent the hell out of her for that, are you really doing her a favor by secretly hating her for this? Wouldn't it be nicer to jokingly say, "I'm on dishes strike for the next week. Either we hire a maid or we take turns."

One more thing: it's an incredibly painful transition when one best friend meets the love of her life and the other best friend doesn't. There's no way around this one; it just sucks for the one who's left behind. Both parties should be aware of this and recognize it as a rite of passage. The lonely one will not be alone forever and the hitched one will not be gazing starry-eyed at her new squeeze for all eternity. If you can both take a long view of this passage, you can maintain your friendship (and living arrangement) for as long as you want to.

How to Get Along With Slimy Landlords, Crazy Roommates and Basically *All* the Difficult Folks in Your Life

After I graduated from college, I felt a little bit furious at the world (and maybe my parents) for training us for a reality that doesn't exist. There are so many infuriating people in the world—they cannot do their jobs properly, cannot communicate properly, are mean. How do we deal with these people? I tried getting angry with them. I thought being direct was the best approach. I was wrong. Patience is a virtue. Also, think before you speak! *—Mary, age 29*

Expectations, it has been said, are premeditated resentments. And resentments, I have learned, while fun to harbor, especially in small groups of people late at night over a bottle of wine or package

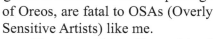

OVERLY
SENSITIVE
ARTISTS

of Oreos, are fatal to OSAs (Overly Sensitive Artists) like me.

There's nothing like spiritual growth to kick the air out of the tires of good old-fashioned gripe sessions. It seems whenever someone irritates the hell out of me and I then complain about that person to another person or group of people, I feel righteous and justified for a good hour or so and then I begin to feel the symptoms of emotional hangover: kind of queasy, sick to my stomach, increased irritation. Sort of like how coffee gives you energy but then you crash, or how sugar feeds your hunger for about twenty seconds before it leaves you wanting to gnaw on your arm (though that may just be me). Or if you have poison ivy how it feels good to scratch the itch, but eventually it just itches more and has turned bloody from the scratching.

A useful question to ask in any sticky spot with any sticky person is, "Is it better to be right or to be in relationship?" And so far, my answer (sometimes well after I've chosen to fight for my rights) is that if the relationship is worth keeping, it's better to be in relationship. If not, it's better to leave the relationship quietly and undramatically. Being right is in the eye (heart, mind) of the beholder, anyway.

What does this mean in real life? It means when my roommate tells me she is going to vote for a particularly corrupt gubernatorial candidate, I don't argue with her. (I used to, and even though I thought my arguments were absolutely brilliant, they got me nowhere with her. She had made up her mind.) It means that when my husband tells me he loves Journey, I smile pleasantly and hum "Don't Stop Believing." (I used to mock him, especially in front of my Rolling Stones-loving friends.) It means when my best friend tells me she's back together with the man who's cheated on her twice, I nod and say "good luck." Why? Because in many situations, no one wants my opinion.

"People with opinions just go around both-ering each other," said the Buddha. When I first read the Enlightened One's statement, I must say I was shocked. It effectively negated a large part of my high school and college education. If I wasn't a person with opinions, who was I? Would I still be a feminist if I didn't argue? Would the world go to the devil if I weren't around to convince people not to vote for bad politicians, not to marry their philandering boyfriends, not to listen to bad 70s bands?

My mother used to attempt to stop fights between Katryna and me when we were little. "You don't have to argue," she'd say. "Just know in your heart that you're right."

It didn't take Katryna having to listen to the Buddha to get this. She would effectively end a verbal argument by looking up at me in the *most* smarmy way and say, "I know in my heart that I'm right." (In the name of full disclosure, I have to tell you, I usually pounded her good after she said this. Can you *imagine* anything more annoying?)

I experimented for a few weeks, and I am here to report that not much actually changed as a result of my non-arguing. My friend broke up with her bad boyfriend on her own, my husband doesn't actually listen to Journey—he just wants to be able to say that they're "wicked awesome"—and my Republican-voting friend would have voted for Romney anyway. In all of these cases, I kept my mouth shut and kept the peace. And I knew in my heart I was right.

Does this mean I am a pushover? No. That's actually not possible given my personal makeup. I'm what a prior and politically incorrect generation would have called a pushy broad. Even when I'm docile, I'm kind of a tough cookie. And I recognize that for some people, the advice I try to heed for myself is the exact opposite advice they need. My friend Lois (not her real name) is a sweet, loving wussbag. She's the kind of person who somehow gets roped into babysitting for her neighbor's two vomiting children. She allows her roommate to take the sunnier bedroom and the closer parking space. She nods patiently while her boss tells her that her marketing plan is old-fashioned, even though every single idea in it was pre-approved by that same boss two days earlier when the boss was mildly soused. For Lois, speaking up for herself is crucial. She needs to work on self-assertiveness, whereas I need to work on self-control. It's all a matter of figuring out your own personal moxie factor and compensating accordingly.

Another good mantra for getting along with people is "Maintain boundaries." Figure out which is your issue and which is the other person's. Don't take anything personally. Most people are pretty self-centered and are reacting to some projection of themselves and not to you at all. If they liked your marketing plan two days ago and dislike it today, for example, you can be assured it has nothing to do with either you or the marketing plan. It's the side of bed they woke up on that day. In any given person, there are a lot of ancient stories and just plain garbage swirling around in that person's head. Also, you might not realize this—being in your twenties and all—but some people over 35, and a few more over 50, have mysterious aches and pains that can make them grumpy for no outwardly discernable reason. Take pity and offer them your seat on the subway.

See Where You Are at Fault and Practice Understanding

This is invaluable! Don't worry about how horrible the other person is. You can't change that person. The only person you have any true influence over is you. So when you are furious at the jerk (and I'm definitely not denying her jerkiness!), ask yourself the following questions:

- Is she triggering me? Am I being totally neutral here?
- Is it possible that I've done the same thing at some point in time myself?
- Did she really mean to hurt me?
- Is she going through something really awful that maybe I don't even know about?
- Did I do anything to contribute to this bad situation?
- Is there anything I can do to make it better?

When we get a handle on another person's bad situation, we loosen our grip on our own bad situation just a little. If I can see that my husband snapped at me because he only got four hours of sleep the night before because I was awake with a hacking cough, I can begin to understand his crankiness, if not forgive it. My sister may have just forgotten the lyrics to the song I wrote, on stage in front of five hundred people, while I'm standing next to her looking stupid, but I can see that she just got off an airplane where she was seated next to a mother with a screaming infant, and meanwhile, she's left her own infant at home, so I'm not going to get angry at my sister. How could I? There but for the grace of the Big Cheese go I.

This Mo Fo Is My Perfect Teacher

The great Tibetan Buddhist nun Pema Chodron says, "This very moment is the perfect teacher."[104] That's a radical stance to take. Who wants their teacher to be some crappy moment when everyone's losing their collective and individual minds? In a way, this is just another version of the New Age idea that God has a perfect plan for each one of us, that even the terrible things in life can be good if we only look for the good, the silver lining, in each and every situation. This may sound Pollyannaish and naïve, but it's an effective way to live, and an especially effective way to live with other people. When I regard everyone who comes into my path as a potential teacher, their annoyingness just becomes a challenge for me to try harder to see the great lesson they have to bestow unto me. After all, we "learn" in school by solving "problems." Therefore, problem people should be terrific ways to advance our knowledge and understanding. That slimy landlord? He probably was abused as a child. Maybe his wife is having an affair. Your crazy roommate? Maybe she really *is* crazy. Be gentle. And move out soon.

I'm not saying you should stick around to enrich your life with lessons, by the way. Sometimes it's better to be quiet about being right *and* it's better to leave the relationship. But leave peacefully. Sweep up after yourself, and always pay your share of the rent.

Dating

In terms of dating, I'd say date lots of people. Learn about who you are when in relationship. Who are you attracted to? Is it the same old pattern over and over again? Reflect. Take the time to know yourself. —Katie, age 34

Romance was where I first noticed that I'd gained Adult self-knowledge. I don't think I really knew what I wanted, in a romantic sense, in college. Part of the reason for this is undoubtedly that I was awfully shy and got a late start on the whole thing. But I think I also just needed some more time to mature. So, even though I'd largely ignored romance for a few years after graduating from college, when I met Mary (at the age of 25), it didn't take long at all for me to realize that I did know what (and who) I wanted. Enough so that when we went to go see Much Ado About Nothing *on one of our first dates, we could laugh at the stupid things the lovers did that I probably would have done myself not long before, but not anymore. —* John, age 39*

At a certain point in our lives, usually between 16 and 30, we fall in love for the first time and then into some form of partnership. We hope and expect this love to be the Real Thing; to bring us back to the Eden we experienced when we were first gazing into our mother's eyes, knowing we were loved unconditionally, or at least that someone was willing to change our stinky diapers without judging us. For a while, this new love sustains us; we make plans for a future together, we explore our sexuality, we get a cat or a shared lease. But at some point, we realize that this wonderful person who has reflected back to us the image we most wanted to see of ourselves—the person with whom we could previously be our "best self"—has changed. Or we've changed. We're not sure. All we know is we used to make love every night, and now we're too tired. Or we're suddenly seeing that our partner's habit of using the couch pillows as a napkin, once charming and totally forgivable, given how he compensated by telling us how beautiful or insightful we were, now grates so much on our nerves that we are tempted to replace his bed pillow with the pizza-scented versions.

Some of us work through these transitional phases with our partners and go on to form family units, learning to live with the new version of our true love, resigning our selves to a life of imperfection and dirty pillowcases. Others decide we were wrong to think we were in love; that there's a better partner for us out there, one who respects furniture coverings (in fact, we will make *sure* that this new, future partner has this attribute, since we have learned that a disrespect for furniture coverings is really a seriously deviant flaw to possess, revealing all sorts of other nefarious inclinations, like a callous disregard for other people's feelings and property, not to mention withholding behavior in bed and a tendency to forget birthdays and anniversaries). We break up, divide the CD collection and the friends we have made as a couple, and spend several months eviscerating our ex to anyone who will listen. We catalogue his or her terrible attributes and wonder aloud how we ever could have fallen for him/her.

We eventually meet someone else who makes us feel like we are finally really *seen*. This person may be similar to the previous partner in all ways but that terrible flaw, or he or she may be quite different on the surface. But after a period of time, we find ourselves behaving in ways we used to behave with partner number one, though perhaps it's different issues that reflect an end to the halcyon years. Maybe now, our new partner (who is extremely neat, by the way) works in a law firm. Great, we thought initially, since partner number one was a drummer in a band who, though knowledgeable about all the same music and films we loved, was constantly broke and sponging off of us (which of course made his abuse of the pillowcases even more egregious since he would *never* think to replace them). Partner number two has a sensible job, the kind your parents approve of, and maybe our parents were right about this one thing after all.

Anyway, the lawyer trip is a good one at first; we get taken out to eat at Maxwell's on Main and he never forgets our birthday. But he also travels a lot and works late at the office and on his off-hours enjoys playing a pick-up basketball game with his buddies from law school. At first, this is a good thing; he's got friends, after all, right? And he stays in shape, right? But why doesn't he want to hang out with us at home sometimes? More and more, he's either working or playing basketball. What about *our needs*? We begin to doubt again that this is the partner for us. The right partner for us would care about our well-being to the point where he'd agree to at least once in a while break his weekly date with his buddies and take us out for a movie. Or go shopping with us. Or propose, for God's sake!

How do you know when you've met the right one? I don't know. I do know that if you aren't really sure, you probably haven't.

Or, to put it a different way, you are probably not ready to declare that this is the right one. From what I've seen, rushing marriage is never a good idea. If one of you is ready and the other one isn't, that means you aren't ready to get married. When you meet someone who really wants to be with you, and you really want to be with that person, and the whole "commitment" question is a non-issue, you will know paradise. In the meantime, have fun dating.

For my shy friends who want to know how to meet the Right Person, I'd give essentially the same advice I have for making friends. Get out there! Look people in the eye and shake hands gently but firmly. Follow your own interests. Don't be afraid to pursue your love interest, and be friendly and nice, but you don't need to bribe someone. (You can be fairly sure it's a bad sign if you find yourself bribing someone in any arena of life). When all else fails, there's online dating, which I've seen work beautifully, although I've also seen some disasters. Put up a well-written, real, honest profile; reveal enough to be intriguing but not enough so the viewer is already sick of you by the time he or she leaves your page. Be sure to put up a really flattering (but again, honest) picture of yourself (and not of Naomi Watts or Denzil Washington). If you don't have one, get someone to take some. Look at other profiles to get ideas about what you want to say. And then, be patient. Check out potential singles on the site and communicate with them via a wink or a message. Don't play coy. When someone writes back who really doesn't appeal to you, send a reply saying, "I'm flattered, but I don't think we're a match. Good luck to you!" This response also works after a first date. There's no need to get into a big defense if you don't like the date; just email or call and say, "It was great to meet you, but I didn't feel the chemistry. Best of luck." No fault; just fact.

And this is the great aspect of dating that unfortunately doesn't apply to would-be friendships: chemistry matters. Actually, it does apply; it's just that you can't use it as an excuse to not be friends. If you realize after a few weeks that the person you thought might make a terrific friend actually leaves you wanting to chew your arm off after your encounters, you can't really say, "You're a really nice person, but I don't think we're meant to be together long term." People are assumed to be able to have hundreds of friends (although you actually can't, given that annoying thing about 24 hours in the day, having to work to earn a living, etc.) but in this country any-way, we're presumed and encouraged to desire monogamy; thus, the chemistry excuse works for dating.

It took me a long time to get the chemistry piece of it. I do know people who felt nothing at first when they were together, and grew to have the hots for each other. So when I first started dating (post-divorce) and I met very nice men with whom I "matched" all over the page, and on the phone, I kept trying to figure out what was wrong with me that I didn't feel attracted to them in person. I'd seek out my friends who took a while to warm up to their sweethearts and listen to their stories as though if I paid close enough attention, I'd crack the code. I waited patiently for desire to arrive. In several cases, I found the time frame to be about eight weeks. I'd usually give up at that point; or rather, some primal part of me would literally revolt, and I would end the relationship, bewildered and a bit con-cerned about my libido.

For me, that primal, physical attraction was (and is) key. Even though I consider my-self to be a highly moral, intellectual kind of gal with standards up to my ears, when it comes right down to it, it don't mean a thing if it ain't got that certain *je ne sais quoi*, as Peter Schickele says.

How to Get Married

At some point, you might get tired of just living together and saying, "No, not yet," when people ask you and your significant other if you are married. And so one of you broaches the subject and the other one agrees. Perhaps there are rings involved. Perhaps parents are consulted and solicited for permission. Perhaps it happens as such a natural occurrence, looking back you can't even recall the moment the two of you "decided." Perhaps you are the same gender and madly in love, and you live in a state that suddenly allows marriage for same sex couples; then, the decision seems obvious. Whatever brings you to the conclusion that you are ready to spend the rest of your life with this one other person, in sickness and health, for richer, for poorer, till death do you part, you are now ready to make the move, and this will involve some planning.

There are as many wedding options as there are couples. Unfortunately, it would be more accurate to say, "as individuals," for many couples discover as soon as they get engaged that their beloved actually has the taste and aesthetic of a flea. Or Zsa Zsa Gabor. Or Flea. Some people keep their mouths shut under great duress. "How could I tell Mark that a carnation was the cheapest, tackiest flower ever?" said my friend Rachel. "My mother nearly had a fit! But he wanted a pink carnation, so he got a pink carnation. It wasn't worth fighting about."

Others are not so sanguine. Lou almost called the whole thing off when his fiancée Tiff thought it would be a great idea to have the bride and groom enter from opposite doors of the church singing "Muskrat Love" (complete with rodent snuffly noises). Deep familial issues come up in the planning of a wedding; expectations are sky high; one or both of the stars of the party may be on a Spartan diet, and effectively self-cannibalizing, and these three factors alone can lead to high dramatics with a lot of tears and temper tantrums.

It doesn't have to be this way. A wedding is actually an excellent testing ground for the marriage. Issues of money come up, and perhaps for the first time the couple has decisions to make together about how to spend that money. There's a guest list to draw up; do you invite your ex-boyfriend since he's still one of your best friends? What if your groom has 85 close relatives and he can't imagine not having them dance the Hora on his big day? What if your father is paying for it, but wants to keep the guest list to a *total* of 85? The couple needs to negotiate difficult issues, and this is a great opportunity to do so.

Having planned and consummated two weddings, I know this much: you don't have to listen to what anyone else tells you about what you "have to have" at a wedding or what you "have to do." During the planning of my first wedding, I was 22 years old and completely at the mercy of the Man (in this case, a woman from Cold Spring Harbor, Long Island, who told me, among other wedding niceties, that if I wanted to have the wedding after 6 p.m., I'd have to advertise the wedding as "white tie"). Halfway through the planning stages, I rebelled and decided to serve Chinese food at the reception and encouraged all my friends from college to wear alternative footwear with their white tie attire (several wore Birkenstocks and one wore bright red Chuck Taylor high tops). For my second wedding, I chose to wear a white dress, though I'd decided it didn't need to be an actual wedding dress. It could have been a flapper dress. Or a big white coat. But I wanted to wear white, and I wanted it to not be so amazing that I'd feel bad if I spilled coffee on it, which I knew I would do. (I did.)

Registering for Gifts

If you get married in your twenties, you will probably need a lot of stuff. Or you may not need it, technically, but you may really, really want it. And some people really want to give you what you want, so it's a good idea to register so you have at least a shot of getting it. Of course, there are more people who don't care what you want at all and will give you crafts from the fair they just went to, or re-gift you with teal-tinted wine glasses they were given for their anniversary. My friend Emily is a master at returning almost anything to almost anywhere, and after her wedding, she cashed in most of her wedding presents, even some of the ones she registered for, and bought a new sleigh bed.

The problem here is that for every gift you get, you are supposed to write a thank-you note, and if you really want to be an adult, you cannot skip this step. So what do you say to the guest who's given you something hideous that you've returned, or stuck in your mother's attic?

> *Dear So and So,*
> *It was absolutely wonderful to see you at our wedding. Bobo and I had a terrific time in Hawaii and thought of you when we hiked Volcano National Park. Have you ever been there? It's an experience everyone should be so lucky to have. We are so grateful for the gift you gave us. We can't believe how blessed we are to have such wonderful people in our lives. Thank you!*
> *Sincerely, You*

To be kind to your guests and to make your life easier, register for things you really want at a store that has internet access and a generous return policy. As a wedding guest, I love to know where my friends are registered and I try to order their gift online and have it shipped directly to them as soon as I get the invitation. In the name of full disclosure, I have to admit that by far my favorite wedding gifts were items we had not registered for but which thoughtful guests had conjured up out of their knowledge and love of us. But these people have a gift I lack: the ability to give the right gift. For those of us with a bit of tone-deafness in the gift-giving division, registries are a Godsend. (Honestly, so are gifts of money. Though my Grand Dame friend from Cold Spring Harbor would be horrified, I'm all in favor of giving and receiving checks. Though here are two fool-proof gifts that the bride and groom might not even know they absolutely need: a cast iron skillet and one excellent extremely sharp knife.)

What matters most? How the two of you navigate the necessary decisions leading up to the big day. After all, this is about a marriage, not one day in your life. Some people care deeply about the big day, so much so that it's really worth it to them to spend $100,000 getting every detail exactly to their liking, and to those people, I say, "Thanks for throwing a swell party!" But for me, what mattered most was having my family and closest friends nearby, looking into my groom's eyes and letting myself feel overwhelmed with the love that flowed our way all day long.

Here are the things I cared about most in retrospect:

1. Getting a great photographer who was both professional and who knew my groom and me well enough to catch the important moments. A wedding is about making memories, to some extent, and I am so happy to have my weddings documented.
2. Having absolutely beautiful flowers, since I love flowers.
3. Having the ceremony be the real focus of the day: choosing a celebrant who knew us and loved us.
4. Having music that meant a great deal to me being performed by people I loved.
5. Having passages read by dear friends and family members.

The things I don't even remember:

1. The food
2. The band
3. My dress
4. Table seating arrangements
5. Who was there

This last sounds a little harsh, and it's not technically true. But it's actually worth noting, as you and your partner haggle over the list, as you inevitably will—after all, at the time, it's a big deal. There were certainly dear friends who traveled many miles to share the day with me, and I rejoiced to see them, and I rejoice seeing them again in the photographs. I mean that if there were people I wasn't keen on having (being that they were my groom's friends from high school and I'd never met them before), I certainly didn't care that they were there once the date was upon us. I also mean that I wasn't ultimately devastated that not everyone could come. People

can get so hurt by not being invited to a wedding that the friendship
might be forever severed. In a way, it's better to frame the question
as "who really wants to come?" rather than "whom do *I* need to be
present?" If you're anything like me, you'll need to be reminded
who was there by photographs.

Extend the invitation to those who really care and not to everyone who ever mattered in your life, especially if you haven't seen
them in fifteen years. I had urges to keep the guest list really small so
that I could "enjoy" my guests. But the truth is, I was so lost in my
own love trip that day, I barely spoke to best friends who traveled
across the country.

How to Get Divorced

Divorce sucks. My friend Jonah wrote me after his and said, "I
wouldn't wish divorce on my worst enemy." When I got divorced, it
felt like my whole world was being cleft in two. Besides the loss of
my husband and partner, I lost people I considered to be members
of my family, along with friends, traditions, habits, identities, not
to mention some of my favorite CDs. I was horrified about how it
would look to the rest of the world. I was horrified to call myself a
divorced person. And mostly, at least at first, I just plain missed the
person I was once married to. I missed having someone who had
shared such a big part of my life, who had known me through so
many stages of life. Who *got it* in a way no one else ever could or
would, or so I thought. Even, I mused, if I were to get married again
and have children, my second husband would always be my "second" husband, and my children would have to learn at some point
that there was a man I loved before Daddy.

When David told me he didn't know if he could stay in the
marriage, I spent the first few weeks in shock. Then I bargained
(behold the stages of grief at work), which meant I agreed to go to
Disney World. This was the ultimate sacrifice for me, and a symbol
of how we had grown apart in the twelve years we'd been together.
When we'd met, we'd both been struggling artists who liked to wear
black turtlenecks, study Brecht and Samuel Beckett, and listen to
Laurie Anderson and Lou Reed. Twelve years later, I had turned into
someone whose ideal vacation was to go to a meditation and yoga
retreat. His was to go to Disney World.

Needless to say, Mickey and Donald did not do it for us, and we spent nine months in couples therapy figuring out the ways in which we'd become hopelessly co-dependent with and hostile to each other. But a lot of good came out of the therapy, specifically that when we did decide to split up, we were very grown up about dividing things like money, housing, property, the dog, even the friends we shared. ("You get Andrew; I get Wendy"—that kind of thing.) I remember the weekend he moved out, I had gigs in the mid-Atlantic region. We were on the phone, figuring out the logistics, dividing up the beds and the equipment (I kept the stereo; he took the TV) and by the time I came home, the house was cleared out. I called him and said, "We are one efficient team." Then we both cried.

Why don't relationships work? For a million different reasons, as diverse as the millions of plays and poems and songs and stories on the subject. But I can offer a few guesses, based on my own experiences and those of my friends.

High Expectations:

Many of us have high expectations of love that are based upon the perfect love we once experienced when we were tiny babies. When we fall in love, we also fall under the illusion that once again, that perfection we experienced long ago is ours at last. This feeling, we believe, is love. In fact, this feeling is what we *define* as love. It's natural that we'd feel that way, since the state of "being in love" is one of the most powerful mind-altering states we can experience. Many of us become physically stronger, lose our appetites for donuts and cans of vanilla frosting and perform much better at the office. Many of us compose poetry. Many of us lose our need to sleep and float about on a cloud of satisfied sex and good wishes for all humankind. But at some point, the bloom is off the rose and we've lost that lovin' feeling. We think love is "gone" and set about looking for ways to get it back. Maybe we're defining love in the wrong way. Maybe love is not that "feeling" but something a lot more substantial, like being willing to empty the garbage. Or going to Disney World when you'd rather be practicing your trichona-asana.

Lack of Respect:

This is a big one. I have seen many relationships disintegrate when partners treat each other with contempt. The renowned marriage expert John Gottman cites lack of respect as one of the "four horsemen of the apocalypse."[105] In couples who would soon be divorced (and he has a 95% success rate in predicting this), he noted a profound scorn emanating from one or both members of the couple. It's very difficult to live with someone who doesn't respect the choices you've made in your life. Conversely, it's very difficult to live with someone whose choices you think are baffling. When this gap is exposed to the salt of ridicule and scorn, the relationship suffers a mortal blow.

Lack of communication:

This is obvious. The less time you spend with each other, the less you know each other, and since people grow and change every day, it's vital for couples to stay in touch with each other, with both quotidian communication (a.k.a. "quality time") and more focused, intense communication (big talks in the car, not to mention physical contact, if not sex). In my first marriage, after eight years of eating, drinking, breathing the same rarified air of a 15-passenger van and the quixotic search for fame and glory via membership in a rock band, David got off the road while I stayed on, touring with just my sister. I would call him from Alaska, from Wisconsin, from Mexico, from Florida: "Is this enough of a marriage for you?" He assured me that it was, convinced that to do otherwise would be to admit a weakness, or try to keep his feminist wife from realizing her full potential— two sins verboten in his personal system of values. But it was not enough of a marriage. I'd be gone for weeks at a time, and when I'd return, I'd find a partner who was immersed in his own life and work, now dramatically different from mine. We had less and less in common, including words and simple experiences.

Expecting the other person to read your mind:

This is another holdover from our infant-idea of love, where it often *did* seem as though our mothers could read our minds. After all, we were preverbal, and they still somehow discerned when the crying was about hunger, when about sleep, when about the state of our diaper, and when about just plain loneliness and the desire to be picked up and cuddled. Because we get confused when we fall in love with M. or Mdm. Right, we subconsciously assume that these amazing soulmates can read our minds too. The trouble is, so many of us co-dependent types really *do* try to read our partners' minds, making the situation vastly more complicated.

Many couples, faced with relationships that aren't working, go to couples counseling. This can be hugely beneficial. The couple can find a safe place to talk about their feelings and expectations and perhaps learn better ways of communicating with each other. Even if divorce is bound to be the outcome, and you suspect this from the start, I would encourage all couples to get into therapy anyway in order to minimize the damage the divorce will cause. Because divorce *does* cause damage no matter how you slice it. Look for a counselor who sees the *relationship* as her client, and not one or the other of the parties. If one of you is already in therapy, ask your therapist to recommend someone to you. Also, keep in mind, the couples therapist is not a judge deciding who is right and who is wrong, and if she acts like one, get a new therapist.

If you are going through a divorce, you will need to work on your anger. Recognize that your partner is in as much pain as you are, even if he or she has taken up with another lover in the meanwhile. I'll admit, this complicates things and makes it much harder to look sweetly across the negotiating table at the bastard, but ultimately, you will fare much better if you are in a calm state of mind. All those suggestions earlier in the book about cheap spiritual practice will come in handy at this point. It will be invaluable to see where you made mistakes; it's altogether too easy to blame your now-absent spouse for the entire mess.

All this being said, know what you need; know what your rights are. If there are not a lot of assets between you, try to hire a mediator instead of lawyers to work through the details of the divorce. Mediators are neutral, and they are a lot cheaper than lawyers. If, on the other hand, you know that you have a hard time sticking up for your rights and/or are emotionally or physically afraid of your soon-to-be ex-spouse, hire a lawyer. At the very least, find a friend who has been through the drill and can help you decipher what the laws are in your state (every state is different). For that matter, find *all* the friends and family you know who have been through the hideousness of divorce, because only those who have been through divorce really understand how horrible it is. Get their sympathy and pity and advice and encouragement. Take their war stories and their recovery stories to heart. Let yourself be cheered by tales of new love, or of new identities found. Nurture yourself through this time, and remember: it's *supposed* to be one of the worst things a person can ever go through. Even so, if you do it with grace and dignity, you will be much happier when you look back on this awful period of your life. And yes, there will come a time when it's in the rearview mirror.

One more thing: it might be that you are doing quite well, even though you might not *feel* well. Facts aren't feelings, as they say. It stinks to end relationships. No one wants to be in that place. But there's not really a way to get around it, if the relationship is really over. The best things you can do are the things you love doing which connect you to yourself. For me, that would be: writing songs, connecting with friends, working on a garden, seeing a lot of sad movies. They are not magical antidotes, but they do help. More importantly, they are bricks in the mortar of your new house.

We are into the quick fix. When our old house burns to the ground, we want to just move into a prefab, beautiful new one. But what if the law of nature tells us that the only real house we can move into is the one we build ourselves? Brick by brick, it sure seems like a long time, like we're still wet and cold night after night as we're slogging away on the foundation. Then one day, there's a roof overhead. But it takes time.

The pain you feel when you lose at love will not destroy you. You can actually live with it. In fact, it makes you a deeper, richer person.

How to Stay Married

The point of marriage is not to create a quick commonality by tearing down all boundaries; on the contrary, a good marriage is one in which each partner appoints the other to be the guardian of his solitude, and thus they show each other the greatest possible trust.—Rainer Maria Rilke

It's a well-known psychological saw that we tend to be attracted to people who will help us work through our problematic issues with our families of origin. Some say this is the very essence of what we like to think of as "chemistry"  between two people: it is simply the stunning recognition of emotional attributes our parents or older siblings possessed that caused us pleasure and pain. There is nothing wrong or stupid in being attracted to these people; it's just hardwired into us. The trick, say the smarty pants sociologists and psychologists, is for us to pick people who are emotionally healthy, loving and who don't force us to sit with them and watch reruns of *Married...With Children.*

As we grow into wiser and kinder people (which is for me the goal, at least occasionally, on good days), we begin to choose our friends and partners and intimates not so much on the basis of attraction but on some other factors as well. Like, can they pay the rent, or at least not punch a hole in your wall each month so that you're adding construction costs onto your monthly mortgage? Or, are they aware enough of their own narcissism so that when your beloved fourteen-year-old cat has died after a protracted battle with her liver, they do not say, "Hey, cheer up—it'll be fun to get a new kitten!"

You will only feel better if you work on yourself, and not the other person. That's the good news and the bad news. No one out there is going to fix us, and we aren't going to fix anyone else. No one out there is going to rescue us, nor are we going to rescue the other guy. If I'm annoyed with my partner, it's usually because he is behaving in a way that reminds me of my own annoying qualities. Or because he's watching *Married...With Children.*

At some point around my divorce, I got that it was no one's job but my own to take care of my needs. I realized that one person couldn't be everything to me, but I could still get everything I needed from the collective of my family, friends, partner and my own resources. Then I took this idea a step further: maybe *I* was the only one who could really take care of me.

This phase of my life was characterized by an almost absurd self-reliance. I didn't want to ask anyone for anything; I wanted to do it myself. Perhaps I was stuck in some developmental phase that was meant to pass around age five, but for whatever reasons, I was working through it in my early thirties. After years of depending on my partner to take care of me, the pendulum swung the other way, and I became Super Independent Woman. This was fine for awhile; I got really good at doing a lot of things I'd never even thought of doing before (like my finances), but the rub was I wasn't a very good girlfriend to the men I dated. Strangely, independence is a very attractive quality to a lot of men, but the problem was, it didn't allow me to be attracted *to* anyone else. Or put another way, perhaps I was only allowing myself to be interested in men who didn't have anything I needed or wanted particularly, for fear I might—well—want or need them.

When I met Tom, I knew he was the right partner for me. I was lucky. I had finally learned, from dating a lot of men and from musing on prior relationships, what I really did want and need (a partner who loved to talk and figure things out and who had an interest in spirituality) and what I didn't need nearly as much as I'd thought I did (someone who was as obsessed with the Beatles as I was). I was old enough to know that there was no such thing as a knight in shining armor, no such thing as a "perfect soulmate"; that falling in love is akin to being on a strong dose of acid for about six months. I have a friend whose girlfriend said to him after they'd been together for a month and were in the madly-in-love phase, "These are our representatives. They will be leaving in three to six months."

But I also knew what to look for, for the traits I knew would weather well with mine for the long run. For me, these included a deep love and respect for family, a yearning and active spiritual life, a willingness to communicate and show warts, and interests that coincided as often as they diverged. In other words, we found plenty we liked to do together, and could agree to let each other have some independence and "me" time to enjoy the activities we each wanted to pursue.

For the first six months, true to form, we were constantly astounded by how well we got along, how similar our opinions were on politics, each other's friends, most music (he made up for his Beatles deficiency with a fierce love of Dylan) and a seemingly endless appetite for self-analysis.

"Where did I find you?" we'd murmur to each other. And, "We must have been separated at birth."

One night, six weeks before our wedding, we watched *What the #$&% Do We Know?* I'd had the movie out for a week, and I'd already watched it four and a half times. It's a heady, groovy movie about quantum physics and enlightenment, complete with state of the arts graphics and Ramtha, a 10,000-year-old sage as channeled by a blond woman named JZ Knight who resembles Zsa Zsa Gabor. The movie is all about creating your own reality, addiction to emotions, and how we miss the point—getting to be alive—on a daily basis.

"Wow," said Tom.

"I know," I said.

We were profoundly moved and certainly forever changed from the experience. Then we got up from the couch to do the dinner dishes. I ran the water over a dirty bowl where the tuna steaks had been marinating. While I was letting the tap water rinse the bowl, I crossed the room to get the dirty flatware from the table. Tom came over to the sink and turned the water off, a familiar dynamic in our clean up rituals.

I felt the hairs on the back of my neck go up, like a pissed-off cat. "Hey," I said. "I had that on for a reason!"

"I know," he said, in a special tone which I did not like one jot. "But we really don't need to waste water."

I fumed. Mr. Spotless Environ-ik was right again, and I hated that. I also hated being bossed around in the kitchen, having my little system of bowl-cleaning disrupted, and most of all, hated the fact that I was still so childish and petty to care that I was being corrected. What would Jesus/Buddha/Muhammad/Gandhi/Mother Teresa/Ramtha do? Surely they would not have bristled at the gentle correction of their partner's turning off of the wasted water.

This is the problem with WW fill in the blank D. Immediately we think we need to *be* fill in the blank, which means we suddenly need to become anything from a saint to the Son of God. But even the Bible says Jesus was occasionally willing to be proven wrong (check out Mark 7:24-30).

I went upstairs and filled the bathtub with warm water, lit some candles, sat in the tub and thought about anger. "Tom and I never used to fight like this," I thought. The Righteous Brothers song "You've Lost that Loving Feeling" came to mind, and I started to cry. I toweled myself off, put on my most comforting polar fleece, and got into bed.

Tom came up and joined me. "I'm sorry I snapped at you," I said.

He shrugged. "No big deal," he said. "We're both tense. In six weeks, we'll be getting married for the second time. It's kind of scary. It's a miracle we aren't screaming at each other night and day."

This made me sadder and angrier. The story I like to believe is that Tom and I were married before *to the wrong people!* And that even though it was sad and painful to break up with those people, *all is well now because we found each other!* So when Tom says something like what he said next: "There's a lot of grief we still have, sweetie, about our exes"—I get angry again. I don't like to be told I have more grieving to do. I want to be done, finito, on to the next wedding cake.

But before I snapped for the second time that evening, I paused. I felt the snap inside, and it felt like a tiny ampoule of medicine pouring a hot Tabasco sauce-like liquid through my veins. Usually when I get this feeling, I *need* to say something out loud, to let the person who made me snap know that his behavior is less than acceptable. I think I will *die* if I don't assert my rights!

But what if I don't? What if I didn't react externally? What if I chose instead to feel that burn of anger that comes from keeping my mouth shut? Is it possible that later on I will just forget about it and not feel as though I abandoned the Equal Rights Amendment?

"I'm angry, but I know it'll pass," I said to Tom. As soon as I said this, I felt liberated. I felt the sky open and a dove settle on my shoulders. Well, not really, but it was a nice feeling. Tom looked at me and smiled.

"You can be angry all you want," he said and kissed me on the top of my head. "That's part of the deal."

The top of my head kept spinning. What if being angry was exactly what I was supposed to be feeling? What if it were as natural for me to feel anger in this moment in my life as it was for a kitten to chase a ball of yarn?

Anger. Even Jesus got angry.[106] Thank God! But anger has its consequences. And its greatest consequences are always leveled back at yourself. My anger is there, and there's nothing inherently wrong with it. It's a fire that wakes me up, points something out. Pay attention! But when I react to it, or act out of it—when I snap at Tom for commandeering my dishwashing program—there will be consequences. There will be burning.

I still want to believe in myths. I want to believe that marriage is a mystical process of finding my soulmate and having him save me, all the while saving him. But I know it doesn't quite work like that. Relationships grow and change; they have a kittenhood and a cathood of their own.

"A woman completes a man," a friend of mine (a man) said to me today.

"No," I said. "You complete you. I complete me. But if I can find someone to share the joke with, I will have a more interesting time in this go-round."

There's a great Buddhist concept called Big Mind. My understanding of it is that when we are grounded and centered and calm—when there's not a lot of turbulence on the journey—we are able to access a collective consciousness. Monotheists might call it the Mind of God. The Buddhist perspective is that of the Four Noble Truths, which are:

1. Life is Suffering.
2. Suffering is caused by grasping (greed, selfishness, wanting: or, we could say, Little Mind).
3. There is a way out of Suffering.
4. That way is the Eight Fold Path, which consists of Right View, Right Intention, Right Speech, Right Action, Right Livelihood, Right Effort, Right Mindfulness, and Right Concentration.

So inhabiting Little Mind, that place where I am concerned with my rights, with doing the dishes my way and not having Tom correct or thwart me, causes me a lot of suffering. The trick, I have found, when I feel like killing Tom, is to first recognize that I am probably operating out of Little Mind (since WW fill-in-the-blank D almost certainly doesn't include the homicide of one's beloved). Next, I sigh, since it's not that easy to just pop into Big Mind when you're in Little Mind. But at least I know that I should be laughing at myself and not making plans to move out, or worse convince Tom to try to make me feel better.

The hardest part about re-marrying and staying that way for me is to practice the reverse of what seemed to split up my last marriage. So even though there's a large part of me that thinks my last marriage failed simply because we weren't meant to stay together forever—that we were somehow mismatched—I also try to learn from what I think I did wrong. It's sort of like that Arabian adage: trust Allah but tie your camel. To wit, I do the following:

Lower My High Expectations:

This is really hard, especially when I'm in one of those crazy-girl-crush moments on Tom, when he just looks adorable and I'm madly in love with him and think he's God's answer to all woman-kind. And I *do* feel that way about him, which is nice, but it's also important to remember that he's not perfect. He's a man who used to be a kid who used to drive his teachers crazy and he has not led a perfect life. When he does something I'm not crazy about, it's easier to sigh and let it go. How important is it really that he leaves his dirty socks under the bedclothes or cheats on self-help tests? Even more important, I need to lower my high expectations about us, about marriage, about my own energy levels and ability to be the perfect partner. To laugh at myself when I am sitting next to Tom in bed reading a book about being in the present moment with your spouse and when Tom leans over to nuzzle me, I say, "Not now, Honey, I'm reading."

Respect Each Other:

This requires a kind of supreme mental yoga sometimes, especially when it comes to things like music. Some of my worst moments of temptation to pull out the old scorn card have been when Tom brings up the subject of Journey. And my work is to calmly nod and smile when he insists that they were a seminal band of the 70s.[107] Just nod and smile, my internal Zen master says as my inner 15-year-old is screaming "Stadium Rock *sucks!*" Again, how important is it really what kind of music he loved when he was 16? Today he listens to Lucinda Williams, Emmylou Harris and Nick Drake. This I can live with.

At my parents' wedding, my brilliant Taoist great-aunt Sally gave my mother this stanza as a tonic for marriage, which I now bestow unto you:

To keep the marriage flowing
With love from the loving cup:
When you're wrong admit it
And when you're right, shut up.

Communicate:

Not so hard for us. We kind of talk each other's ears off, and we like it that way. But some days when I get into a funk, it feels like pulling taffy to say why, mostly because I don't even know why I'm feeling funky. Sometimes I need to do some work on my own to get at the tangle. In this case, I'll journal, call a friend, book an appointment with my therapist or life coach, lie on the carpet and cry, listen to Bob Dylan, or go for a walk. Usually after some digging, I can get at the tip of the iceberg. Often, when I begin to talk to Tom, the whole issue emerges. That's when I feel like the luckiest woman on earth. It's one thing to be lucky enough to have a support system to help you work through your stuff. To be able to work out your issues with the person you love the most—well, this is just what I always wanted.

Don't expect the other person to take care of your needs:

I fell into this trap a lot, especially when Tom needed to go away for a job (he was, until recently, a freelance writer and reporter). Ironically, this was the way he paid his share of the household expenses, so you would think I would have welcomed this little foray out into the plains to conquer and collect our weekly wildebeest ration. Instead, I felt abandoned and thought things like, "How could he leave me tonight of all nights? Doesn't he care that it's *The West Wing* night?" Or, "He better at least bring me back some Lung Ching Dragonwell tea from the Peet's near his mother's house!" As if I've ever once told him I'd like him to do that. I fell into that pre-verbal "if he loved me he'd be able to read my mind" state.

This state signals the need to channel Super Independent Woman from my single days. This is when I need to make phone calls to my girlfriends, catch up on my email correspondence, clean my office, play the guitar, read *The New York Times* cover to cover and try to make space also to let myself feel a little lonely too. I practice my cheap therapy and I lick my ancient wounds and usually by the time he comes home, I am cheerful and one with Big Mind again.

In the end, I really don't know why some couples stay married and some don't. This is what works (and what didn't work) for me. Like I said before, marriage might fail because couples disrespect each other, but then again, look at Archie and Edith Bunker. It seems logical that couples need lots of together time, but I've seen many long-distance arrangements work, not to mention all those marriages that survive years of child rearing in which the parents can count on one hand the number of times they've had nights out alone. And we all know severely co-dependent marriages that seem to work the way a key turns a lock: she takes care of him, and he lets her; or vice versa. Plenty of people make seemingly difficult situations work beautifully. There's a lot of mystery involved here, just as there's a lot of mystery involved in all these facets of adulthood. Though the roads have all been walked on before, we're making our own paths, creating our own itineraries. That's the fun of it. You get the hang of it by just doing it, by living it. The child psychologist Jean Piaget believed that children learned in stages, and could only learn in a developmental sequence. We're the same as we age, even into our thirties, forties, fifties, sixties and beyond. The feeling of bewilderment passes just as the terrain changes from mountain to desert to plain to grasslands to forest and back again as we travel across a continent. The goal, as always, is to enjoy the changing scenery, to "touch, taste, smell your way to the holy and hidden heart of it" (as Frederick Buechner says); to notice the disappointments, but above all, to notice the grace.[108]

Parenthood

The moment Lila arrived my life turned inside out, like one of those silk scarves magicians use, with one color inside and the other outside. I felt completely skinless, as if there were no amniotic sac protecting me  from the incredible joy and incredible pain of the world. I looked down at her lovely little face and the tears welled up in my eyes at the thought that she and I wouldn't be together forever and ever, that I will die, that my parents will die, that she will grow up and have to go through the sixth grade, that she would get too heavy for me to hold in one arm, the way I could when she was just five pounds. In short, I didn't want anything to change from those moments of pure perfection.

Nothing could have prepared me for the overwhelming physical love for my child which gripped me from the moment I set eyes upon her. She was placed in my hands, and I instantly felt my heart grow at least three sizes, like the Grinch's. Then she was whisked away and placed under oxygen to help her little lungs adjust to the world outside her watery womb. I didn't hold her again for 36 hours, but once I got my hands on her, I didn't let go much.

My friend Melany is a neonatal nurse, and she explained the motherhood gig like this: you take in, you take on, you take over. I liked the sound of that, especially the take over part. So I diligently tried to learn everything the nurses told me to do, particularly in the breastfeeding department. As I was resting in the postpartum room, one of the post-labor nurses informed me that I was anemic following the delivery and needed to eat more foods with iron. "Beef, spinach, and yams," she said, and of course, wanting everyone to like me and think I'm a good little patient, I immediately began my iron rich regimen, complete with an iron supplement. Another nurse, whom Tom swore was an ex-nun, wielded her authority cleverly by telling you that all the other nurses were incorrect and/or liars, and only she really cared enough about you to give you the straight truth. Then she terrified you with the consequences of doing anything other than what she recommended. Her method of making sure Lila was awake enough to breastfeed properly (an issue as Lila was 4 pounds 13 ounces at the time) was to vigorously pinch her tiny ears and rub her head so forcefully that I was afraid she'd give my daughter whiplash. Initially. I took this in, and then tried to take it on once home, only to find that there were other more humane ways of getting Lila awake enough to eat. This same nurse also said the reason Lila was gassy was because of all the spinach I ate.

"Iron," she sighed, shaking her head. "Babies just don't like it."

My *How to Be an Adult* training served me well here, as did my little Spiritual Ablutions practice. No one's fault; this was just one of those situations. And here's where the parental transformation reveals itself: caring much more about her well-being than my own, I immediately stopped taking the iron supplements (though I continue to eat spinach. The idea that spinach has a lot of iron is a conspiracy perpetuated by the creators of *Popeye*).

My whole life quickly became about breastfeeding. No one really tells you that your body completely stops being your body once you have an infant. I eagerly signed up for breastfeeding when I heard that breastfed babies have way fewer colds, flus, have lower obesity rates as adults, are more likely to be young Einsteins and Michael Jordans, can leap tall buildings in a single bound, etc. Plus, the idea of spending thousands of dollars on formula didn't appeal when the good Lord gave me plenty of what my child needs for free. But I somehow slept through the part about how you breastfeed for a good half-hour at a time and have to do a feeding every two hours, three max. Figuring into this equation the fact that premature babies don't really want to do anything passionately besides sleep, there was a good fifteen minutes devoted to rousing our teeny child for each feeding. This meant I really was spending more than half my life focused on feeding my baby during the first three or four months. Once she was latched on and grooving at the job, I had huge impulses to multitask. I wanted to talk on the phone, check my email, read my Dr. Sears baby book, have a meal, get Tom to entertain me, watch TV, listen to the Bruce Springsteen *Seeger Sessions* CD which had just come out, and fantasize about doing the laundry and rearranging all the furniture in my house. But if I did these things, I inevitably failed to notice that my baby had fallen off the breast and was dangling half-asleep from her little nursing cushion (marketed as—I kid you not—"My Brest Friend"). Yet another annoying lesson in the virtues of mindfulness.

I wanted to end with the topic of parenthood, for obvious reasons. Becoming a parent can seem like the final frontier in adulthood, after which one has a much harder time justifying the eating of cereal for dinner or refusing to sort socks (though I know plenty of parents who do both of these). Many are parents who are still children, either biologically or emotionally. Still, once you have a child, you will never see the world the same way again. You are now responsible for someone else, and the boundaries get very blurry.

I wasn't one of those women who felt incomplete without a child. Sure, I liked kids; and I had my share of doll babies whom I rocked to sleep and wheeled around in the basket of my banana seat bike. I taught music at a day camp for four years and knew every kid by his or her favorite song. But by the time I got into my twenties, I was much more interested in having a career, and since that career was singing in a rock band that traveled around the country in a dirty van (with attached trailer), adding a diaper bag and car seat to the mix just wasn't very appealing.

I had a dream around that time of driving a car through a war zone with my then-husband. We were white knuckles to the steering wheel, grimly passing through showers of bullets, when behind me I heard a little voice saying, "Why are we here?" I turned and saw two red-haired children huddled in the backseat. Somehow that image was enough for me to postpone motherhood till my thirties.

And I'm glad I did. There's no way I had enough patience and acceptance when I was younger to deal with the kinds of contortions motherhood has already put me through (seven years worth, as of today's writing). When I was in my twenties, I figured I would lose everything by becoming a mother. What do I mean by everything?

- My figure
- Sleep
- Time to exercise
- Time to write
- A sex life

- My dignity (because of all the plastic toys I feared
  would fill my house, not to mention bad CDs like
  Baby Einstein and Raffi)
- All my childless friends
- Any chance of seeing any movie in the theaters
- My music career

After Lila was born, and later her brother Johnny, all these so-called losses either proved themselves not to be losses or else took on a different cast in the face of those toothless miracles. I did have to face some losses, and I felt some part of myself in step with my toddlers, wanting to tantrum right along with them as I kept noticing all the ways in which I had to compromise. I moaned, in my best imitation of a whiny Buddhist, "And this too?" Still, Lila and Johnny seemed to come not so much with the proverbial loaf of bread tucked under their arms but rather with a magic spell, which (mostly) lulled me out of my grief.

That said, after Lila turned two, Tom and I have regularly taken time away, sometimes as a couple, and sometimes alone. We find it crucial to our emotional health to do both. I was crippled for awhile by the thought that if I really loved my husband and children I would never want to leave them, even for a night. Today, even though I often have to wrench myself away, I know I will come back rested and refreshed and with my attitude of gratitude repaired. And I know this about Tom, too: he will be a much more cheerful co-parent if he gets some alone time.

I did know from firsthand experience that motherhood would put a crimp in my touring. Other musician moms said so, and of course, since my singing partner/sister Katryna had had Amelia, our own touring had been reduced substantially. Adding my own children to the mix would only decrease the number of gigs we'd be able to do per year (we went from 340 annually to 150 after Amelia was born, and now we're down to about 48).

And yet, the year Lila was born we released a CD, and since then, three more, plus two books and a DVD. I have an additional album's worth of songs in demo form, and I play my guitar and sing for and with my kids all the time. Katryna and I created and now teach a music class called HooteNanny[109], for little ones and their parents, which has flourished and continues to thrive in our area, providing us with more than enough additional income. (An excellent breadcrumb we followed there!) Both my kids play Suzuki violin, and getting to watch my children fall in love with music is substantially better than living off of Subway salads and Diet Coke, and well worth the jungle of plastic toys that I was unable to completely fend off.

This isn't to say that I don't have pangs of thwarted ambition or regrets or wistful memories. I would love to have the freedom to accept gigs in Colorado or Winnipeg, to take a three-week tour of the West Coast, or even drive around the Michigan peninsula, or connect with our delightful, eclectic audience in Tampa, Florida. Not to mention, I miss the road life where you leave your hotel bed unmade and eat take-out. Life for a time seemed measured by loads of diapers and scoops of dishwashing liquid, and more recently by drop offs and pick ups and Suzuki Play-ins. I have traded the thunderous applause at folk festivals for the twinkly sound of my children's laughter.

And I would never trade back. What I couldn't have understood, what no one can tell anyone, is the degree to which I fell in love. And love changes everything. Love forces you to re-examine all your priorities; no, that makes it sound like decisions come from the head when in fact they come from the heart and from the gut. When Lila came out of me and I first held that wet, wonderful miracle of a person, my covenant was forged. There was no decision—it was pure desire. I wanted to be with this person, to serve her and nurture her and honor her struggles and victories for the rest of my life. It felt like my wedding day, like the moment when I took the vows, only I didn't look as good in the pictures afterwards.

When I watched Lila move from a seated position to pre-crawl pose, I was amazed at the way we grow up. I get to watch it first hand, in high speed. In November, when I put her in a tripod sitting position, she wobbled around like a Weeble and eventually tottered to the carpet, sucking her fist happily in her mouth and not caring a whit about her balance or dignity. A few weeks later, she was a regular sitting professional. Nothing could shake her game. These days, I get to watch her master multiplication and start to read the Harry Potter series to herself. I listen in wonder as a Beethoven minuet comes to life under her bow and fingers. Watching her develop like this brings me great peace around my own journey toward adult-hood, a journey Lila is already on, even though it will be years be-fore she has to think about health insurance or changing the oil.

The great Swiss psychologist Alice Miller says, "The sun does not need to be told to shine. When the clouds part, it simply shines."[110] So much of our growth depends on us just doing instinc-tively what comes next, letting the growing happen, and having the support of those around you—or at least having those around you know when to shut up and keep their sticky fingers off your back. When Lila was a baby, she cried when she was frustrated, and then I understood what that meant: she wanted me to help her out, by feeding her, changing her diaper, picking her up out of her crib and comforting her. Now that she can speak, she still communicates her desire to get from point A to point B. I hope she'll ask for help with how to do whatever it is she doesn't know how to do. I hope there won't be a lot of questions about the new New Math. I hope there'll be a lot of questions about bird symbols in King Lear and various meditation techniques and how to make a really great roast chicken. But she'll have other people to ask when I can't help her.

Twenty Parenting Tips

I really am tempted to write an entire book on parenthood, but until then, I will end with the best advice I was given when becom-ing a parent and I will pass it on to you, here.

1. Don't try to be a good parent. Try to be a good enough parent.
2. Sleep when the baby sleeps. Sleep when the child sleeps.
3. Don't check your iPhone all the time. It's one thing to miss your child's first steps because you were at work. It's another to miss your child's first steps because you were watching a YouTube video of the Kardashians.
4. The hours drag, but the years fly by.
5. When your child has a temper tantrum, or is angry, or sad, don't try to reason with him. Start by nod-ding and saying, as compassionately as possible, "It sounds like you're angry." You will be amazed at how

this changes your child's behavior. Simply know-ing that you understand the feeling he is having does wonders in terms of calming him down.

6. Write down the cute things your kids say. Take a lot of photos and video. You think you will never forget this phase, but you will. The next phase obscures the last one. Take the time to organize your photos and videos. They will prompt a lot of hidden memories.

7. Write a letter to your child on her birthday. Seal it up and keep in a special place. Give it to her 18 years later. My friend Joan's dad did this for her, and it's one of the coolest things in her life. She kept getting letters even after he had died.

8. Be light and funny and fun as much as possible. Kids are so funny; let their kookiness inspire you.

9. Play as much music as possible. Enroll them in music classes. Make family playlists and play them. Daily if possible.

10. There's no such thing as a vacation for you once you have kids. Don't even use the word "vacation." Say, "We are going on a family trip." Remember: expecta-tions are premeditated resentments.

11. Find good babysitters and take a regular weekly date night, even (especially!) if you are a single parent. Find a trusted friend or family member, train them well, and go for an overnight or even weekend away once in awhile. This will be your vacation.

12. Send your kids to a great school. If your school is not great, see if you can participate to make it better.

13. Don't give up everything for your kids. Model a bal-ance, fulfilled work life.

14. Don't lose touch with your friends. Model a life that's full of strong friendships. Make friends with your kids' friends' parents.

15. If you are going to let your kids watch TV, watch with them (sometimes).

16. Spend as much time with them outdoors as possible. Teach them about the planet.

17. Put the oxygen mask on yourself before putting it on your child.
18. You can do *anything* you want, but you can't do *everything* you want. Parenthood makes this abundantly clear. Choose wisely.
19. Don't ever refuse your child when he wants to snuggle.
20. Read to your child every night. While you are snuggling.

Epilogue: 2013

One spring day, as I was walking with my two kids down a Northampton street, I saw what can only be called an example of knitting graffiti. It was a kind of round scarf knitted in place around a traffic meter. I almost didn't stop, but the colors in the yarn caught my eye. Upon closer inspection, I saw that the artist had not only cozied up the meter pole, she had also stitched us a message: "You Are All Beautiful."

It was the first day where we could take off our shoes and let our tender pale feet begin to develop their summer calluses. It was the first day where the bugs were more than a curiosity to my kids; the first day we had lunch and dinner outside. I took the kids over to a friend's house and the two of us moms watched our older ones swing on her swing set while we cuddled and breastfed our little ones. She was telling me about a friend of hers who was expressing some distress about the fact that she was choosing to pursue her career full throttle at the expense of spending time with her kids. It seems like there's always some new variation on this one. In her friend's case, the mother was wistful about all that she was missing in order not to compromise her very successful career. My friend said, "The hard part is, in the beginning you are feeling bad for your child. All the 'mommy' your baby doesn't get. But later, you feel bad for you—all the child and child-time *you* don't get."

A Catholic friend of mine told me she'd given up negative thinking for Lent. How hard could that be? I thought. Way easier than giving up caffeine. I always like to take something on rather than give something up. And so I adopted the practice as well, and found almost immediately that, just as with meditation, I cannot do it anywhere close to perfectly, or even 25% of the time. But, again like meditation, the practice is actually in the noticing that you are not present, not positive, and then gently steering your mind back to a friendlier turf. You do this over and over and over, as Jack Kornfield says, the way you train a puppy to pee on the newspaper instead of on your rug. And while I hadn't had a single day that was truly free from negative thinking, let alone complaining—which is the audible version of negative thinking— I had never been happier in my life. I didn't feel as compelled to make everyone do what I wanted them to do. I seemed to be happy just observing and participating when called upon. People delighted me. Everything seemed fresh and amazing. Best of all, I stopped beating myself up. I wasn't wasting my time being annoyed with myself for failing so miserably at the task of thinking positively. I just said, "Oh, well. I am learning. Nice trying!"

The difference might also have been that because I had to drop the thought, I didn't get to fondle it, nurture it, explore all the intricate nuances of how right I was and how wronged I had been, how things really would have been so much better if they'd gone the way I'd wanted them to go, how rotten it was that the beautiful 77 degree day we had yesterday has morphed into 45 and drizzly today.

This is my practice, not my perfect. When I start to feel my jaw tighten and my eyes get hard like a lion about to pounce, or when I feel that queasy feeling in my gut, I know that this is not good for me. I think about something joyful—usually my kids or Tom or the writers in my weekly groups and seasonal retreats making great literature and telling some crucial bit of truth—and my mouth turns up, my forehead uncrinkles, my heart feels peaceful and the cycle is broken. It's as if I have a screened-in porch, where before I was at the mercy of the mosquitoes and yellow jackets. I still see them, but now they can't get at me.

Jesus said, famously, "Judge not that you be not judged." He didn't say this in a wagging-a-finger, Law-of-Congress kind of way. He said it as the Law-of-Physics-kind of fact that it is. When we judge, we enter a state of judgment and judgmentalism. The opinions start ricocheting off any available surface; they are like little arrows stabbing us constantly. Judgments create pain. This reminds me of the Buddha's "Opinions just go around bothering people." I am so lucky to have work I adore, work that feels more like a calling than a way to make a paycheck. There are moms who, when they give up their paycheck gig, feel very clear and good about their decision. And some moms are able to keep doing the work they love while missing very few beats in the saga of their kids' lives. I wanted to be so comfortably famous and successful by the time I had kids that I'd be able to chuck them in the back of the tour bus with a full time excellent nanny who would also be one of my best friends and a traveling Kodaly or Dalcroze teacher who also loved to play soccer, and maybe my bandmates would have kids my kids' age and we could all go around the country together, one gigantic preschool on the road. Katryna and I would be selling out shed dates and big theatres and then spending the mornings in the lobbies of the hotel, chasing our kids up and down the elegant carpets past flower arrangements the size of my Jetta. My kids would see the country, pooling into Yosemite and Yellowstone and the Grand Canyon whenever we toured these areas. I would have it all.

And that didn't happen. And what I have today is so much better, so much richer, primarily because it is real and not a projection of What If. The projection misses the mosquitoes and the yellow jackets—rarely do such commonplace villains get written into fantasy. But why begrudge the mother who has this, my projected fantasy? And why pity the mother who doesn't? How could I have predicted that the best moment of my recent life was getting to watch my daughter play a variation of "Twinkle Twinkle Little Star" onstage with a bunch of other kids on a Sunday afternoon while my son ran around on the grass outside? The best parts are always your real life. The best parts are when you stop, wherever you are—be it in the middle of your detested job, the middle of your never-ending afternoon, the middle of your peak moment onstage or in the operating room, the middle of your walk down Crafts Avenue—and let the voice tell you the truth. You are beautiful.

Appendix A- HTBAA Spiritual Ablutions Form

I resent_____ for _____

They should not have _____

I should not have_____

This is how it should have gone _____

Forgiveness Work

Greed/Wanting/Control

Where was I trying to play God? _____

Where was I being selfish? _____

What did I want?_____

Would it have been the best outcome for everybody? _____

Delusion/Dishonesty/Not seeing the full picture

Have I ever done what I resent X for doing? _____

What are three possible forgivable reasons X might have done this?

1. _____

2. _____

3. _____

What are three ways that life is better because of what *did* happen?

1. _____

2. _____

3. _____

Are you *sure* your life would be better if things had gone your way? _____

Fear

Am I afraid of losing what I already have? If so, what? _____

_____

Am I afraid of not getting what I wanted? _____

Am I afraid of what people might think of me?_____

Who would I be without my anger? _____

Who would I be without my fear? _____

Appendix B- Spending Plan Worksheet

Expenses	Planned	Actual	Carry over for next month
Mortgage/rent			
heat			
phone			
phone			
cable			
subscriptions			
gas for car			
car maintenance & taxes			
car payment			
Medical/ dental			
visits to psychics			
charitable contributions			
new gadgets			
coffee			
Pilates			
grocery			
restaurant			
clothing			
computer/office			
books			
movies			
Internet access			
Insurance: health			
Insurance: car			
Insurance: home			
total expenses			
total income			

Bibliography

Beck, Martha N. *Finding Your Own North Star.* New York: Three Rivers Press, 2001.

Beck, Martha N. *The Joy Diet.* New York: Crown Publishers, 2003.

Brown, Brené. *The Gifts of Imperfection.* Minnesota: Hazeldon, 2010.

Chodron, Pema. *When Things Fall Apart.* Boston: Shambala Publications, 1997.

Cilley, Marla. *Sink Reflections.* New York: Bantam Books, 2002.

Dacyzcyn, Amy. *The Complete Tightwad Gazette.* New York: Villard Press, 1998.

Dominguez, Joe and Robin, Vicki. *Your Money or Your Life.* New York: Penguin Group, 1992.

EarthWorks Group. *The Recycler's Handbook: Simple Things You Can Do.* Berkeley: EarthWorks Press, 1990.

Gottman, John. *The Seven Principles for Making Marriage Work.* New York: Three Rivers Press, 1999.

Gladwell, Malcolm. "The Moral Hazard Myth." The New Yorker, August 29, 2005. www.gladwell.com/2005/2005_08_29_a_hazard.html

Hanh, Thich Nhat. *Peace is Every Step.* New York: Bantam, 1992.

Kingsolver, Barbara. *Animal, Vegetable, Miracle: A Year of Food Life.* New York: HarperCollins, 2007.

Kobliner, Beth. *Get a Financial Life.* New York: Fireside (Simon & Schuster), 1996.

Lamott, Anne. *Bird by Bird: Some Instructions on Writing and Life.* New York: Pantheon Books, 1994.

MacEachern, Diane. *Save Our Planet.* New York: Dell Publishing, 1990.

Mitchell, Byron Kathleen and Mitchell, Stephen. *Loving What is: Four Questions That Can Change Your Life.* New York: Three Rivers Press, 2002.

Mitchell, Stephen. *Bhagavad Gita: A New Translation.* New York: Three Rivers Press, 2000.

The Monks at New Skete. *How to Be Your Dog's Best Friend.* Boston: Little, Brown and Company, 1978.

The Monks at New Skete. *The Art of Raising a Puppy.* Boston: Little, Brown and Company, 1991.

Morgenstern, Julie. *Organizing from the Inside Out.* New York: Henry Holt & Co., 1998.

Morganstern, Julie, *Time Management from the Inside Out: The Foolproof System for Getting Control of Your Schedule—And Your Life.* New York: Henry Holt and Company, 2000.

Pollan, Michael. *The Omnivore's Dilemma.* New York: Penguin Press, 2006.

Pressfield, Steven. *The War Of Art.* New York: Black Irish Entertainment, 2002.

Rilke, Rainer Maria. *Letters to a Young Poet.* Translated by Stephen Mitchell. New York: Vintage Books, 1986.

Rubin, Gretchen. *The Happiness Project: Or, Why I Spent a Year Trying to Sing in the Morning, Clean My Closets, Fight Right, Read Aristotle, and Generally Have More Fun.* New York: HarperCollins, 2009.

Seligman, Martin. *Authentic Happiness: Using the New Positive Psychology to Realize Your Potential for Lasting Fulfillment.* New York: Simon & Schuster, 2002.

VanderKam, Laura. *168 Hours: You Have More Time Than You Think.* New York: Penguin, 2010.

Volhard, Jack and Bartlett, Melissa. *What All Good Dogs Should Know.* New York: Simon & Schuster, 1991.

Wilson-Schaef, Ann. *Living in Process.* New York: Ballantine, 1999. (I didn't actually read this book, but a friend took her training program and told me about carpet therapy, which is her idea.)

Endnotes:

[1] Brené Brown, *The Gifts of Imperfection* (Minnesota: Hazeldon, 2010), 24-26.

[2] Arthur Fry

[3] http://www.gretchenrubin.com

[4] Dame Edith Sitwell said this.

[5] Marla Cilley is a force, a wonderful thinker, and a blogger par excellence. Check this out: http://www.flylady.net

[6] For an excellent discussion of resistance, read Stephen Pressfield's *War of Art*, see bibliography.

[7] By "I" I actually mean Julie Morgenstern. If I, Nerissa Nields, were to actually do this step, I'd be so evolved and productive that I would probably not be writing this book, having realized that it's impossible to both write How To books and write songs and novels, which is my actual life goal. But I have not planned well, and so here you have this book.

[8] http://lauravanderkam.com/books/168-hours/

[9] The Pilates Studio of Hadley http://www.thepilatesstudioinhadley.com/

[10] Stretching: http://well.blogs.nytimes.com/2011/11/16/theright-reasons-to-stretch-before-exercise/

[11] http://www.valleyayurveda.com

[12] Maybe not such a crackpot idea: that having a lot of colds is a sign of health: http://http://www.rethinkingcancer.org/resources/articles/no-cure-for-the-common-cold.php

[13] There's a movement nowadays in my crunchy granola town to refrain from immunizing kids from measles, mumps, rubella and the like. Partly this is due to the erroneous belief that vaccinations might give a child autism. THIS IS NOT TRUE! Here, read this: http://www.dailykos.com/story/2011/03/25/959994/-Be-a-GoodParent-Vaccinate-Your-Kids

[14] I recommend OmEyes, the best most luscious treat for tired eyes ever: http://www.omeyes.com/

[15] Emerson, RW *The Complete Prose Works*. New York: Ward, Lock and Co, 1891.

[16] From Leonard Cohen's song "Anthem," from the 1992 album *The Future* on Columbia.

[17] http://www.kentalan.com

[18] Substance Abuse and Mental Health Services Administration. (2002). *Results from the 2001 National Household Survey on Drug*

Abuse: Volume I. Summary of National Findings (Office of Applied Studies, NHSDA Series H-17, DHHS Publication No. SMA 02-3758). www.enotes.com/mental-disordersencyclopedia/anti-anxiety-drugs-abuse.

[19] Somatic Experiencing is a very cool technique developed by Peter Levine. To learn more: http://www.traumahealing.com/somatic-experiencing/

[20] Read this excellent book by Les Fehmi to learn more about the amazing techniques in this book. http://www.shambhala.com/the-open-focus-brain.html

[21] *Living in Process* by Ann Wilson-Schaef.

[22] *Peace is Every Step*, p. 6-7.

[23] See http://www.laughteryoga.org.

[24] Martha Beck, *The Joy Diet*, p.168.

[25] *Peace is Every Step*, p. 62.

[26] According to this excellent Garbage exhibit from the Annenberg Foundation, ask.yahoo.com/20020606.html.

[27] Gandhi: http://www.cybernation.com/victory/quotations/authors/quotes_ gandhi_mahatma.html

[28] To find out more about Byron Katie and The Work (which I encourage you to do!), read her excellent book *Loving What Is*, or visit http://www.thework.org.

[29] My copy editor Lori didn't know what ablutions were. "Ablutions" is a great term, which you should adopt, meaning "washing" in a kind of ritualistic, daily way. Originally meant as a kind of religious purification, my college roommates and I used to the term for the time of day (night) when we took out our contacts, washed our faces and brushed our teeth.

[30] For more information about Byron Katie and The Work, visit http://www.thework.org.

[31] http://www.Yoga-sanctuary.com

[32] Our book, All Together Singing in the Kitchen: Creative Ways to Make and Listen to Music as a Family, came out in 2011 on Roost Books, a division of Shambhala.

[33] *Bhagavad Gita* http://www.krishna.com/dharma-bhagavadgita

[34] *Bhagavad Gita* ch. 11 verse 54 Stephen Mitchell translation

[35] Flow: http://server1.noblenet.org/merrimack/wiki/index.php/Positive_P sychology

[36] Martin Seligman and the three theories of happiness: http://www.authentichappiness.sas.upenn.edu/newsletter.aspx?id =49

[37] Right Livelihood http://www.buddha101.com/p_path.htm

38 Plastic Angel is here: http://www.amazon.com/Plastic-AngelNerissa-Nields/dp/043970913X. The song is here: http://www.amazon.com/This-Wrong-Nerissa-KatrynaNields/dp/B00016MT2U. My writing retreats and groups are here: http://www.nerissanields.com.

39 http://www.nields.com

40 Although rumor has it the Rolling Stones manager only included bad press in his band's press kits.

41 Wilson Mizner, US screenwriter, said this.

42 Sing "Row Row Row Your Boat." That lasts seventeen seconds.

43 http://www.doesgodexist.org/JanFeb04/AbrahamLincolnOftenAFailure.html

44 Here is the full poem: http://www.poetryfoundation.org/poem/176657

45 From *Letters to a Young Poet*, Letter Four (16 July 1903)

46 NYTimes on twenties transience: http://www.nytimes.com/2010/08/22/magazine/22Adulthoodt.html?pagewanted=all

47 Okay, the truth is Tom takes the garbage to the dump.

48 The Recycler's Handbook, page 13. http://www.learner.org/exhibits/garbage/solidwaste.html.

49 Snack Taxis: http://www.snacktaxi.com.

50 About rodents: Most people have an innate distrust of rodents, and for good reason. They have extremely sharp teeth, which were evolutionarily pre-determined to chew through things like acorns (which cannot be penetrated even with a ginsu knife and cable wires). Their teeth never stop growing, made with enamel on one side and soft dentine on the other, so they are constantly being worn away and sharpened like, well, ginsu knives. Also, rodents, contrary to what d-con would have you believe, are extremely hard to get rid of. I cannot stress this enough: *stay away from rodents*. Our minister Stephen Philbrick (bona fide adult who has worked, in his life, as a poet, a shepherd, a General Store clerk and now a Congregational parson) who is practically *married* to the peace movement, says that trying to get rid of rodents is akin to waging a yearly battle of Antietam.

51 Here's a great, clear article elucidating the financial crisis of 2008: http://www.cbsnews.com/8301-505125_162 28244229/the-financial-crisis-for-dummies/

52 Jennifer Taub: http://www.vermontlaw.edu/our_faculty/faculty_directory/jennif er_s_taub.htm

[53] Euthanized rates: http://members.aol.com/tipoftexk9rescue/PetOverpopulationand OwnershipSt.html

[54] Pet Insurance: http://www.aspcapetinsurance.com/

[55] My first cat, Ristleberry, actually did this.

[56] We recently bought a beta fish. He died within 2 days.

[57] Of course, a Habitrail, made out of plastic, is a poor choice, both from an environmental perspective (generally, plastic=bad) and also from a practical one. In my experience, rodents are easily able to chew through the tubes of their modular home and make an expedient escape. Choose a much more boring, but cheaper, aquarium instead.

[58] Marla Cilley: http://www.flylady.net

[59] Potter Stewart: http://www.law.cornell.edu/supct/html/historics/USSC_CR_037 8_0184_ZC1.html

[60] On how to fix a toilet: http://ks.essortment.com/howtofixtoile_rurc.htm

[53] Bad Teflon: http://therantersrant.blogspot.com/2007/12/teflon-pans.html

[54] On how to season and clean a cast iron skillet: http://whatscookingamerica.net/Q-A/castiron.htm and the back of the Lodge Logic Cast Iron Skillet Box

[63] Kingsolver, *Animal, Vegetable, Miracle.*

[64] Dirty Dozen: http://www.ewg.org/foodnews/list.php.

[65] CSAs: http://www.localharvest.org/

[66] Actually, it's my grandmother's chicken recipe. She handed it down to her daughter, who handed it down to my two sisters and me. My grandmother lived to be 103. Coincidence? I think not.

[67] Helpful Sources for raising chickens: *Storey's Guide to Raising Chickens* by Gail Damerow. Practically a textbook loaded with information on breeds, setting up facilities, caring for chickens, and preventing and diagnosing illness. *Living with Chickens* by Jay Rossier. A good introduction to raising chickens, focused on backyard hen-keeping. *Keep Chickens!: Tending Small Flocks in Cities, Suburbs, and Other Small Places* by Barbara Kilarski www.backyardchickens.com. A great place to start online, with specific information on local ordinances, coop designs, information on breeds, and a forum for chicken keepers to seek and share knowledge. pioneervalleybackyardchickenassociation.weebly.com Excellent community forum with friendly information from both new chicken-keepers and well-experienced small-scale poultry farmers. Based in Western Massachusetts but open to anyone interested as a hobbyist.

[68] McCarney R, Warner J, Iliffe S, van Haselen R, Griffin M, Fisher P (2007). "The Hawthorne Effect: a randomised, controlled trial". BMC Med Res Methodol 7: 30.doi:10.1186/1471-2288-730. PMC 1936999. PMID 17608932

[69] Buycott App: http://www.buycott.com/ about: http://www.forbes.com/sites/clareoconnor/2013/05/14/new-app-lets-you-boycott-koch-brothers-monsanto-and-more-by-scanning-your-shopping-cart/

[70] UW's website about college grads earning more than high school grads: http://www.uwcu.org/planning/goodvsbaddebt.asp

[71] "Why Consumption Matters," by Dave Tilford. http://www.sierraclub.org/sustainable_consumption/tilford.asp

[72] Jane Bryant Quinn: http://janebryantquinn.com/

[73] Experiences vs possessions: http://www.cnn.com/2009/HEALTH/02/10/happiness.pos sessions/

[74] Today, Massachusetts' tax rate is a flat 5.3% and Connecticut's is 5% for those making between $10,000 and $500,000 a year. Above $500,000 citizens pay 6.5%.

[75] 1040 online: http://www.irs.gov/pub/irs-pdf/f1040.pdf.

[76] Downloadable tax forms: www.irs.gov/pub/irspdf/f1040es.pdf

[77] Tax Software: http://www.taxact.com

[78] Malcolm Gladwell, *The New Yorker*, Aug. 29, 2005.

[79] According to the Blue Cross web site: http://www.bcbs.com.

[80] Malcolm Gladwell, *The New Yorker*, Aug. 29, 2005 p. 45.

[81] About COBRA: http://www.dol.gov/dol/topic/healthplans/cobra.htm

[82] I know, right??!!!??!! http://www.foxnews.com/opinion/2012/03/28/5-reasonsobamacare-is-already-good-for/

[83] Kelly Blue Book: www.kbb.com

[84] Conventional wisdom (and the stickers oil companies put on your windshields) tells us to change the oil every 3000 miles. But that's just not necessary: http://www.edmunds.com/carcare/stop-changing-your-oil.html

[85] *The Complete Tightwad Gazette*, p. 366, contributed by Susan Kuhn

[86] Re: new car smell in a bottle. Really! Here's the link: http://www.lanescarproducts.com/newcarscent.html

[87] The Automobile Association of America; www.aaa.com; 1 800-AAA-HELP

[88] For changing the oil: http://meme.essortment.com/carsoilchange_ruio.htm

[38] For jumpstarting car: http://www.geminicarcare.com/howto/jumpstart.html

[90] Zipcar: http://www.Zipcar.com

[91] NYtimes Article: http://www.nytimes.com/2006/06/27/science/
earth/27cool.html? pagewanted=all&_r=0

[92] http://www.nytimes.com/2006/06/27/science/earth/27cool.html

[93] "Since 1972, Freedom House, an independent private organization,
has published Freedom in the World, which assesses the state of
democracy and civil liberties of every country. A determination is
made whether the country is 'Free,' 'Partly Free,' or 'Not Free.' For
2007, Freedom in the World placed 90 countries, representing 46
percent of the global population, in the 'Free' category. Some 60
countries, 18 percent of the world's population, qualified as 'Partly
Free.' And 43 countries, 36 percent of the world's population, fell in
the 'Not Free' category. China constitutes about half of the 'Not Free'
population." Epoch Times, Freedom House: Democracy and Freedom
Declines for Second Year," By Gary Feuerberg. http://en.epochtimes.
com/news/8-1-20/64399.html.

[94] Youth Vote: http://www.civicyouth.org/youth-turnout-at-least49-22-
23-million-under-30-voted/

[95] Why you shouldn't watch Fox News: http://www.americanprogress.
org/issues/race/news/2011/11/29/1 0637/race-and-beyond-dumbing-
it-down-on-fox-news/

[96] This actually did happen in 2010. Read this excellent article
in Mother Jones: http://www.motherjones.com/politics/2012/11/
republicansgerrymandering-house-representatives-election-chart

[97] Harvey Milk: http://en.wikiquote.org/wiki/Harvey_Milk

[98] Read Michael Pollan's excellent *The Omnivore's Dilemma* to get a
more extensive explanation of how commercial farms are destroying
the planet and your health.

[99] Gay Daly, "Bad Chemistry: A Special Report" http://www.nrdc.org/
OnEarth/06win/chem1.asp

[100] For more information about the garment industry and sweatshop
labor, see http://www.sweatshopwatch.org/index.php?s=59. For a
report on which companies are attempting to sell clothes that are
sweatshop free, see http://www.monitor.net/monitor/sweatshop/ss-
actions.html.)

[101] There's a fabulous online video out called The Story of Stuff, made
by a woman named Annie Leonard. I urge you to watch it! http://
www.storyofstuff.com.

[102] Better World Shopper: http://betterworldshopper.com/

[103] "Bob Dylan's Dream" by Bob Dylan, from *The Freewheelin' Bob
Dylan*, Columbia Records, ©1963. Used by permission. How cool is
that???

[104] *When Things Fall Apart*, Pema Chodron

[105] Gottman, *Seven Principles for Making Marriage Work*, p. 27.

[106] The Bible, Mark 11:15-16.

[107] Dave Chalfant says they actually were a seminal band of the '70s. My bad.

[108] *Listening to Your Life*, Frederick Buechner (Random House, 1989) © 1988 by Frederick Buechner.

[109] Hootenanny! http://www.hootenannyfamily.com

[110] *For Your Own Good: Hidden Cruelty in Child-Rearing and the Roots of Violence*, by Alice Miller, p. 248-249.

About the Author

Nerissa Nields has been a member of the legendary band The Nields since 1991. She has toured North America, been on major labels, played to tens of thousands from stages all across the continent and has passionate fans all over the world. Between the Nields and her duo with sister Katryna Nields, she has recorded and released sixteen CDs. Her first novel, *Plastic Angel,* was published by Scholastic Press in 2005.With Katryna, she wrote A*ll Together Singing in the Kitchen: Creative Ways to Make and Listen to Music as a Family* (Roost Books, Shambhala 2011). She is currently working on her second novel, *The Big Idea,* the story of a rock band who is also a family. She maintains three blogs: May Day Café (www. nerissanields.blogspot.com), Singing in the Kitchen (www.nields. wordpress.com) and *How to Be an Adult* (www.howtoebeanadult. org). A graduate of Yale University, she has taught creative writing, songwriting and the art of living well for her entire adult life. Trained as a life coach by Martha Beck, she runs writing workshops and retreats out of her home in Northampton, Massachusetts where she lives with her husband and children.

For more information, and to sign up for her newsletter, visit www.nerissanields.com.

Follow her on Twitter @NerKat.

Praise for *How to Be an Adult*

A friend of mine once said, "In college I studied Shakespeare, calculus, molecular biology. What I really wish I had learned was: How long do eggs keep in the refrigerator?" How to Be an Adult *is packed with information required to make it in the real world where a person needs to rent an apartment, vote, set up a 401(K) and buy those eggs. If you know anyone who is graduating soon, buy them a copy of this book. It might be more useful than a car.*

—Gay Daly, Environmental Journalist,
author of Pre-Raphaelites in Love.

This is a magical book—I wish I'd had it when I graduated from college!

Nerissa Nields manages to combine the essence of "Hints from Heloise" with a spiritual wisdom reminiscent of Sharon Salzburg or Byron Katie, leavened with the humor of Anne Lamott. Even if you have no street smarts and have spent the past ten years living under the North Pole, you will be ready for adult life with this engaging earth manual. Whether telling you how to pay taxes, change a flat tire, navigate a relationship with a housemate, or stop beating yourself up with the club of perfectionism, Nields is amusing, smart, lively, and full of surprises. She is at her best when discussing psychological self-care, conscious living, self-acceptance, and the search for meaning. Every twenty-something (and many 40- or 50-year-olds, as well) should own and read How to Be an Adult.

—Judith Hooper, author, Of Moths and Men
and The 3-Pound Universe

Spend LESS time on the mundane stuff, using Nerissa's beautifully written how-to guide, while spending MORE time experiencing the FABULOUS world of all-the-way-grown-up life—and make no mistake, being grown up IS a blast; Nerissa has some vital words to add there, too!

—Dar Williams, singer-songwriter

As someone who works with college students on a daily basis, I have been waiting for this book to be written! With wit and wisdom, Nerissa Nields provides practical guidance and wise counsel for young people on their journey towards adulthood. She is the big sister and coach we all need when embarking on such an adventure.

—Jill Stratton, Associate Dean of Students,
Washington University in St. Louis

Made in the USA
Lexington, KY
05 May 2017